IMAGES
of America

MISSOURI VETERANS
MONUMENTS AND MEMORIALS

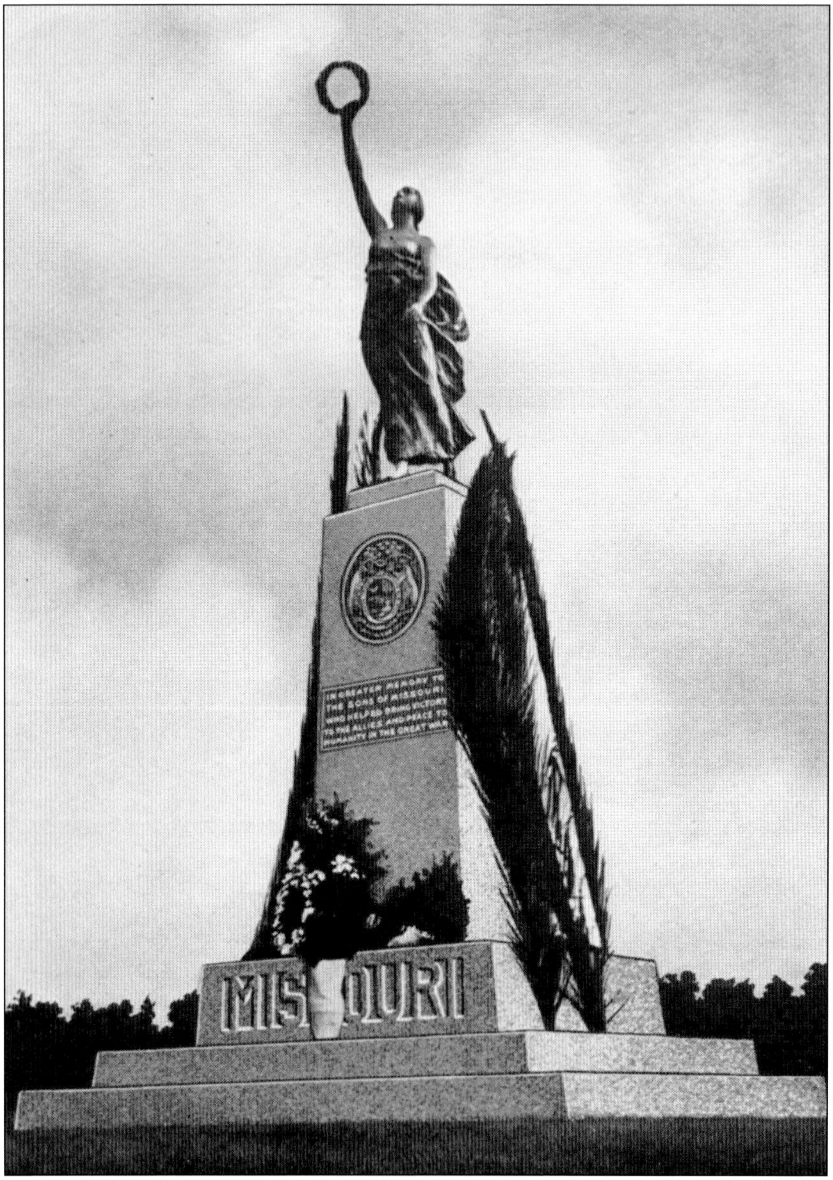

The Missouri Legislature appropriated $25,000 on May 5, 1919, for the purpose of building a memorial to commemorate the heroism of Missourians who served in France during World War I. Nancy Coonsman Hahn of St. Louis was chosen to create the monument, which was named *Victory* and dedicated on November 5, 1922, on a site near Cheppy, France. Missouri became the first state to erect a memorial in France to honor her sons who perished in the war. (Author's collection.)

On the Cover: On September 14, 1953, in a roadside park on Ten Mile Drive west of Jefferson City, the dedication a Blue Star Memorial marker was held. Pictured in the unveiling is Augusta Voss, Blue Star chairman of Hawthorn Garden Club. During the construction of the Capital Mall in the late 1970s, the marker was moved for expansion of the roads in the area and placed in the roadside park on Missouri Boulevard; however, the marker has since been moved and placed at the entrance to Washington Park. (VFW Post 1003.)

IMAGES
of America

MISSOURI VETERANS
MONUMENTS AND MEMORIALS

Jeremy Paul Amick

ARCADIA
PUBLISHING

ISBN 978-1-4671-2824-7

Published by Arcadia Publishing
Charleston, South Carolina

Printed in the United States of America

Library of Congress Control Number: 2017953999

For all general information, please contact Arcadia Publishing:
Telephone 843-853-2070
Fax 843-853-0044
E-mail sales@arcadiapublishing.com
For customer service and orders:
Toll-Free 1-888-313-2665

Visit us on the Internet at www.arcadiapublishing.com

I must first thank my Lord Jesus Christ, through whom all things are possible. Secondly, my wife, Tina, for accompanying me on many of my journeys throughout the state and using her eye and camera to supply me with several superb photographs.

Contents

ACKNOWLEDGMENTS

I cannot extend enough appreciation for the expertise my friend Dennis Hall, who is not only a veteran of the Coast Guard but also greatly assisted in the formatting of the photographs used in this book. I am also thankful for the assistance of Charles Machon and Douglas Sheley, with the Museum of Missouri Military History, for digging into their archives of military photographs. Also, I would like to thank the Veterans of Foreign Wars Post 1003 for providing the cover photograph for this book.

Unless otherwise noted, all images are from the author's collection.

Introduction

The citizens of Missouri have long sought to honor the legacy of their veterans through memorials and monuments erected in communities throughout the state. This is military heritage that predates statehood in 1821 and includes the burials of such frontier heroes as Daniel Boone. During the Revolutionary War, Boone expanded upon his reputation as a frontiersman when serving as a captain in the militia and defending settlements in Kentucky. In later years, he chose to move his home to Missouri, where he passed away in 1820. Although Boone was laid to rest in a cemetery near Marthasville, there remains much academic dispute as to whether his remains still reside in Missouri or if they were moved to Kentucky. Regardless, the Daughters of the American Revolution continue to honor the service of this great American frontiersman and veteran, and they have dedicated a stunning memorial at his original gravesite in Missouri as a tribute to his military service.

In the years after the Revolutionary War, Missouri's military tradition carried forth with William Clark, who served as a cocaptain during the famed Lewis and Clark Expedition. The expedition made its brief passage through area that would later become the state capital in June 1804, but Clark would maintain ties with the state for decades to come. In the years after gaining fame as an explorer, the soldier was appointed as an agent for Indian affairs in the West, became a brigadier general in the militia, and served as governor of the Missouri Territory before it became a state. Following his death on September 1, 1838, Clark was laid to rest in the historic Bellefontaine Cemetery in St. Louis.

A monument dedicated to the memory of Capt. James L. Callaway—a veteran of the War of 1812—demonstrates the impact of yet another interesting individual whose service to the state and nation lives on well past his passing. Though Callaway was killed in 1815, a memorial unveiled on the grounds of the Callaway County Courthouse in Fulton on August 29, 1905, helps in perpetuating his legacy. In the years following his death, Callaway was also honored through the naming of Callaway County.

The state's military traditions took a more temperamental turn during the years of the Civil War due to divided loyalties of those who were struggling with the issue of secession. Guerilla fighters such as William Quantrill and "Bloody Bill" Anderson rose to the level of celebrity during the war and helped train future outlaws such as Frank and Jesse James. The gravesites of these men are honored through simple military markers. On the Union side, the state also influenced William T. Sherman, whose March to the Sea helped crush the South's ability to wage war. He was so impressed with the state that he requested burial in Cavalry Cemetery in St. Louis. In nearby Bellefontaine Cemetery, Confederate general and former governor Sterling Price has been memorialized through a large obelisk at his gravesite.

In the years preceding World War I, a young Harry S. Truman from the rural community of Lamar made the decision to enlist as a private in the Missouri National Guard in 1905. The future president remained with the National Guard until receiving his discharge in 1911. He later reenlisted with Battery B, Missouri Light Artillery in 1917 and was elected as lieutenant. The Missouri National Guard battery was federalized in August 1917, and Truman served overseas as an artillery officer during World War I, eventually rising to the rank of captain. After the war, he became a member of the Organized Reserve Corps and retired at the rank of colonel. Truman's military legacy and that of his service as a senator and president are memorialized through monuments and displays at the Harry S. Truman Presidential Library and Museum in Independence.

World War II presented entirely new opportunities to honor specific groups of veterans, which is demonstrated in a monument in Jefferson Barracks Historic Park dedicated to those who participated in the Battle of the Bulge. Military bases and camps within the state, such as Whiteman Air Force Base, are themselves lasting memorials to specific veterans. Named for George Allison Whiteman—a pilot from mid-Missouri who became the first Missouri resident to lose his life in World War II following the attack on Pearl Harbor—Whiteman Air Force Base began its life as the Sedalia Glider Base in late 1942.

As the nation became embroiled in later conflicts, many communities banded to together to honor and recognize its citizens who served in Korea, Vietnam, and the Cold War. More recently, cities such as St. Joseph have worked diligently to memorialize specific individuals who perished in more recent conflicts in Iraq and Afghanistan by erecting individual monuments on a sprawling lawn across from city hall. Throughout the state, there are also many examples of towns and cities that have erected both simple and elaborate monuments honoring all veterans, regardless of the branch of the military in which they served or the timeframe of their service.

Although it would take volumes to exhibit all of the magnificent monuments and memorials chronicling the service and sacrifice of veterans throughout our state's history, this book highlights a small segment of our state's rich past and pays homage to those who have assumed the mantle of military service on behalf of our state and nation. Welcome to the rich military traditions shared in *Missouri Veterans: Monuments and Memorials.*

One

Central Missouri

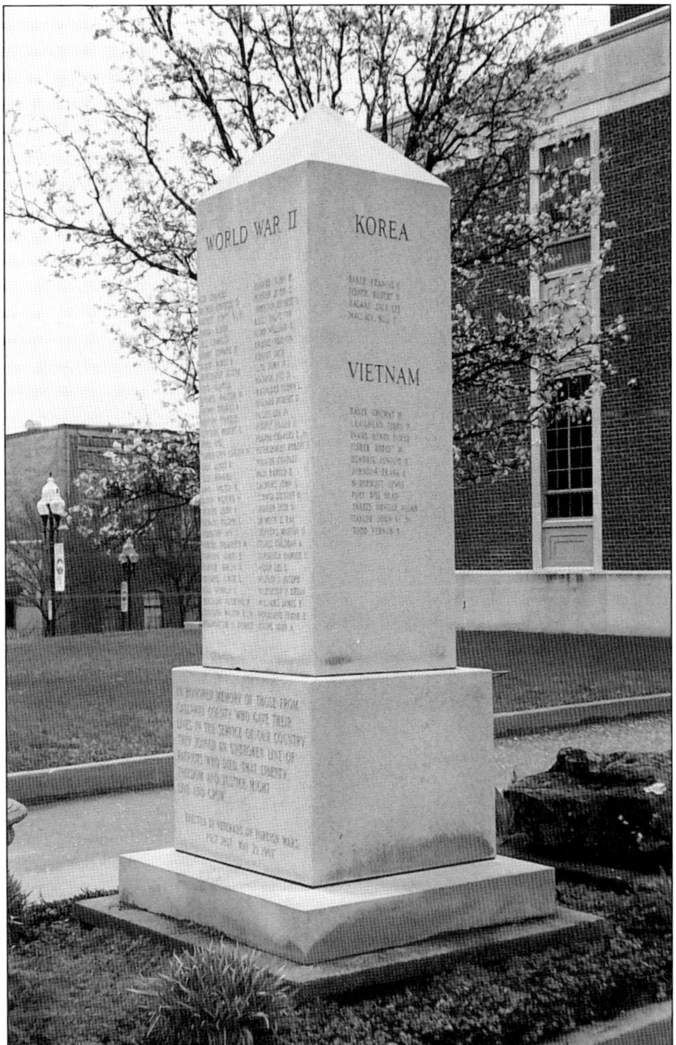

The Veterans of Foreign Wars Post 2657 sponsored a Callaway County Veterans' Memorial that stands boldly on the grounds of the Callaway County Courthouse in Fulton. Dedicated on May 29, 1989, the memorial honors "an unbroken line of patriots" who gave their lives in the defense of liberty, listing the name of each casualty from the county from World War I through the Vietnam War.

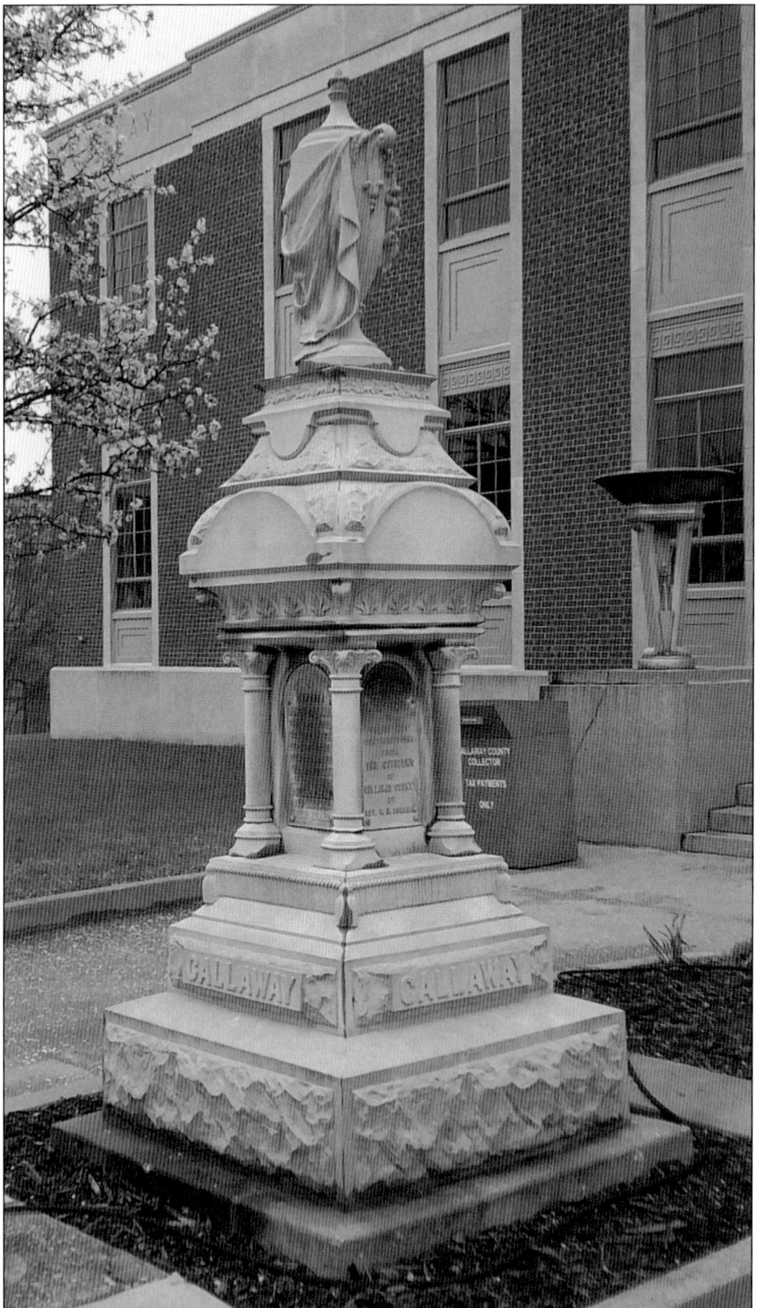

A monument dedicated to the memory of Capt. James L. Callaway—a veteran of the War of 1812—was unveiled on the grounds of the Callaway County Courthouse in Fulton on August 29, 1905, in a ceremony witnessed by 3,000 to 4,000 people, reported the August 31, 1905, edition of the *Mexico Missouri Message* newspaper. A grandson of Daniel Boone, Callaway commanded several companies of rangers who were engaged in fighting Native Americans; however, he was killed on March 7, 1815, during a skirmish on Loutre Creek in what is now Montgomery County. Callaway County was named in his honor in the years following his death. (Tina Amick.)

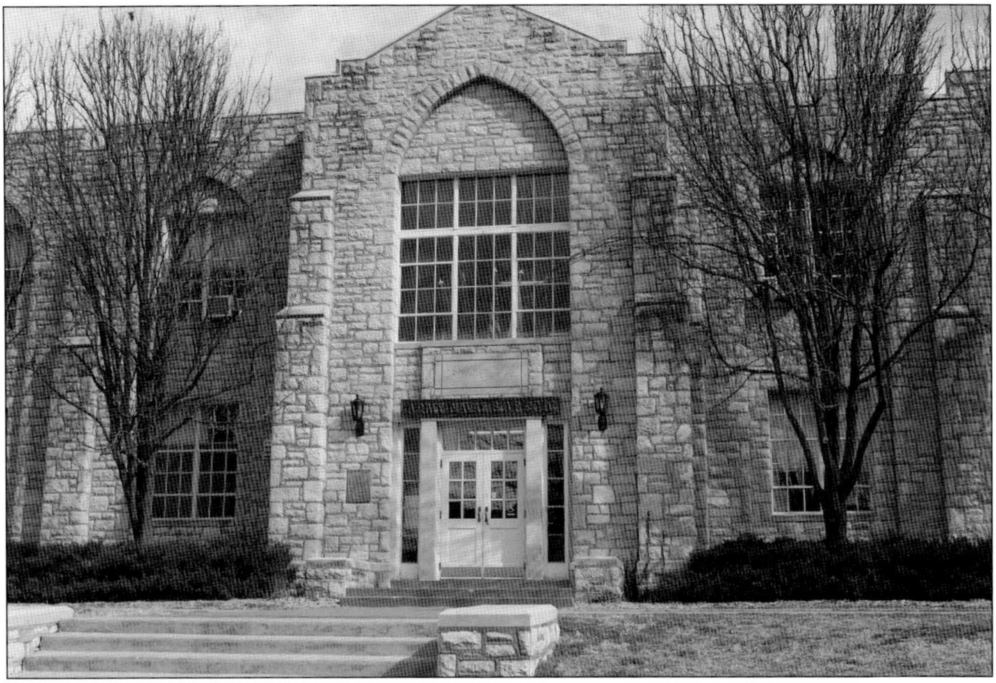

During a dedication ceremony held on May 10, 1940, and attended by Missouri governor Lloyd C. Stark, an armory for the Reserve Officers' Training Corps (ROTC) on the campus of the University of Missouri in Columbia was christened Crowder Hall. The stone building was named for the late Maj. Gen. Enoch H. Crowder, a native of Grundy County, Missouri, who served as commandant of cadets at the university from 1885 to 1889 and helped draft and implement the Selective Service Act of 1917 during World War I.

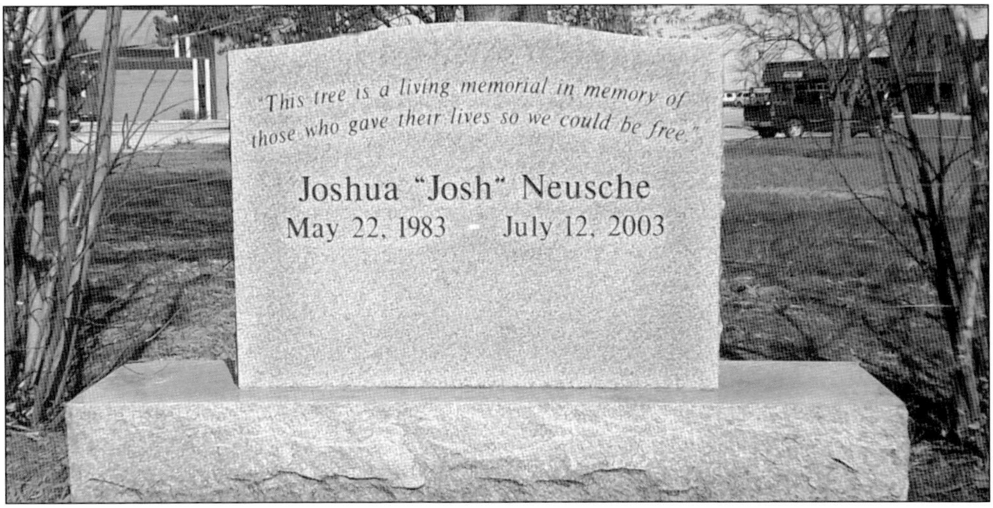

Specialist Joshua Neusche—a 2002 graduate of Camdenton High School—was deployed to Iraq in May 2003 with the Missouri National Guard's 203rd Engineer Battalion from Joplin. Sadly, the young citizen-soldier became seriously ill and passed away at a military hospital in Germany on July 12, 2003. The community gathered on the square of the Camden County Courthouse on October 26, 2003, to celebrate Neusche's life and to dedicate a tree and a marker in memory of his service.

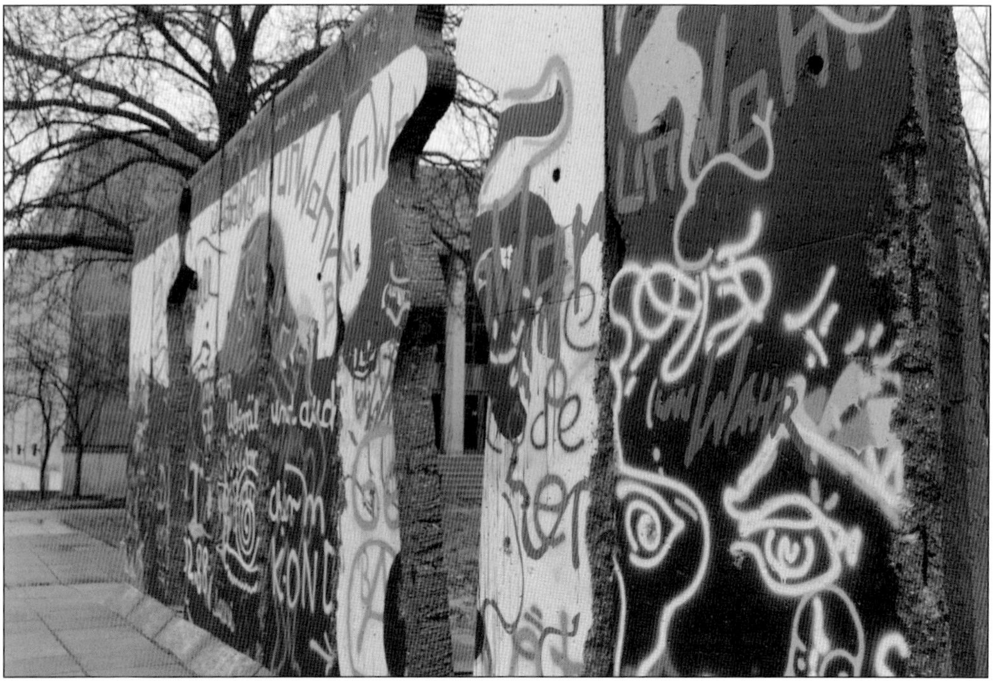

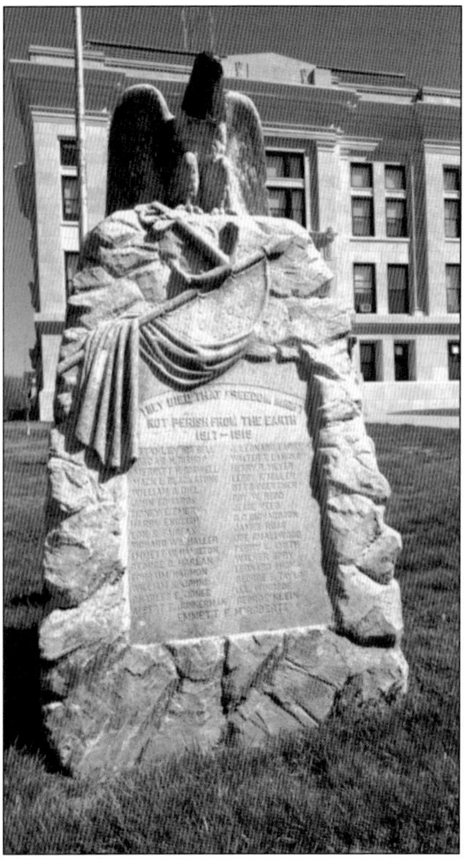

A section of the Berlin Wall stands as a memorial to the Cold War near the National Churchill Museum on the campus of Westminster College in Fulton. The 11-foot-high by 32-foot-long structure is a sculpture by artist Edwina Sandys—granddaughter of Winston Churchill—and is made from eight sections of the Berlin Wall that were removed from an area near the historic Brandenburg Gate. Titled *Breakthrough*, the sculpture was introduced on November 9, 1990, during a ceremony attended by former president Ronald Reagan. (Tina Amick.)

On the northwest grounds of the Cooper County Courthouse in Boonville is a limestone marker denoting the ultimate sacrifice made by local residents during World War I. The memorial is topped with an eagle; the upper section of the memorial features the carving of an anchor and a spear, the latter of which has a banner wrapped around the shaft. In addition to a list of the names of Cooper County residents who died during World War I, the following is inscribed upon the three-foot monument: "They died that freedom might not perish from the earth, 1917–1919." (Tina Amick.)

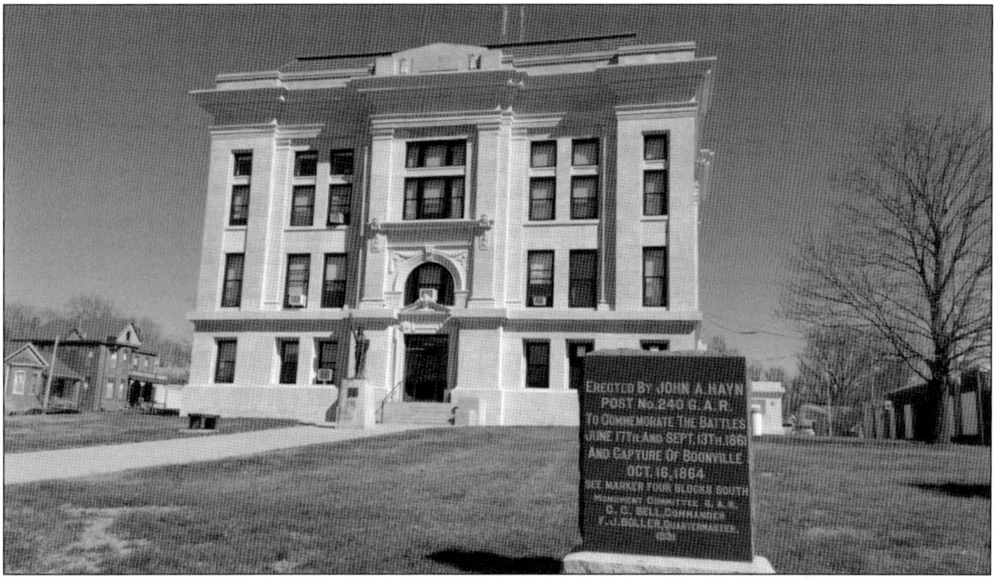

In recognition of the brave men of the Union who fought during the Civil War battles and skirmishes that took place in and around the community of Boonville, the John A. Hayn Post 240 of the Grand Army of the Republic erected a memorial on the grounds of the Cooper County Courthouse in Boonville in 1931.

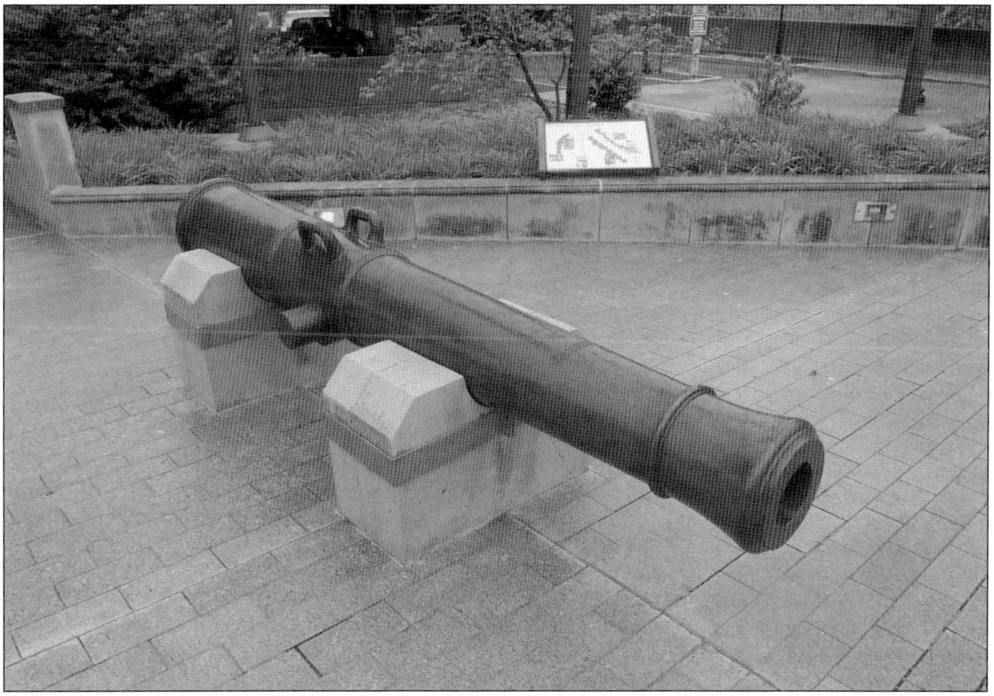

This eight-inch brass gun is 12 feet long, weighs 6,000 pounds, and was built in 1769, according to an article appearing in the September 26, 1901, edition of the *St. Joseph Gazette-Herald*. The cannon was captured by the US Navy in Cuba during the Spanish-American War and on September 25, 1901, arrived at the Missouri State Capitol in Jefferson City, where it currently remains on display on the northern grounds.

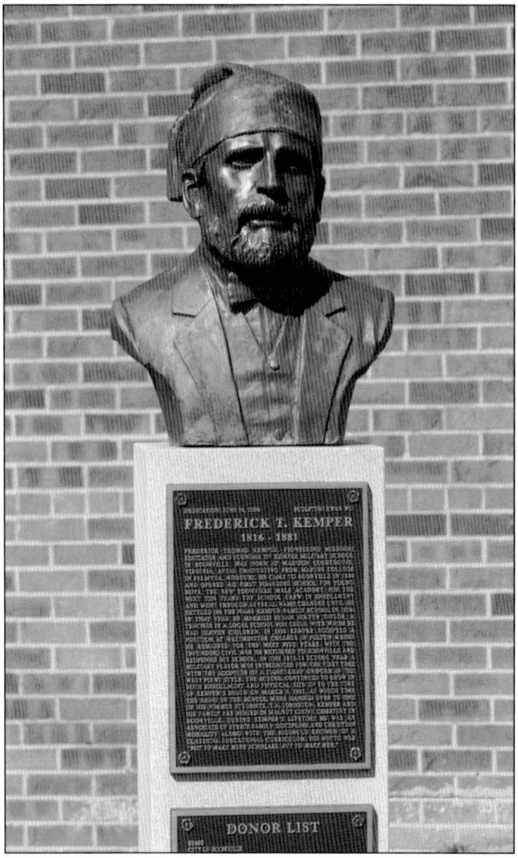

A bronze sculpture bust honoring the memory of Frederick T. Kemper is located in Morgan Street Park in Boonville. Kemper was born in Virginia in 1816 and eventually found his way to Missouri while in pursuit of an education. In 1844, Kemper opened the Boonville Male Boarding School, which, after undergoing several name changes, became the Kemper Military School under the guidance of his successor, Thomas A. Johnston. (Tina Amick.)

A column at the entrance to the Kemper Military School serves as a memorial and testament to what was once a thriving military academy. The school provided an education to students for 158 years, remaining in operation from 1844 until its bankruptcy closing in 2002. The campus was purchased by the City of Boonville, and although the iconic Administration Building has been demolished, much of Kemper's charm has been preserved through a local college and YMCA utilizing some of the original buildings. (Tina Amick.)

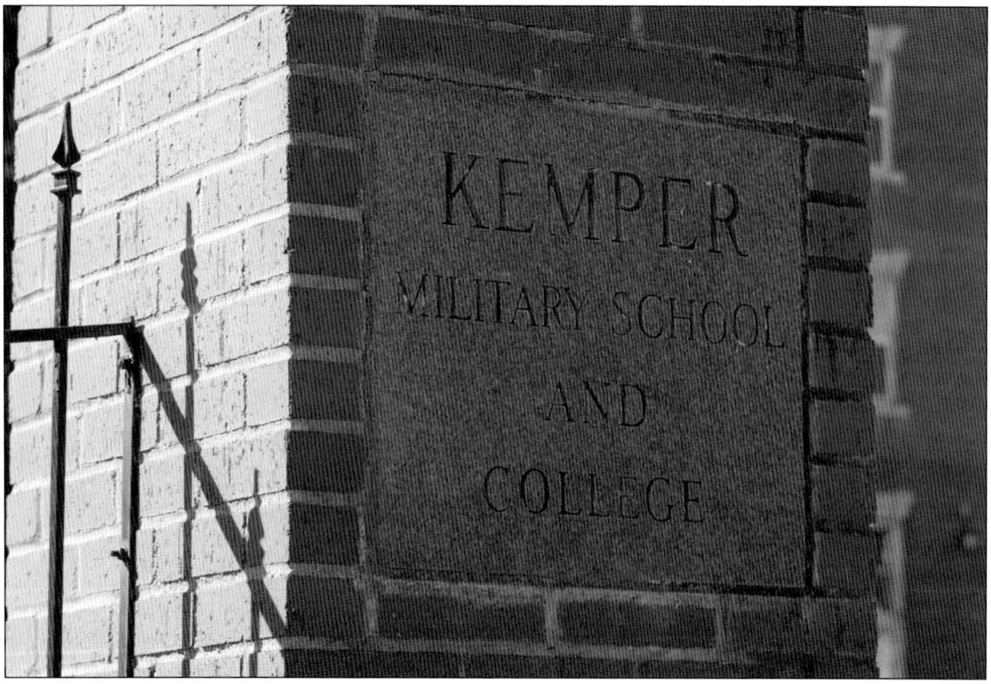

Thomas Alexander Johnston was born in rural Callaway County and served with the Confederate forces of Gen. Sterling Price during the Civil War. After the war, he attended what would become Kemper Military School, from which he graduated in 1871. Following the death of the school's founder, Frederick Kemper, Johnston was chosen to serve as the school's president. Much of the school's success has been associated with Johnston's leadership, and he later became Kemper's superintendent, a position he held until his death in 1934.

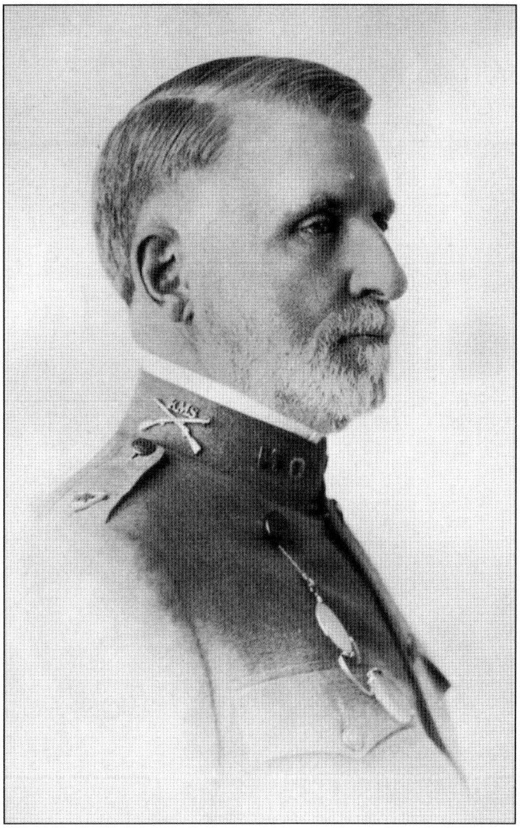

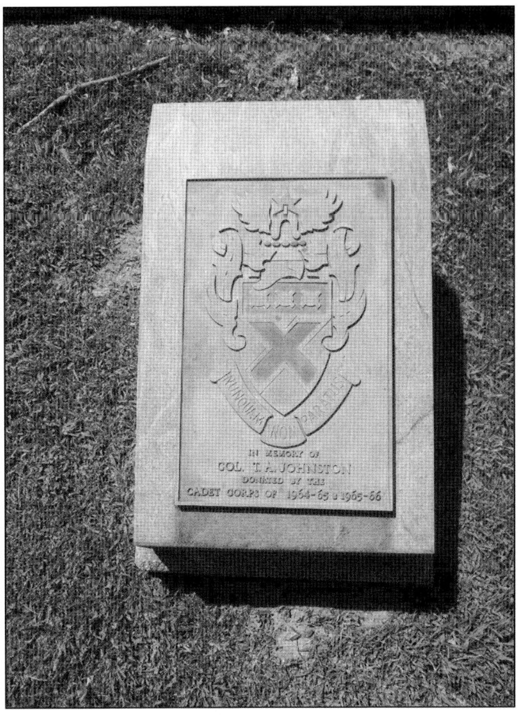

Col. Thomas Alexander Johnston was well respected by the students at Kemper Military School—an interesting list that included cowboy humorist Will Rogers, who attended the school for two years. Thirty years following Johnston's death, classes at Kemper honored the late school president by donating a memorial plaque with the school seal that is situated at the base of the flagpole.

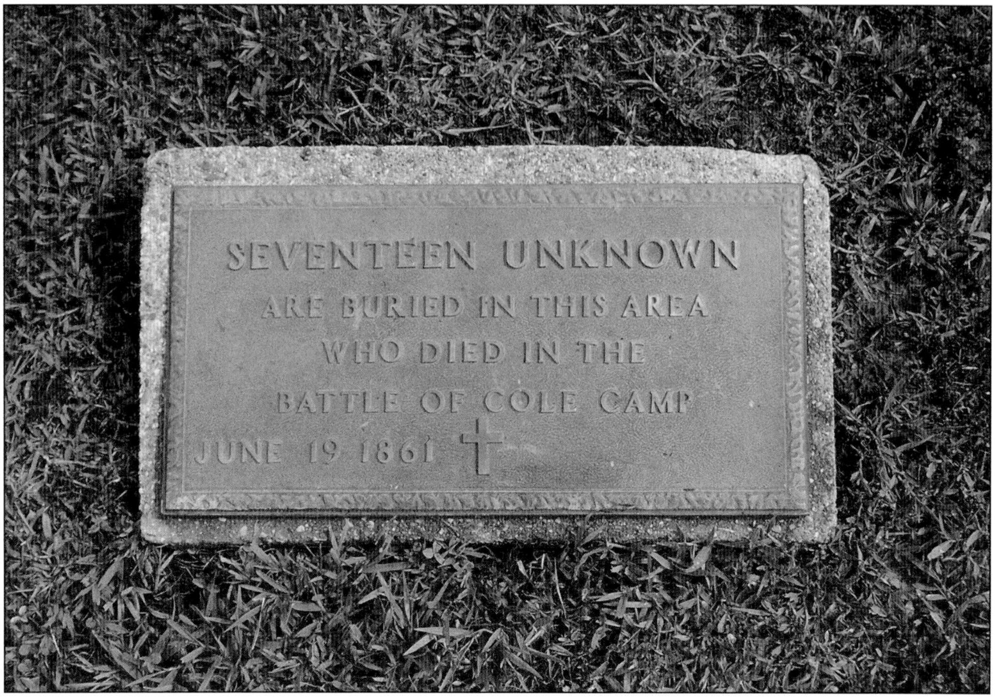

This simple marker in Monsees Cemetery near Cole Camp is all that designates the final resting site of 17 unknown Home Guard members killed during the Battle of Cole Camp. The skirmish took place east of Cole Camp during the early morning hours of June 19, 1861, when the sleeping Home Guard was overrun in a surprise attack by Confederate forces from the nearby community of Warsaw.

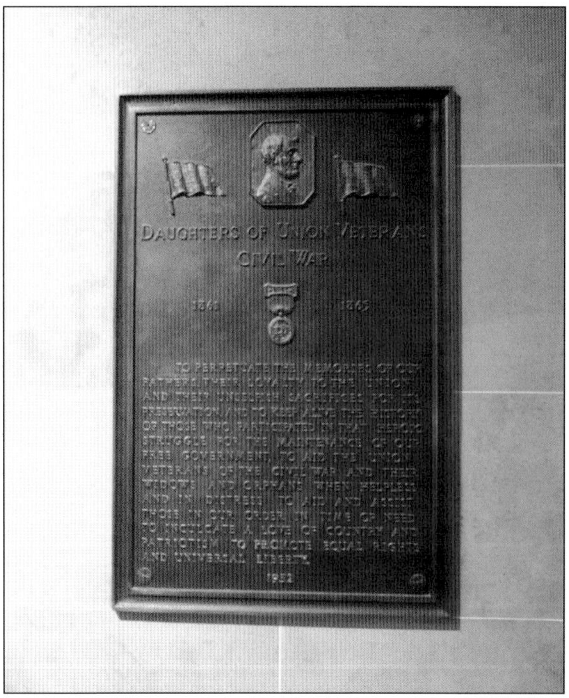

During a patriotic ceremony held in the state capitol in Jefferson City on April 9, 1932—the 67th anniversary of Gen. Robert E. Lee's surrender to Gen. Ulysses S. Grant at Appomattox—a bronze tablet was unveiled in honor of the Grand Army of the Republic (GAR). The tablet contains the profile of Pres. Abraham Lincoln, the American flag, and the GAR badge and was sponsored by the Daughters of Union Veterans of the Civil War.

A native of the Sedalia area, George Allison Whiteman trained as a pilot with the Army Air Corps and was the first Missourian killed in World War II when the Japanese attacked Pearl Harbor on December 7, 1941. He was laid to rest in the Schofield Barracks Post Cemetery in Hawaii on December 9, 1941, but his remains were later returned to Missouri and reinterred in Sedalia's Memorial Park Cemetery.

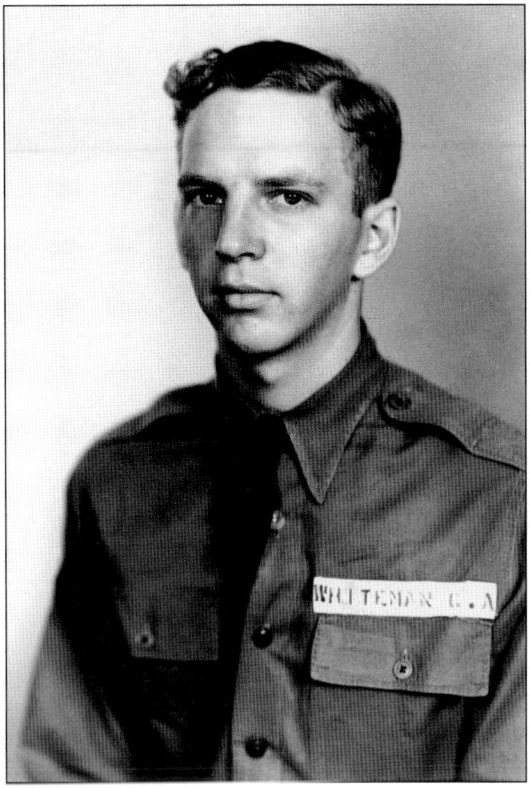

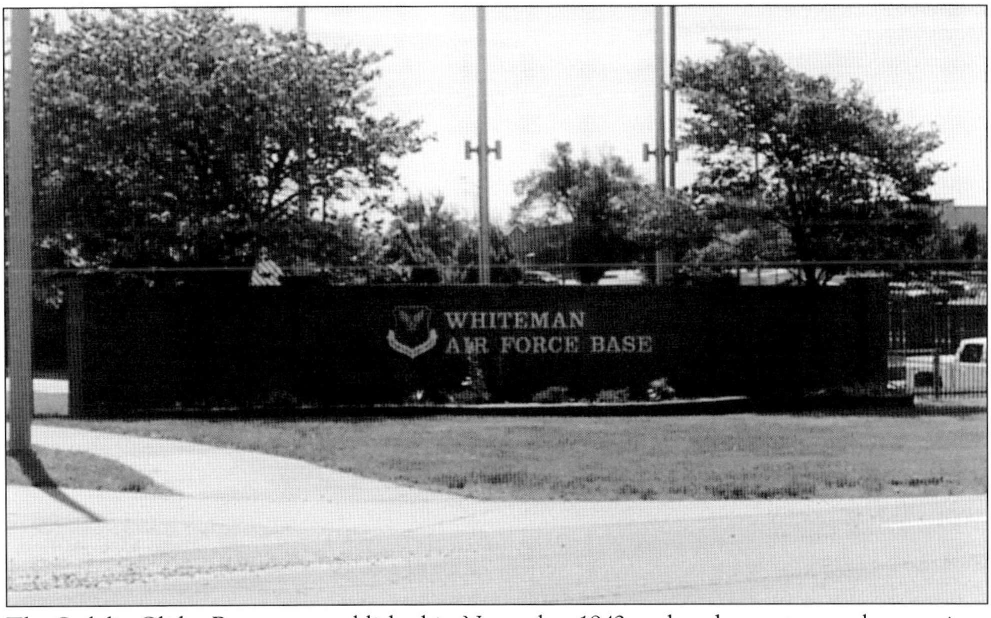

The Sedalia Glider Base was established in November 1942 and underwent several expansions and changes in the ensuing years. In 1954, the Air Force announced it was seeking nominations from civic groups for the renaming of the airfield. During a dedication and renaming ceremony on December 3, 1955, the Sedalia Air Force Base underwent the official transition to Whiteman Air Force Base, nearly 14 years following the death of its namesake.

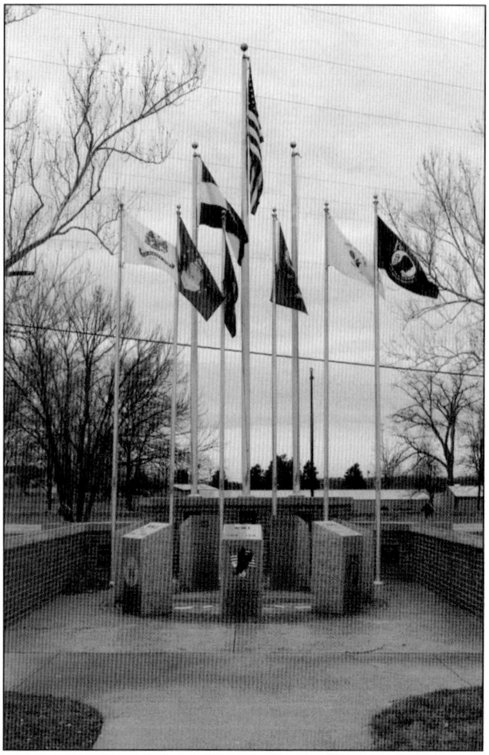

Located off of Highway 50 in Legion Park in the Franklin County community of Gerald is a magnificent veterans' memorial comprised of a walkway, nine flags, six memorial pillars, and benches. Dedicated in 2004, the memorial serves as a beautiful location to reflect on the men and women who gave their lives in the defense of freedom. (Tina Amick.)

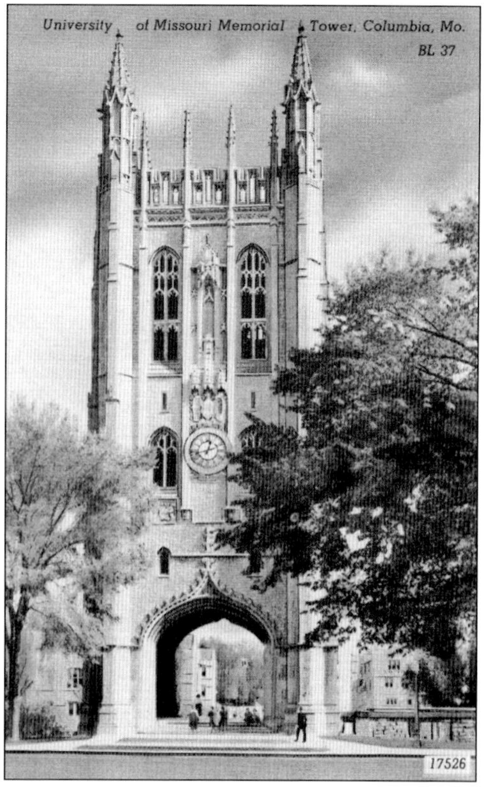

Although discussion began prior to World War I regarding the construction of a student union on the campus of the University of Missouri–Columbia, the idea did not come to fruition until after the war. Memorial Tower, which is pictured in this vintage linen postcard, was the highlight of the student union and was completed in 1926. The tower cost $288,000 to construct and is dedicated in honor of university students who died in World War I. (Tina Amick.)

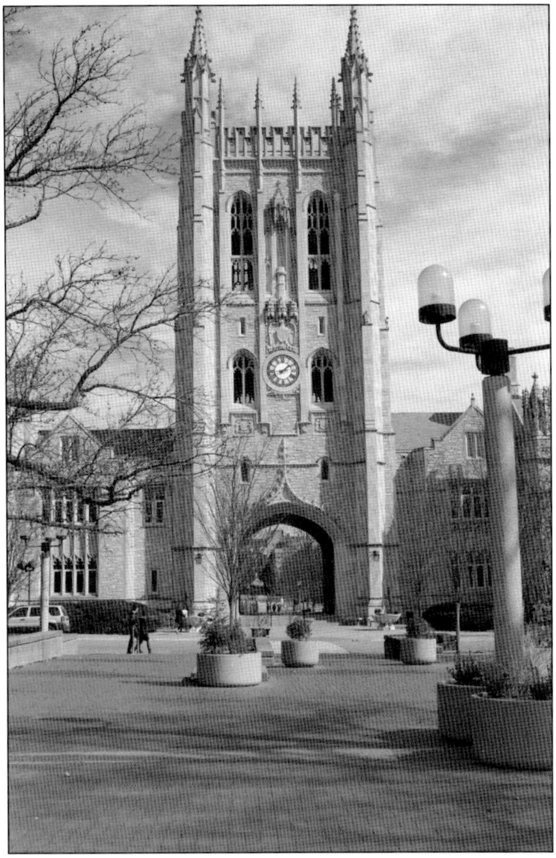

Memorial Union, as it appears today, once consisted of only Memorial Tower, which was one aspect in the grand construction plan for a building to house the student union. The same year the tower was dedicated (in 1926), so too was Memorial Stadium, but it would be many years later before the construction was completed on Memorial Union. In September 1952, the north wing was added to the Memorial Tower, with the south wing being completed in August 1963. (Tina Amick.)

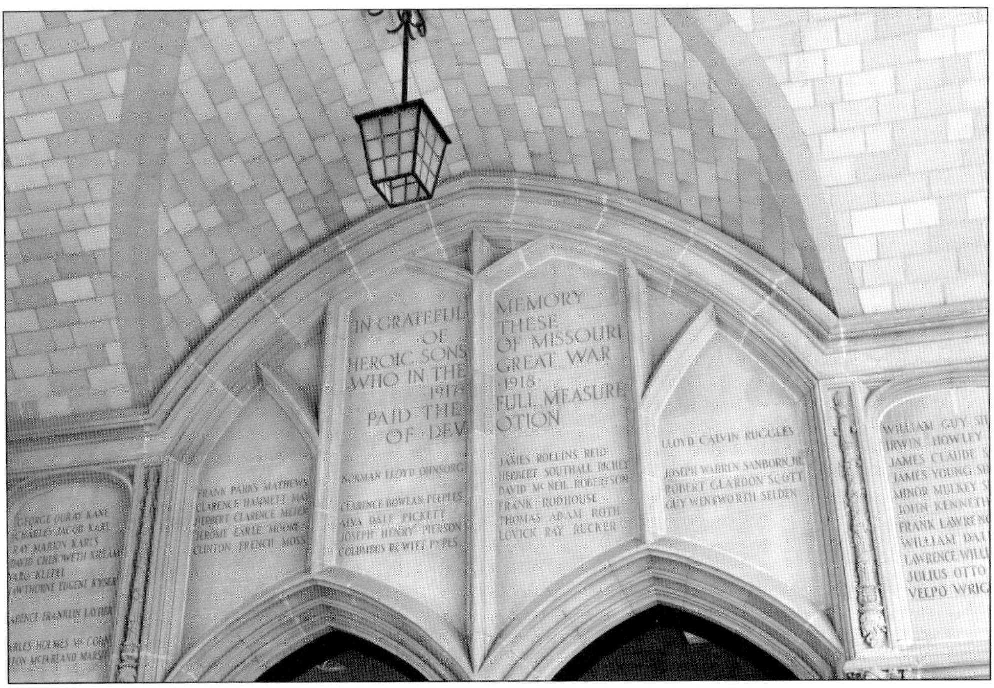

Inside the archway of Memorial Tower are the engraved names of 117 university students who died during their service in World War I. Additionally, there is a small plaque mounted within the archway as a gentle reminder to those passing through of the tradition of tipping their caps as sign of respect for the men whose names are inscribed above. (Tina Amick.)

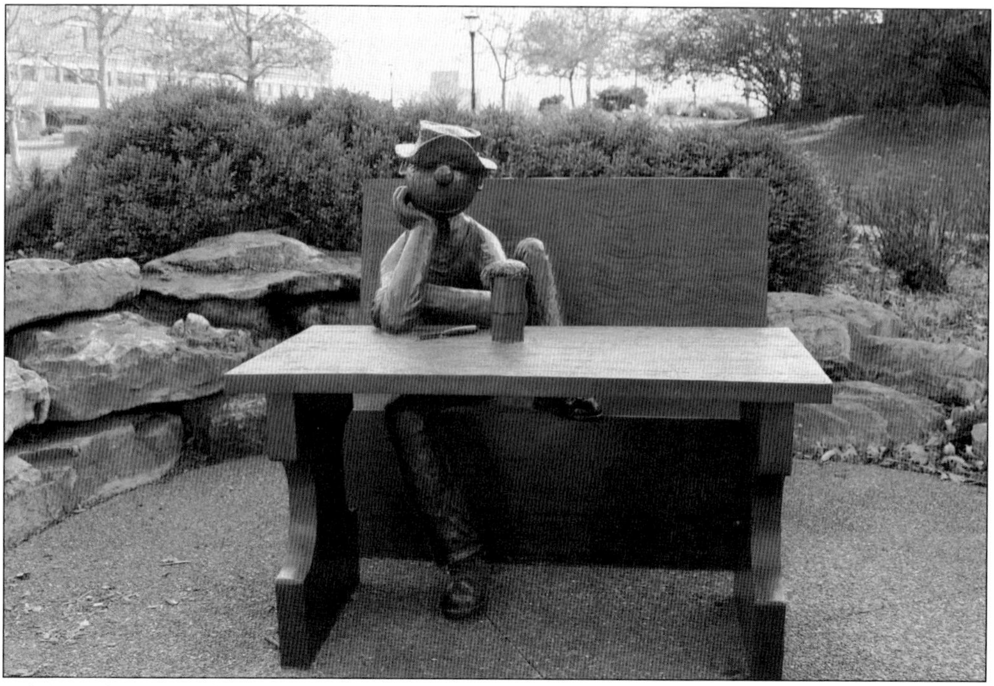

A life-size bronze sculpture of Beetle Bailey was dedicated outside Reynolds Alumni Center during the homecoming celebration at the University of Missouri on October 23, 1992. Mort Walker, the creator of Beetle Bailey, introduced the character while he was attending the university in the early 1940s. Walker was later drafted into the Army during World War II, and his wartime experiences at Missouri training locations inspired characters and locations later used in his *Beetle Bailey* comic strip. (Tina Amick.)

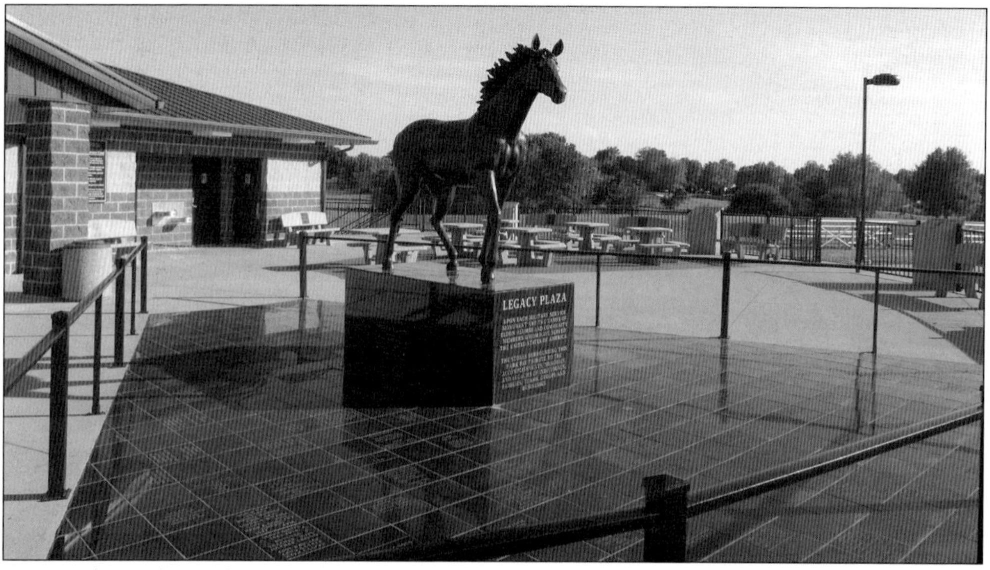

Legacy Plaza is located in Mustang Memorial Park behind Eldon High School in Miller County. Situated in a semicircle around a bronze sculpture of a mustang within the Legacy Plaza area is a collection of monuments representing each branch of service, upon which the names are inscribed of Eldon alumni and residents who served in the armed forces.

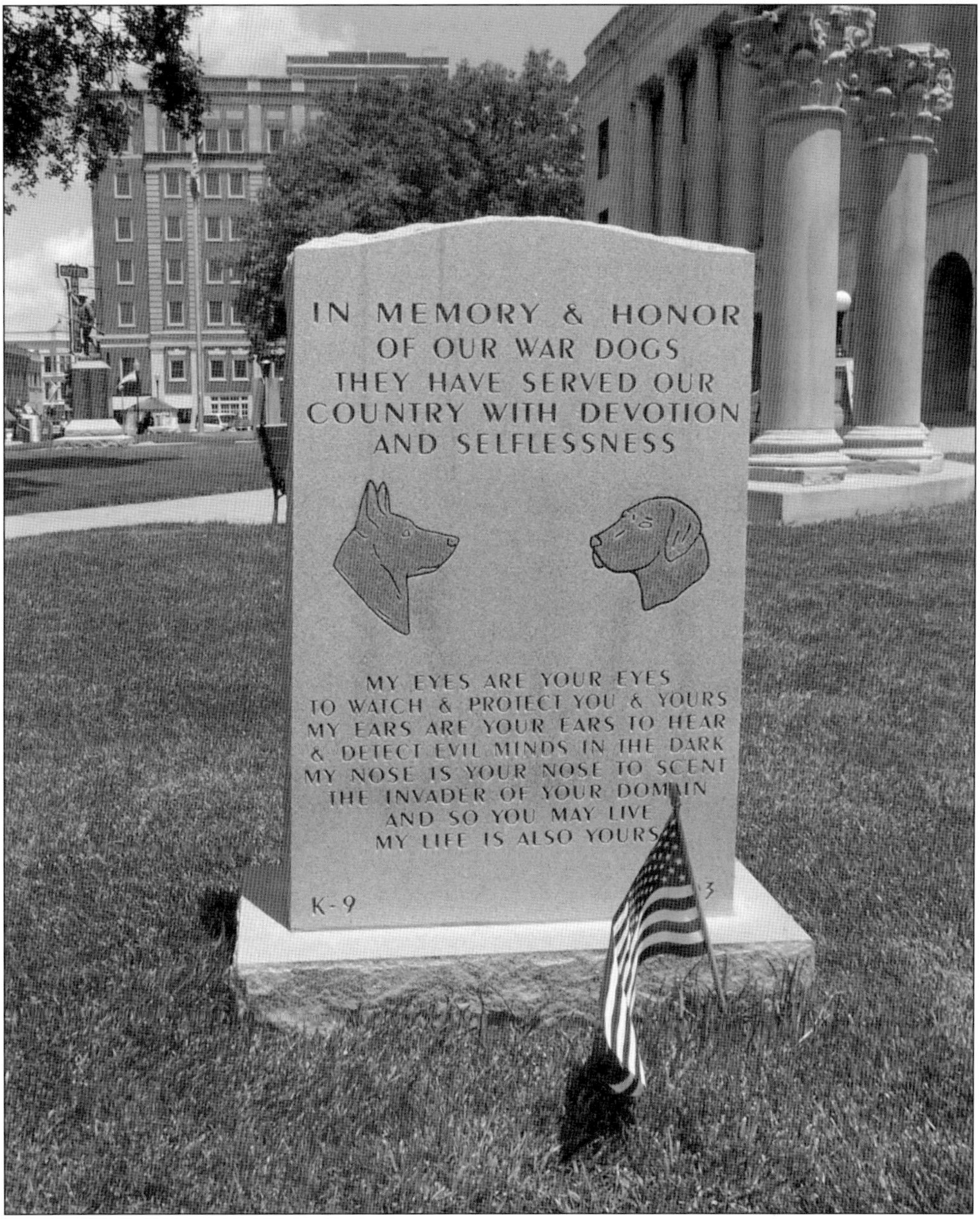

The War Dog Memorial is a small granite marker located on the southwest corner of the Pettis County Courthouse in Sedalia and was dedicated on May 17, 2003. During the dedication, then Sedalia police commander Jim Gaertner discussed his two tours of duty in Vietnam and described how war dogs saved his life by preventing him from springing a booby trap while also warning of approaching enemy forces.

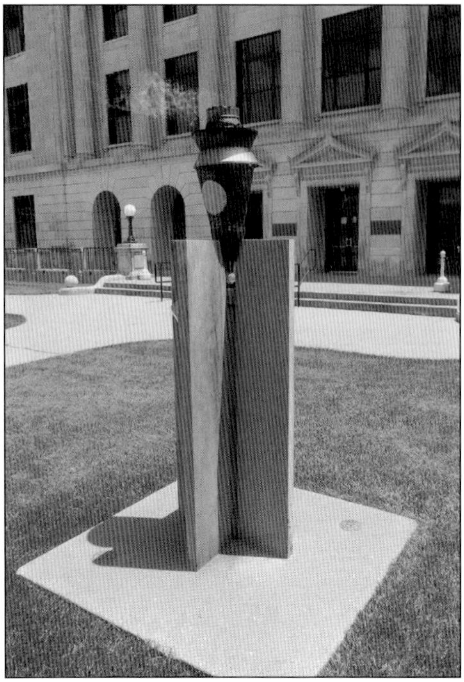

This six-foot-high monument designated the Eternal Flame was officially dedicated on the western lawn of the Pettis County Courthouse during a ceremony held on November 10, 1973. The monument was erected through the efforts of American Legions Post 16 and the county court to honor all veterans, and despite its name, the flame does not remain lit at all times but is only used on special occasions.

A Vietnam War Memorial was dedicated on the south grounds of the Pettis County Courthouse in Sedalia on November 5, 1988. Built at a cost of $24,000, the memorial consists of a 14,000-pound slab of academy black granite topped by an empty pair of boots, a helmet, and a rifle made of bronze, which symbolizes fallen warriors. In addition to a display of the seals of four branches of the military, inscribed upon the monument are the names of the 12 Pettis County citizens who lost died in the war.

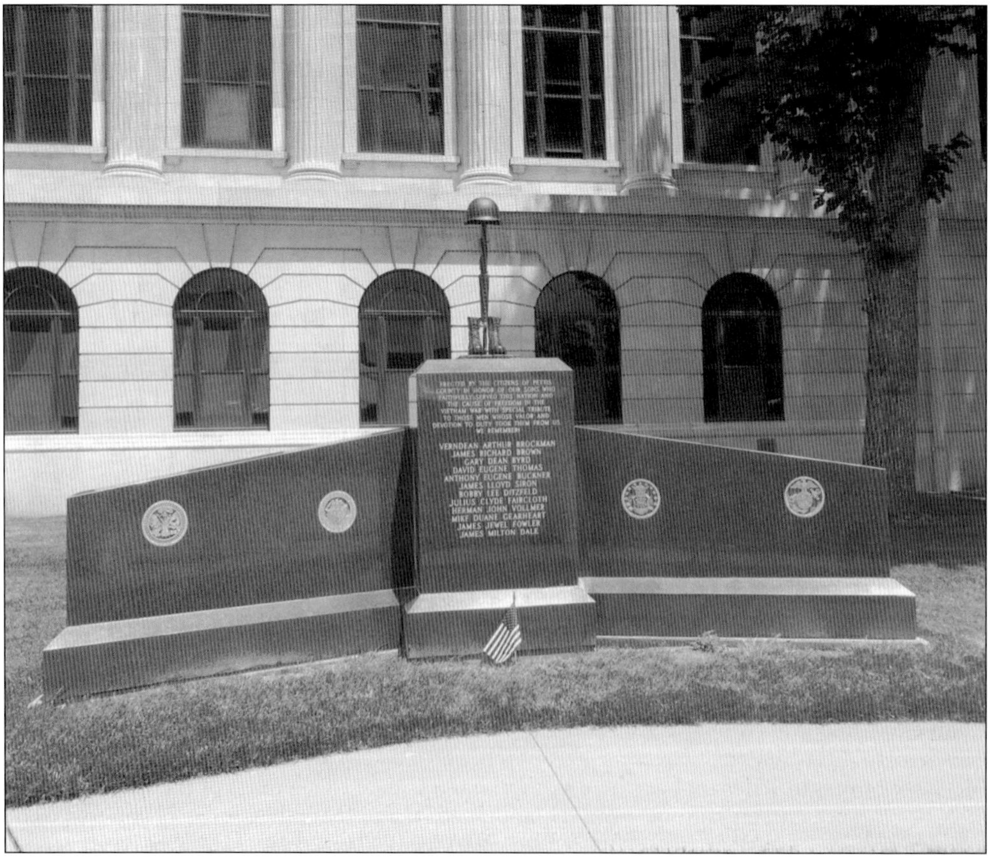

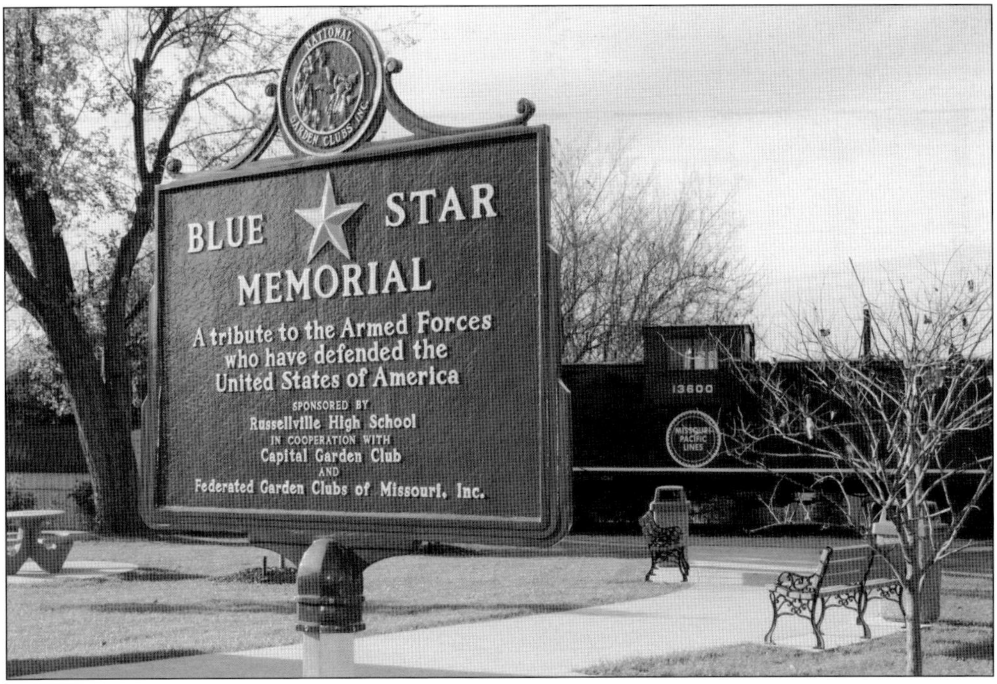

Three student groups from Russellville High School banded together to conduct a fundraiser for a Blue Star Memorial marker in early 2016. The marker was placed in Railroad Park across from city hall in Russellville and unveiled during a patriotic ceremony led by the Capital Garden Club from Jefferson City on Veterans Day, November 11, 2016. (Tina Amick.)

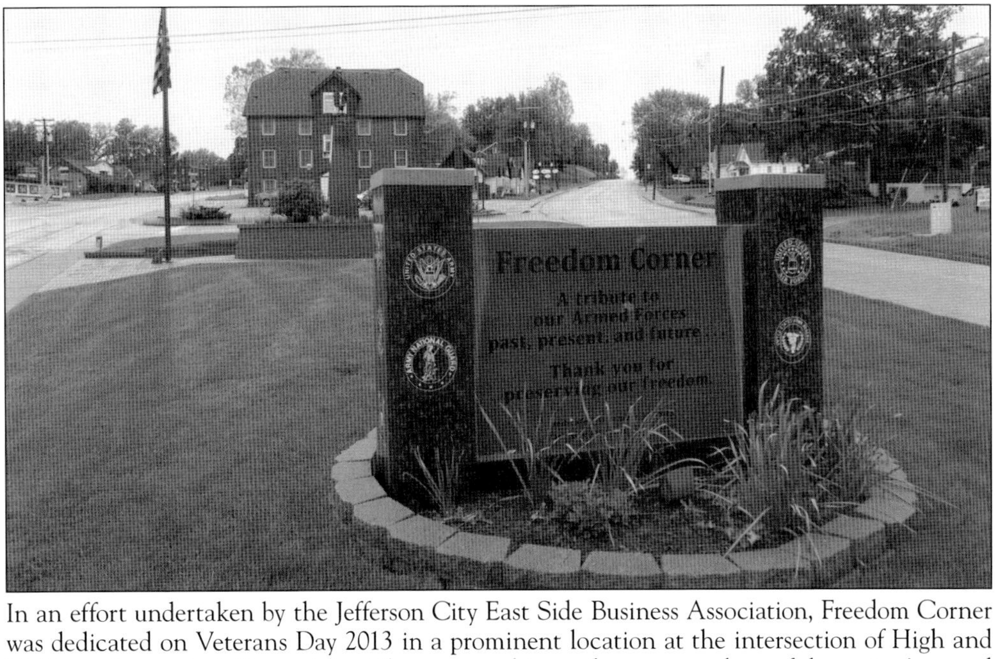

In an effort undertaken by the Jefferson City East Side Business Association, Freedom Corner was dedicated on Veterans Day 2013 in a prominent location at the intersection of High and McCarty Streets in Jefferson City. The memorial is a tribute to members of the nation's armed forces—past, present, and future—and is highlighted by a 14-foot-tall granite column topped by a bronze bald eagle in flight.

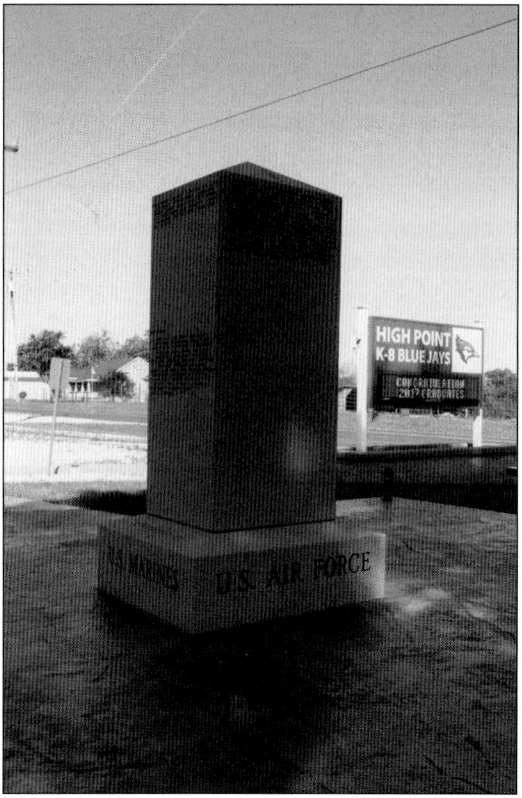

Through the use of social media, church bulletins, and other sources, the High Point Community Renewal Association secured donations of money, materials, and labor to construct a memorial to military veterans. Placed on the grounds of the High Point Elementary School in Moniteau County, the memorial was dedicated on July 4, 2013, and lists the names of area veterans from the Civil War to the present.

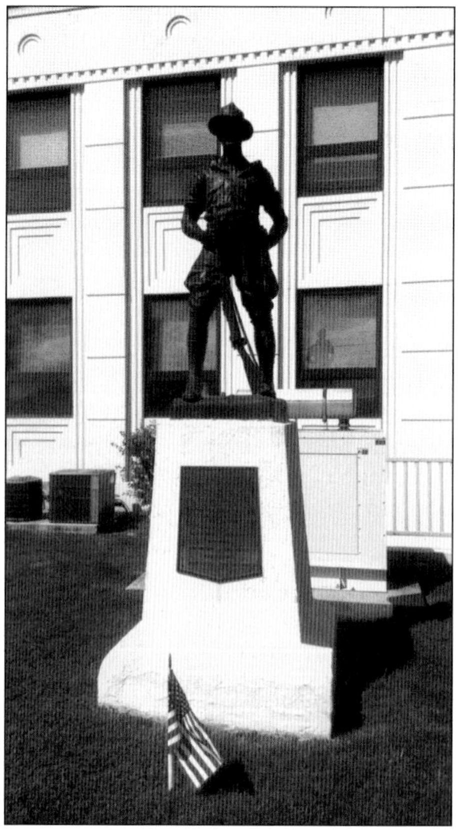

Flanked by memorials dedicated to those who served in World War II and Vietnam, this World War I monument is displayed on the back lawn of the Maries County Courthouse in the community of Vienna. It was dedicated by the citizens of Maries County "to those of their sons who served the nation and the cause of humanity," and the base of the memorial lists the eight county citizens who lost their lives during World War I.

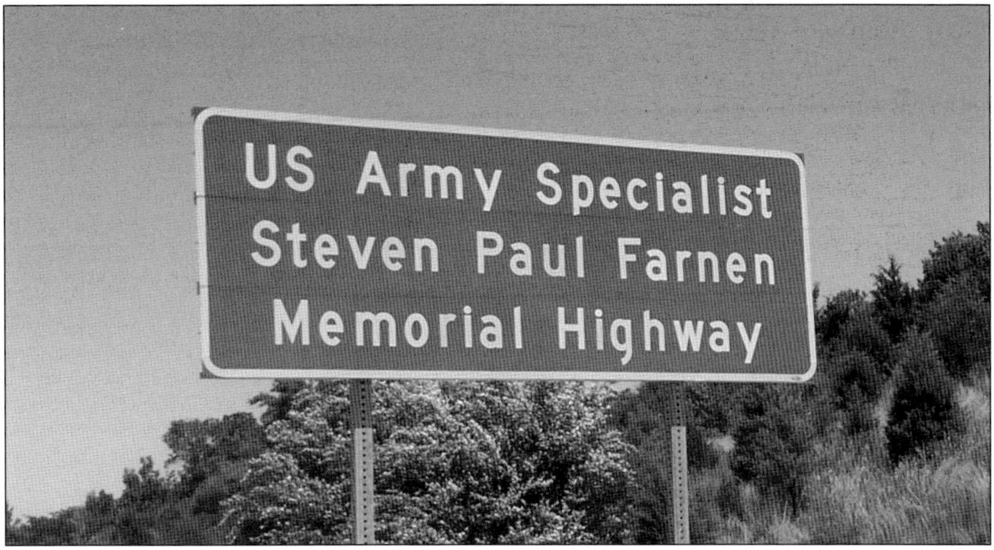

North of Columbia is a stretch of US Highway 63 that was dedicated in honor of Army specialist Steven Paul Farnen on November 5, 2016. Farnen was serving in the Army Reserve when he was recalled to active duty during Operation Desert Storm. The 22-year-old reservist was one of 28 US soldiers killed on February 25, 1991, when sections of an Iraqi Scud missile struck the barracks in which they were housed.

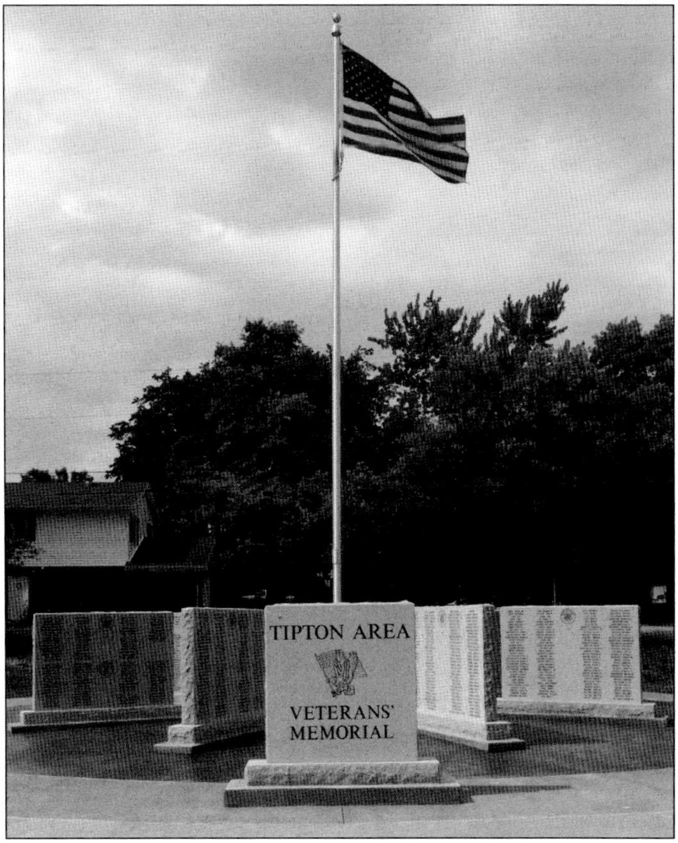

Situated inside the beautiful Tipton City Park, the Tipton Area Veterans' Memorial was dedicated in 2015 in honor of past, present, and future members of the armed forces from around the community. The monument consists of eight granite markers, each dedicated to a specific branch of the military and engraved with the names of local veterans who served in that branch. (Tina Amick.)

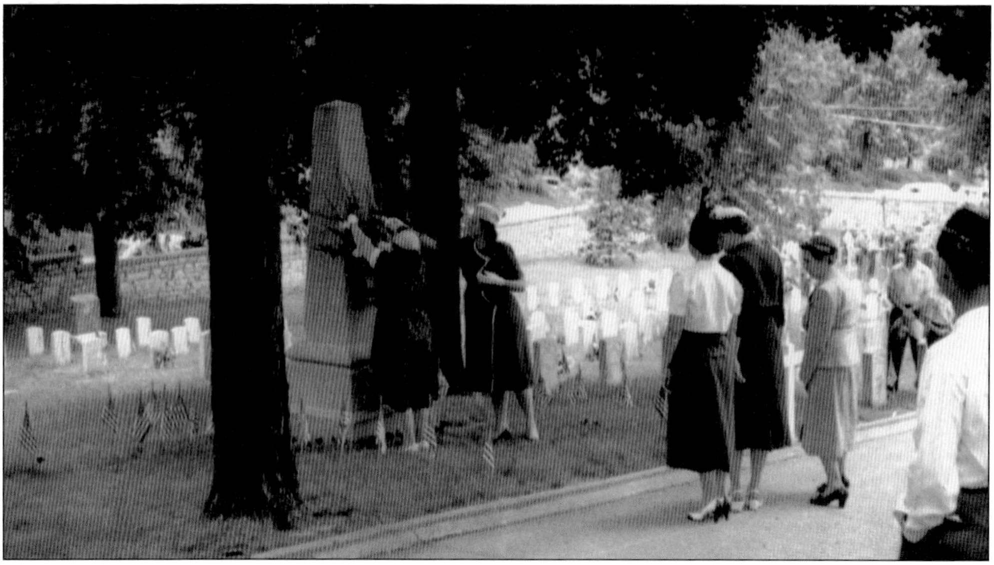

During the Memorial Day ceremony held at the Jefferson City National Cemetery in 1956, members of the local American War Mothers chapter lead a portion of a ceremony during which they place a memorial wreath on a monument honoring soldiers of the 39th Missouri Volunteer Infantry killed in action near Centralia on September 27, 1864. Beneath the monument, in a mass grave, lie the remains of 118 Union soldiers killed by "Bloody Bill" Anderson's bushwhackers. (VFW Post 1003.)

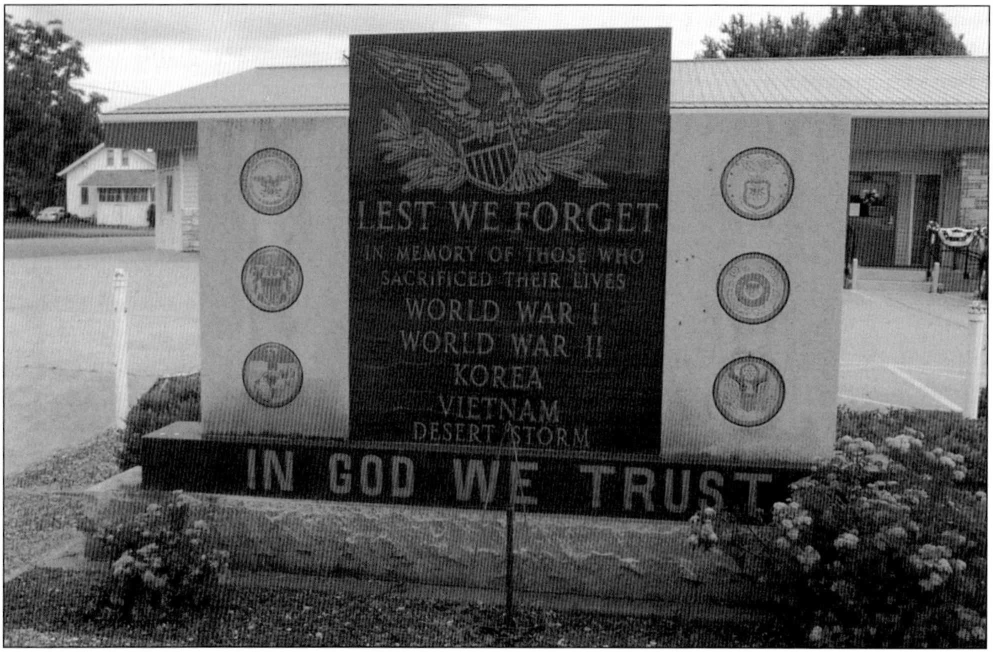

In front of the Bledsoe-Bulas Veterans of Foreign Post 6133 in the Gasconade County community of Owensville stands a memorial to veterans, which was dedicated on May 30, 1988, by the VFW and local members of the community. Behind the memorial are markers honoring the post's namesakes, Wilbur O. Bledsoe and Theodore J. Bulas, both local residents killed while serving with the US Army in World War II.

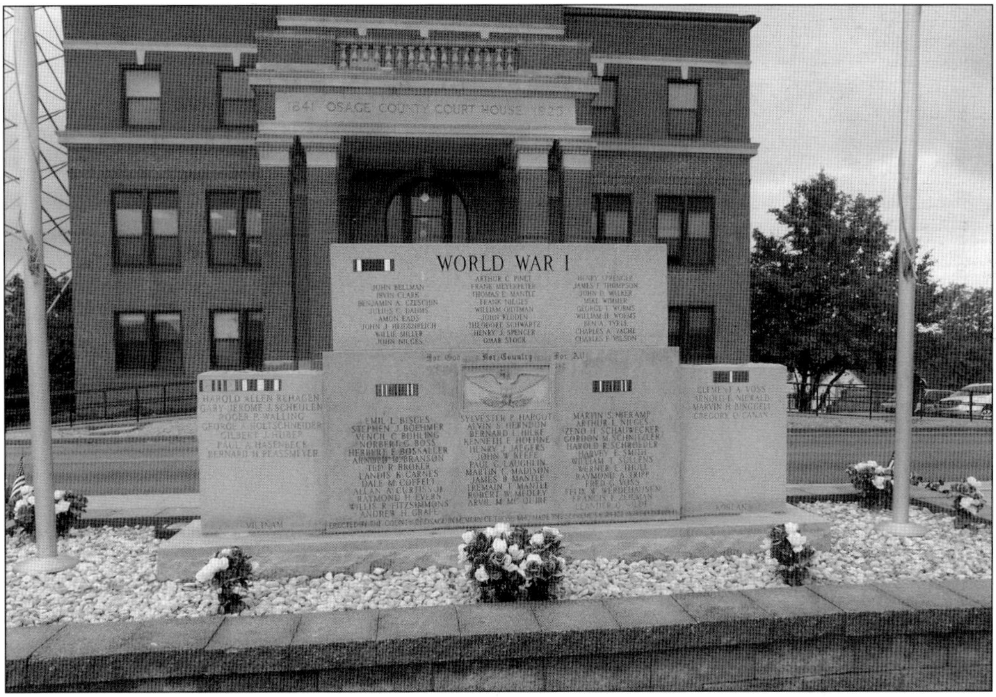

The Veterans of Foreign Wars Post 4756 in cooperation with the county government maintains the Osage County Veteran Memorial located in the square across the highway from the county courthouse in Linn. The memorial was first located next to the courthouse but was moved in 2004 because of the construction of a 911 communication tower. The memorial lists the county's fallen veterans from World War I through the Vietnam War.

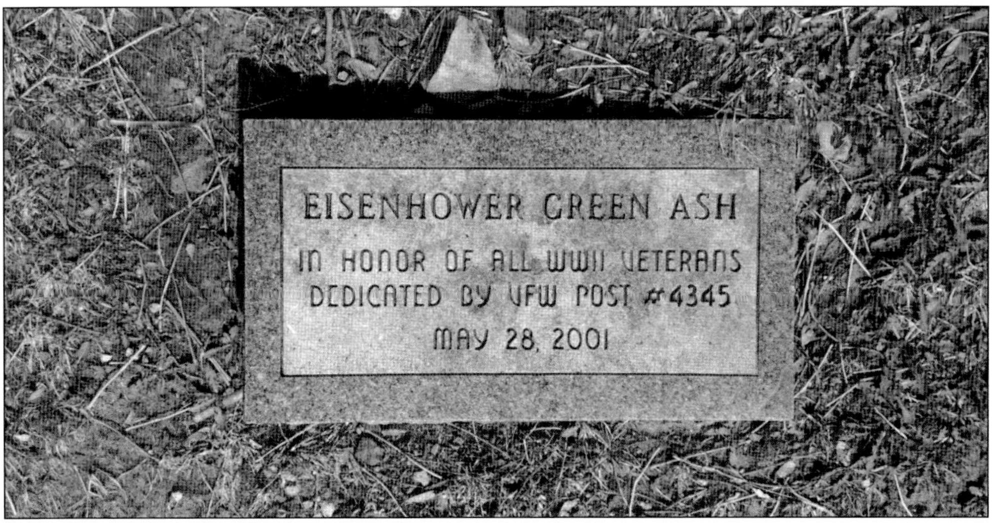

On the south lawn of the Moniteau County Courthouse in California, the Veterans of Foreign Wars Post 4345 planted an Eisenhower Green Ash tree and dedicated a marker "in honor of all WWII veterans" on May 28, 2001. This was part of a program between Scotts Company, Wal-Mart, and the VFW Foundation to plant thousands of Green Ash Trees to recognize veterans. Each tree planted was a direct descendant of the Green Ash tree located at the birthplace of Pres. Dwight D. Eisenhower in Dennison, Texas.

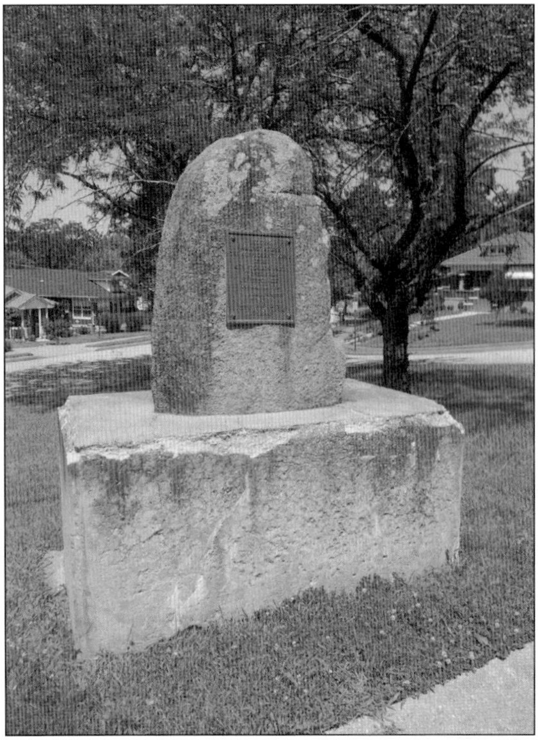

A crowd gathered at a small grassy area at the intersection of Moreau and Hough Park Drives in Jefferson City on April 6, 1933, to dedicate a granite marker with a bronze plaque affixed. The marker, sponsored by the Winnie Davis Chapter of the United Daughters of the Confederacy, designates the area near which Gen. Sterling Price, a Confederate commander, chose to turn away his troops in October 1864 rather than make an attempt to capture Jefferson City.

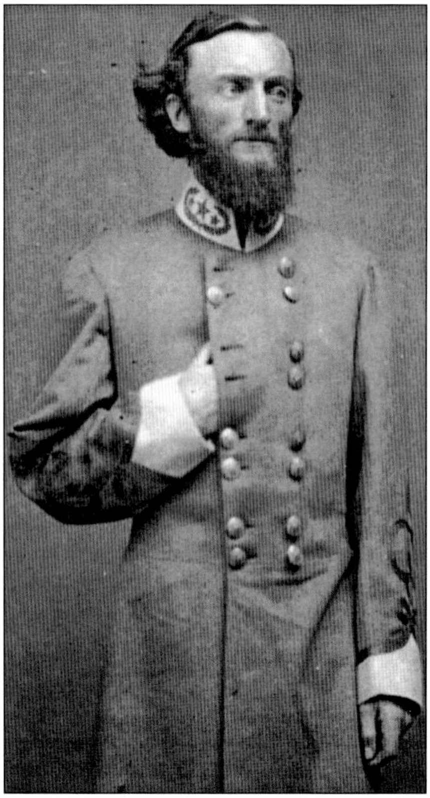

John Sappington Marmaduke was born near Arrow Rock, Missouri, in 1833 and attended college before receiving appointment to the US Military Academy. Following his graduation from West Point in 1857, he served with the Army in Utah and New Mexico but returned to Missouri in 1861 to receive his commission as a colonel in the Confederacy. He was wounded during the Battle of Shiloh but went on to fight in several major campaigns of the Civil War, eventually rising to the rank of major general. (Museum of Missouri Military History.)

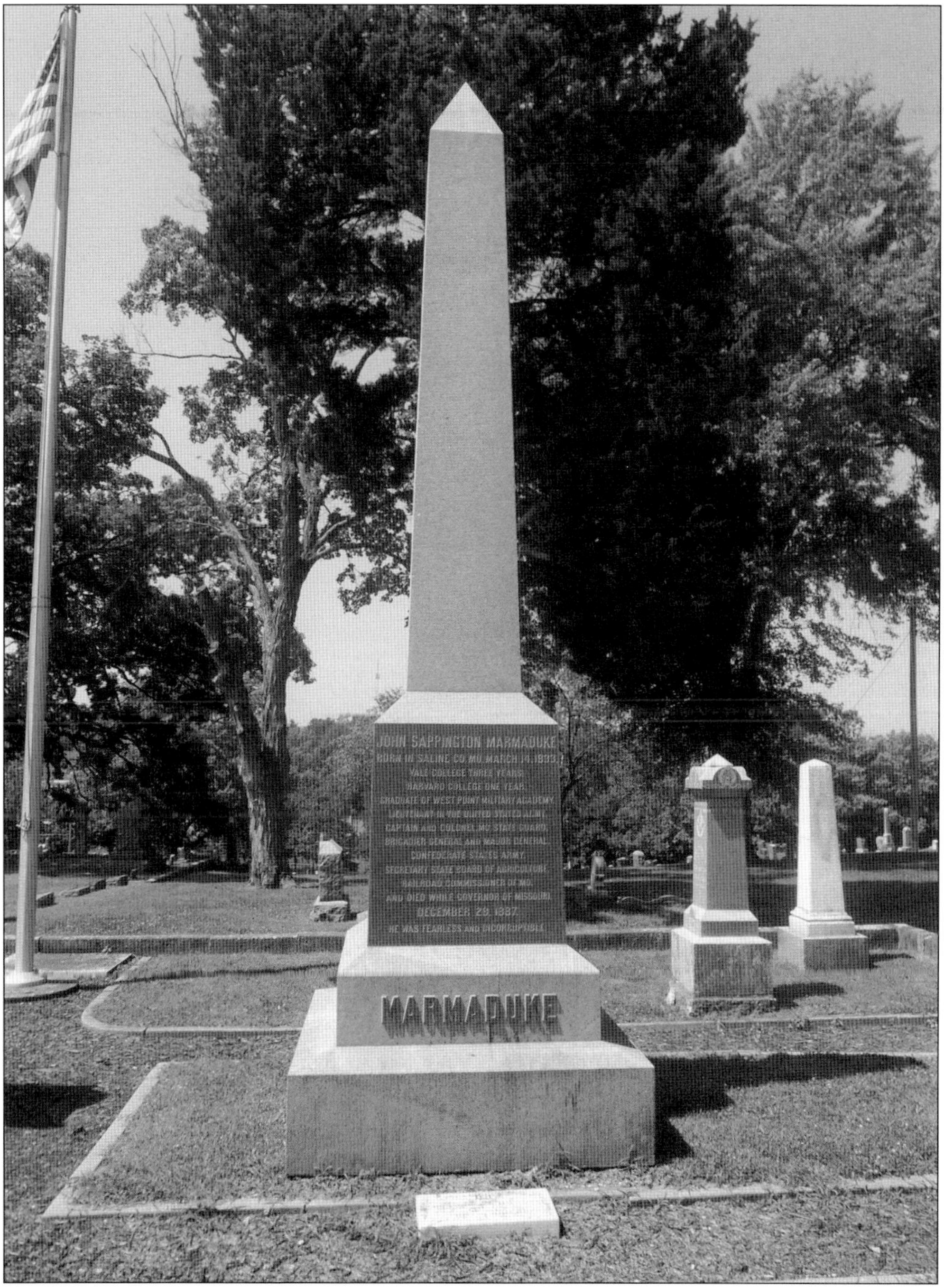

After the Civil War, Marmaduke served on the Missouri Board of Agriculture and the Missouri Railroad Commission before his election as the state's governor in 1884. Marmaduke died from pneumonia while in office on December 28, 1887, and was laid to rest under a massive pink granite obelisk in the Woodland–Old City Cemetery in Jefferson City.

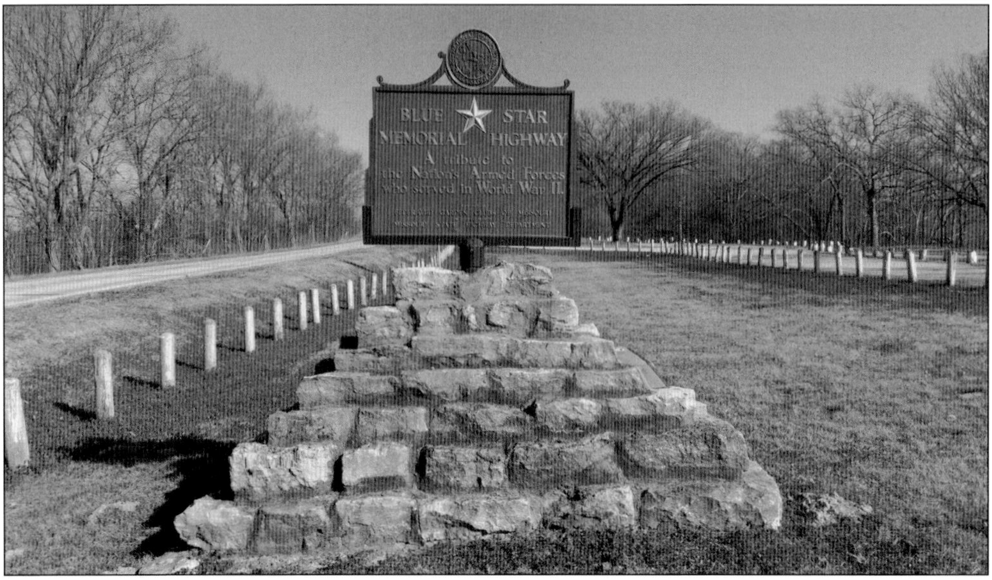

Within the Bradford Roadside Park on Old Highway 50 a couple of miles east of Otterville is the state's second Blue Star Memorial, which was sponsored by the Otterville Garden Club and dedicated on October 20, 1950. According to the Federated Garden Clubs of Missouri, Inc., the memorial was rededicated in 2006. (Tina Amick.)

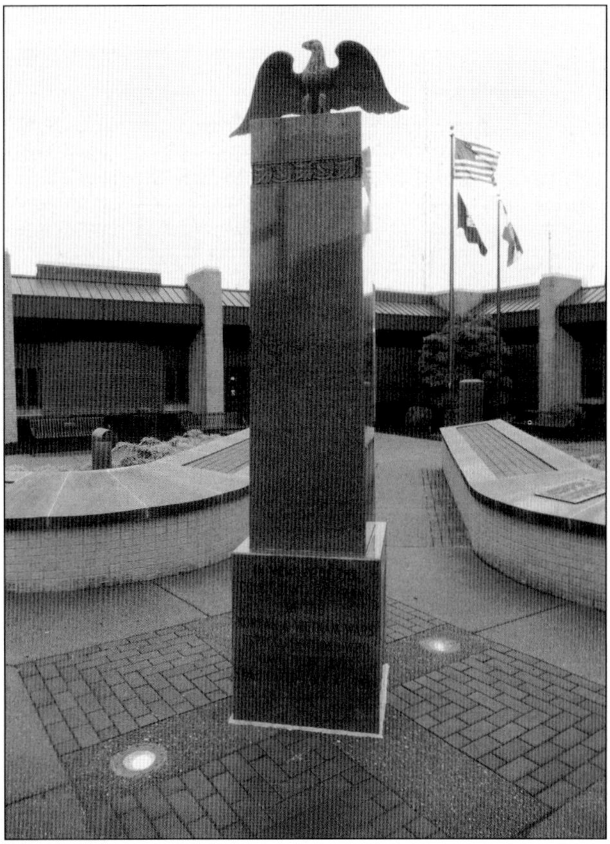

Through the efforts of the Jefferson City Veterans Council, a memorial to veterans of the Korean and Vietnam Wars was dedicated July 4, 1983, on a site provided by the City of Jefferson. The memorial was moved and dedicated at its current location in front of the Jefferson City Police Department on October 9, 2006, and re-designated Veterans Plaza, honoring all veterans who served honorably in the US military.

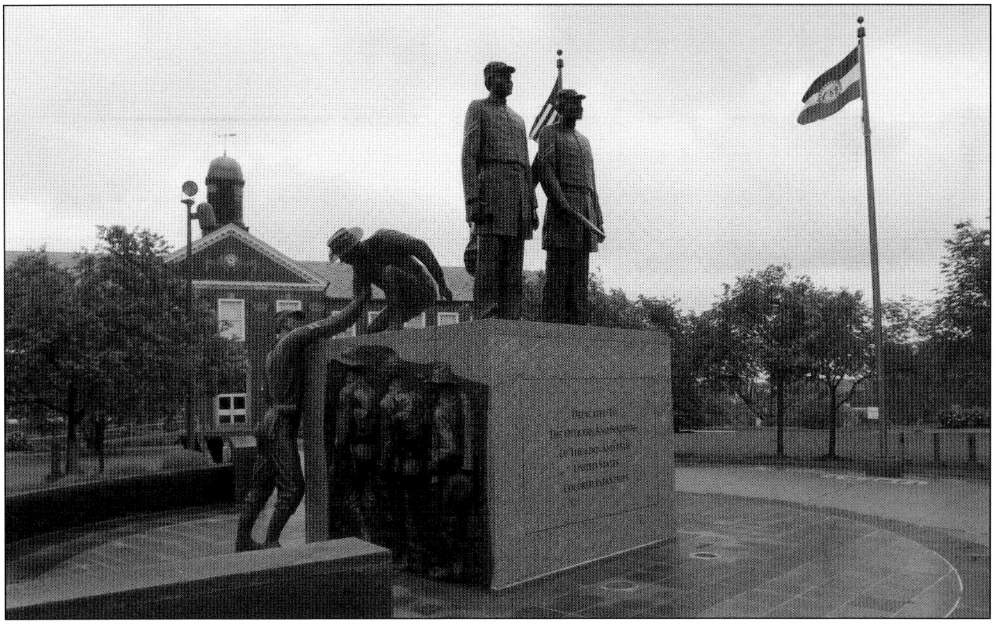

The Soldiers' Memorial Plaza on the campus of the historic Lincoln University in Jefferson City serves as a tribute to the members of the 62nd and 65th Colored Infantry Regiments who founded the educational institution after the Civil War. The monument was dedicated in 2007 and sculpted by Ed Dwight Studios of Kansas City, Missouri.

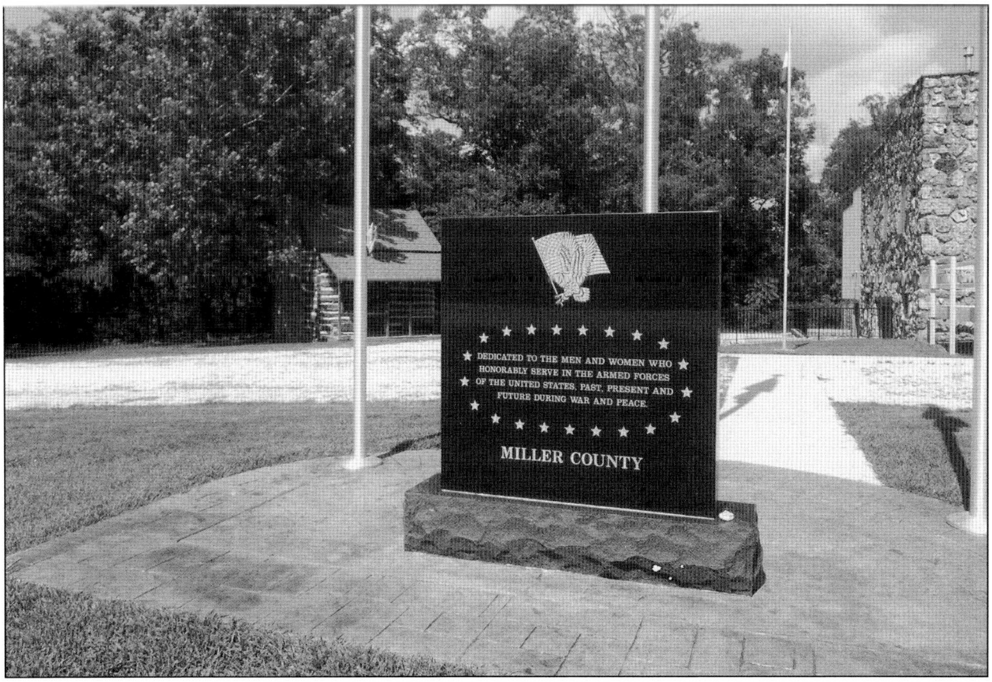

A memorial honoring the veterans of Miller County was dedicated in May 19, 2012, in front the Miller County Museum in Tuscumbia. Local soldiers and members of the Veterans of Foreign Wars Post 2442 participated in the ceremony during which the American flag and the five flags representing each branch of the military were raised.

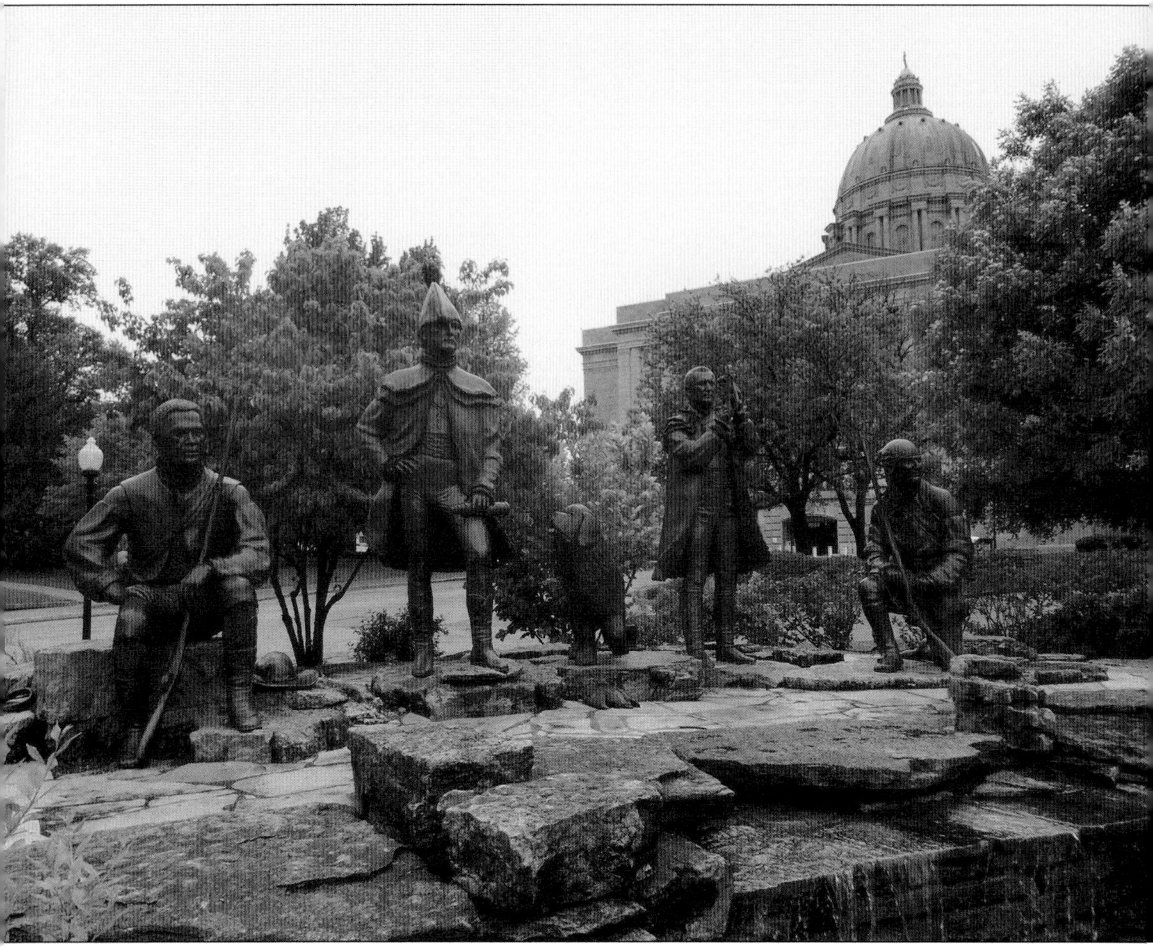

The Lewis and Clark Trailhead Plaza is situated east of the Missouri State Capitol and pays homage to the famed Lewis and Clark Expedition, which passed through Jefferson City. As part of the memorial, bronze statues of the following expedition members are featured looking toward the Missouri River: (from left to right) York, servant to Captain Clark; Capt. Meriwether Lewis; Seaman, Lewis's Newfoundland dog; Capt. William Clark; and George Druillard, hunter and interpreter.

Two

Northern Missouri

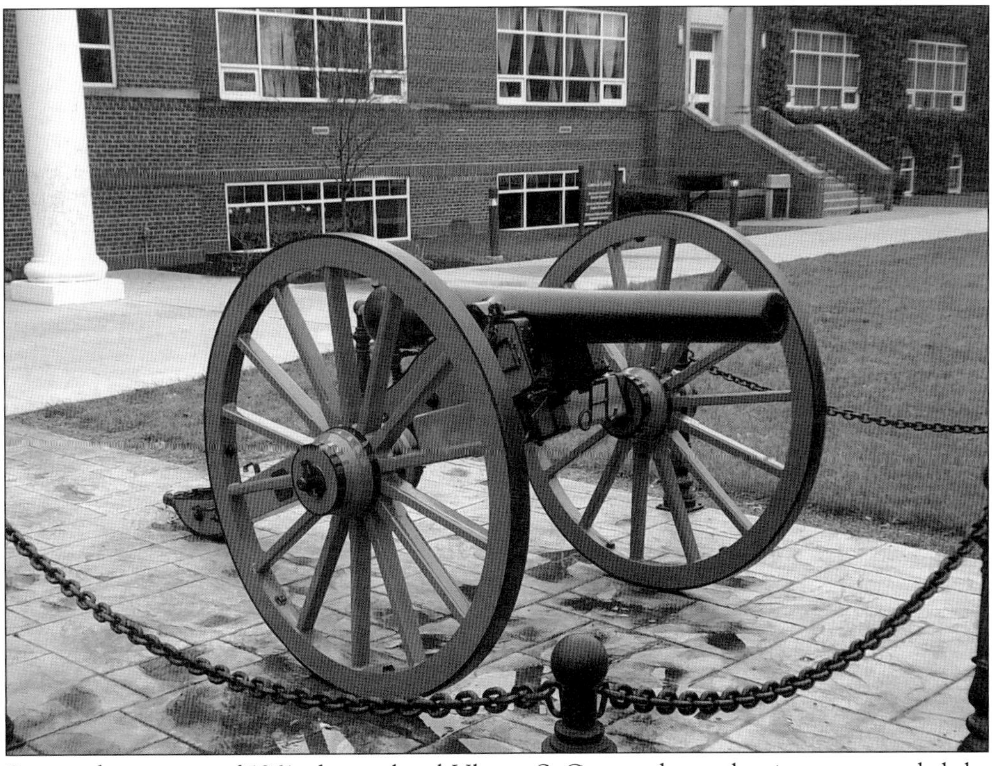

During the summer of 1861, then colonel Ulysses S. Grant, who at the time commanded the 21st Illinois, was stationed in Mexico, Missouri, to help guard railways in the area. In 1964, the Missouri Military Academy in Mexico was celebrating its 75th anniversary when the classes of 1962, 1963, and 1964 dedicated a cannon used by the 21st Illinois during the early days of the Civil War. The cannon was rededicated on September 27, 2014, during the school's 125th anniversary celebration.

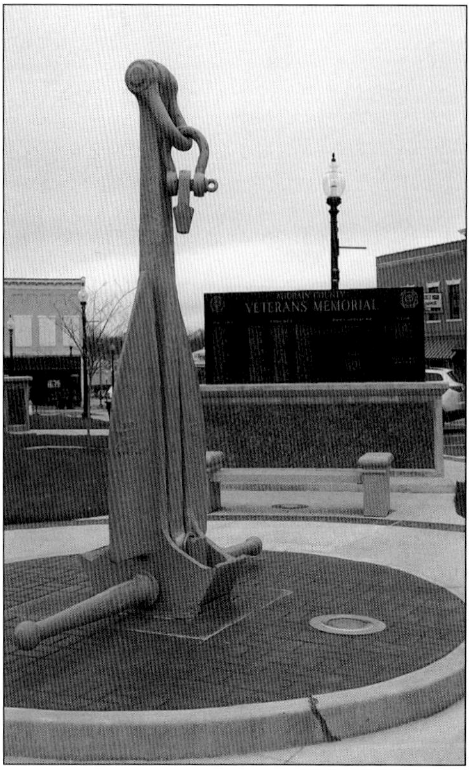

The Missouri Exercise Tiger Army and Navy Anchor Memorial was dedicated on the grounds of the Audrain County Courthouse on April 28, 2000. This memorial honors the brave US soldiers and sailors killed on April 28, 1944, when attacked by German torpedo boats off of Slapton Island in England while conducting a large-scale exercise in preparation for the D-day landings. Many of those killed were Missouri residents of the 3206th Quartermaster Service Company who were serving aboard LSTs (Landing Ship Tanks) destroyed in the attack. (Tina Amick.)

A memorial to all veterans "who served in the country in both war and peace" was dedicated on the lawn of the Saline County Courthouse in Marshall in 1991. It was constructed from angled red granite columns with black plaques. A dominant feature of the memorial is a bronze bald eagle with spread wings atop a pedestal.

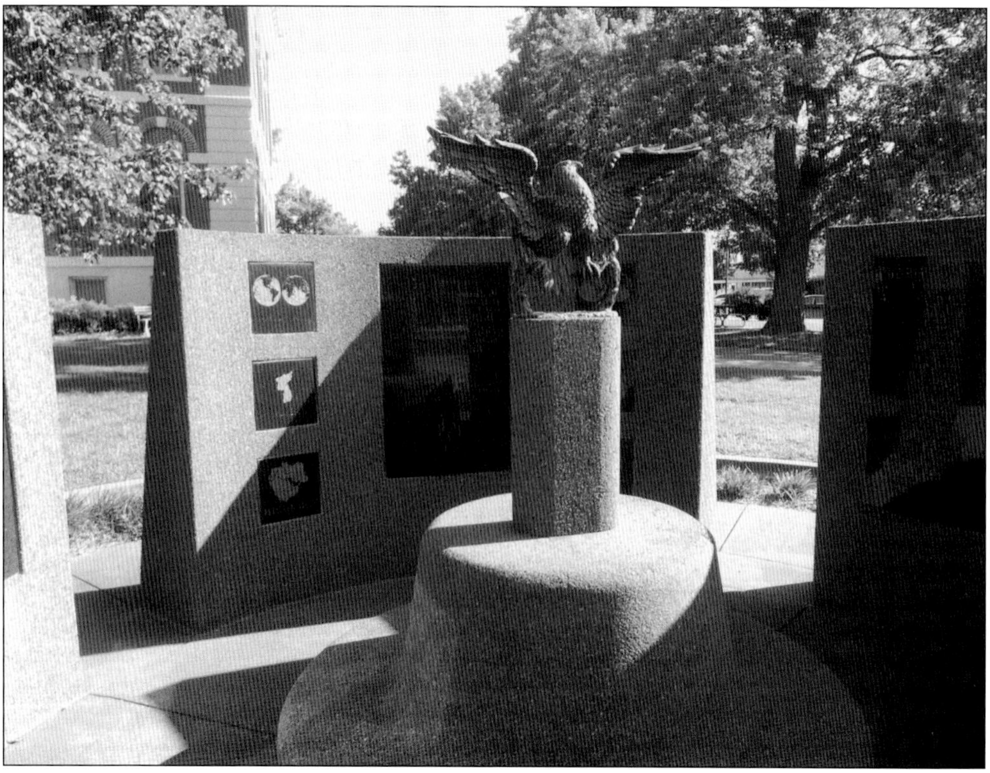

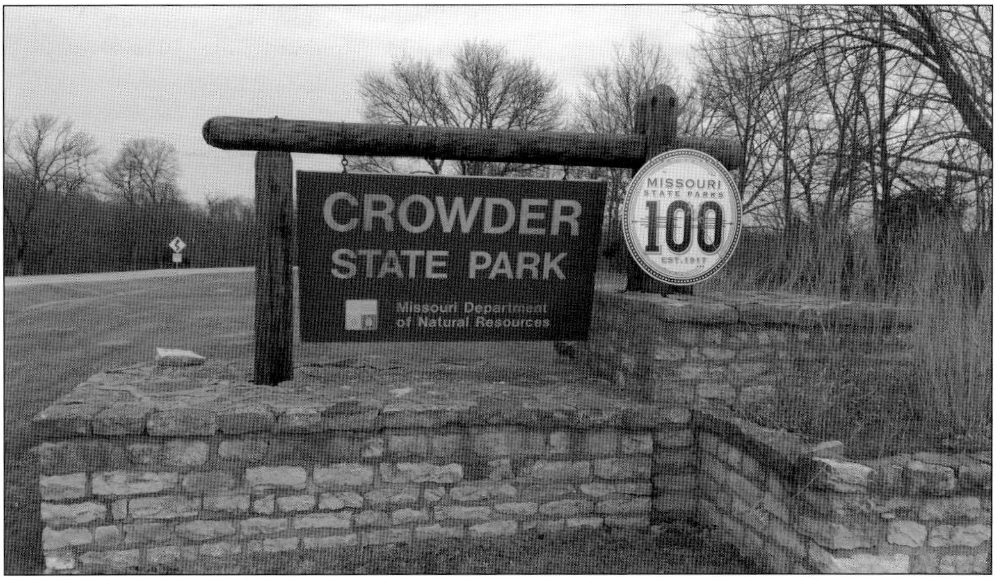

Located west of Trenton is Crowder State Park—an expansive memorial to the memory of the late Maj. Gen. Enoch H. Crowder. Development of the 650-acre tract that would become the state park began in 1939 through work performed by the Civilian Conservation Corps. In later years, the park has remained a Missouri state park, has grown in size to 1,912 acres, and now includes the 18-acre Crowder Lake.

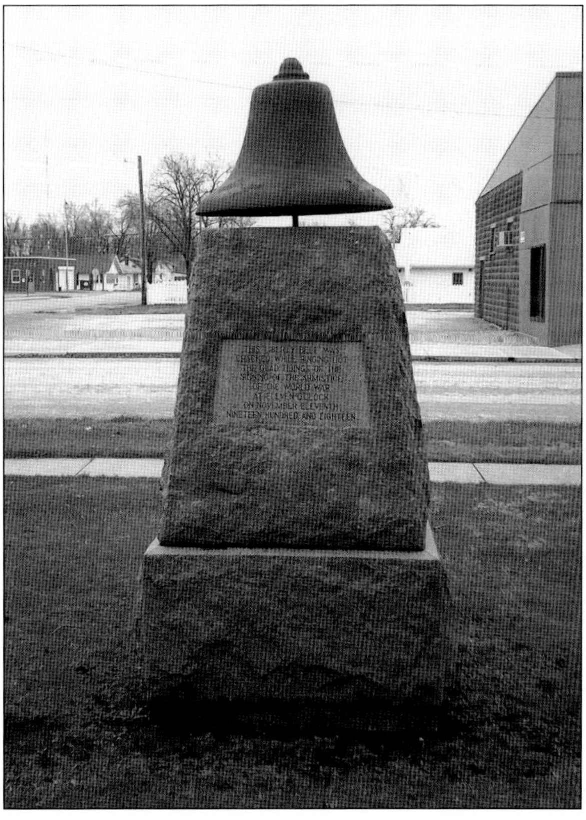

In the northwest corner of Stone Street Park in Vandalia is this Liberty bell that is displayed on a granite shaft. Although it used to be a city fire bell, it cracked in a fashion similar to the original Liberty Bell in Philadelphia when being rung in celebration of Armistice Day, November 11, 1918. The citizens of Vandalia dedicated the bell on November 11, 1938, as a memorial to the memory of those who had served in the military. (Tina Amick.)

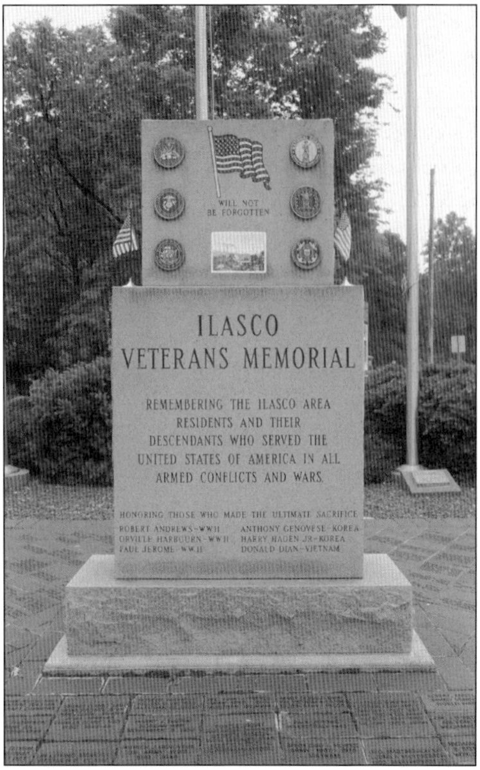

The Village of Ilasco was a once-thriving immigrant community located a few miles south of Hannibal. Established as a company town, the village was at one time home to 3,000 residents who came from Romania, Slovakia, Italy, Poland, Croatia, Hungary, and Ukraine to work at the nearby Atlas Portland Cement Plant. Although the community was dissolved in 1963, the descendants of Ilasco have erected memorials to preserve the former village's rich history, including a tablet to honor their local veterans of the armed forces.

The Marion County Veterans Memorial, erected in 1962, is a concrete structure with tablets listing the names of local citizens who served in World War I and II. Located in Central Park in downtown area of Hannibal, the memorial was sponsored by the Service Mothers of World War II, the local American Legion post, the City of Hannibal, Marion County, and the State of Missouri. A commemorative plaque has since been added to honor the service of local men and women who also served during the Korean and Vietnam Wars.

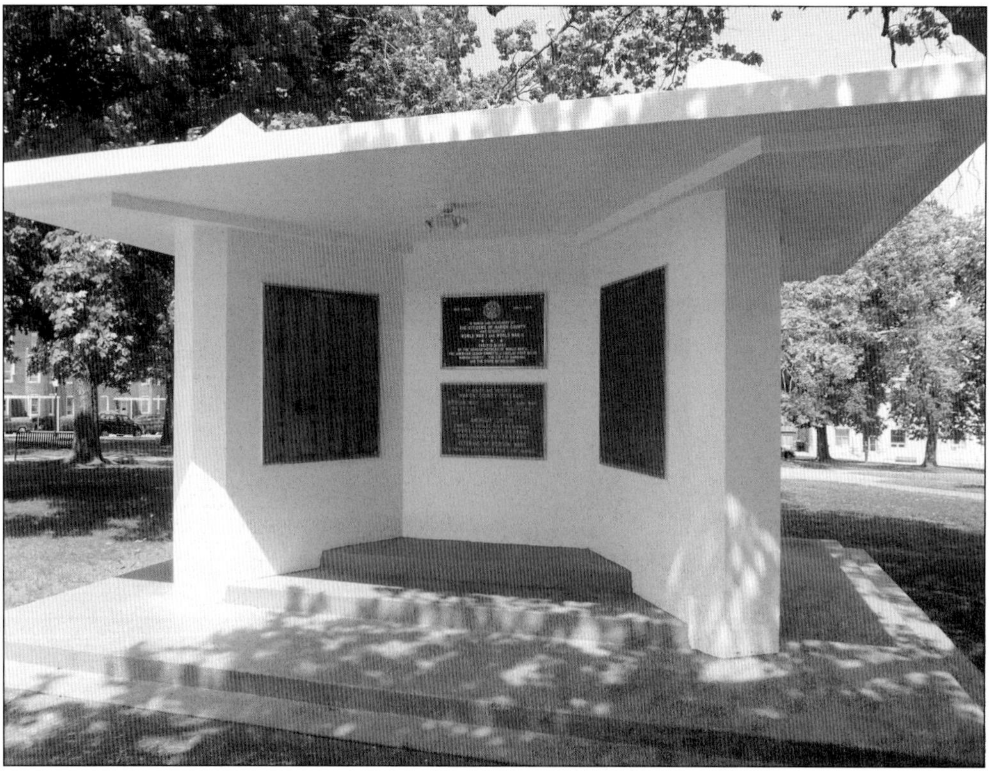

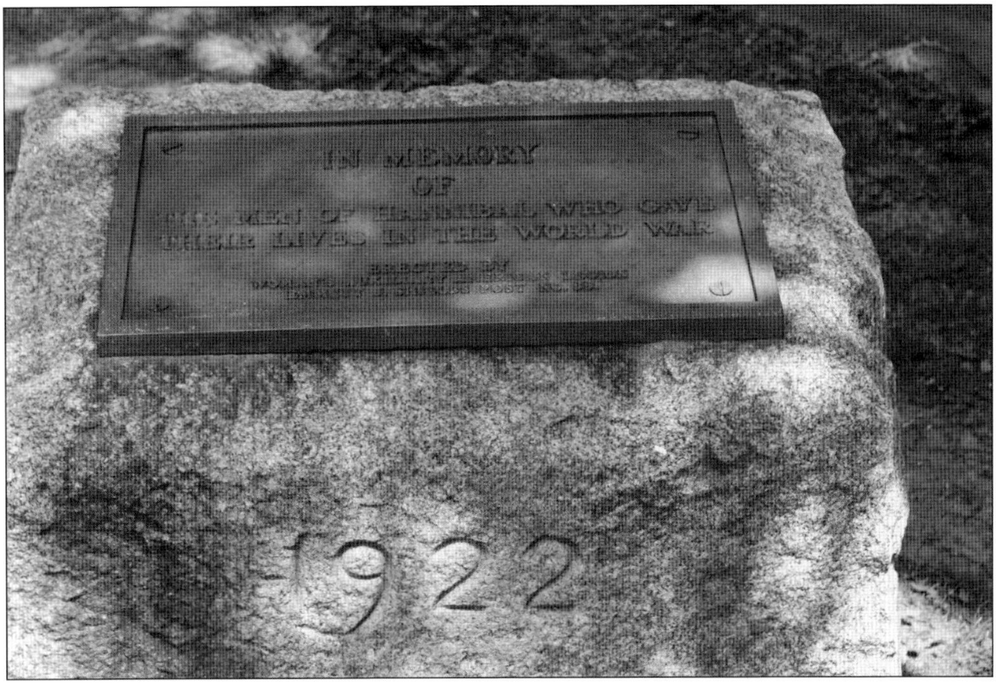

Although it has been virtually eclipsed by the prominent stature of the Marion County Veterans Memorial, the World War I memorial in Central Park in Hannibal predates its companion military memorial by four decades. Erected in 1922 by the local American Legion Emmet J. Shields Post 55 and its auxiliary, this small, square, and unadorned memorial consists of a bronze tablet on a stone and was dedicated in honor of the men of Hannibal who served during World War I.

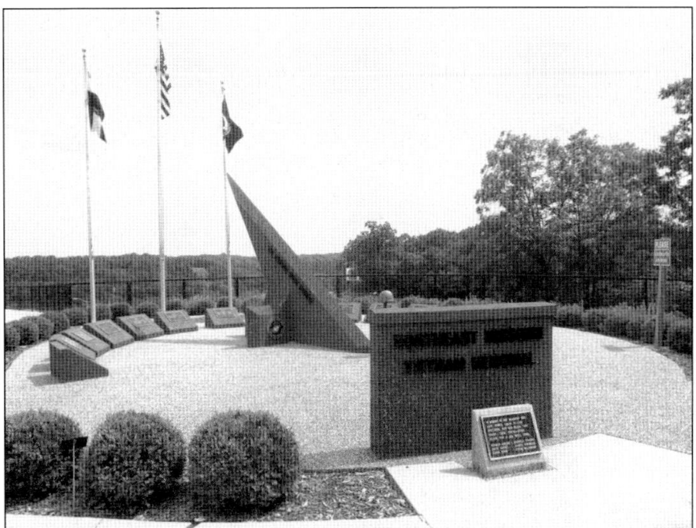

In 2010, on a site at the US Army Corps of Engineers' M.W. Boudreaux Memorial Visitor Center overlooking the Clarence Cannon Dam and Mark Twain Lake near Perry, the Northeast Missouri Vietnam Memorial opened to the public. The expansive memorial has been used as the site for "Welcome Home Vietnam Veterans" celebration events and features a 12-month sundial. (Tina Amick.)

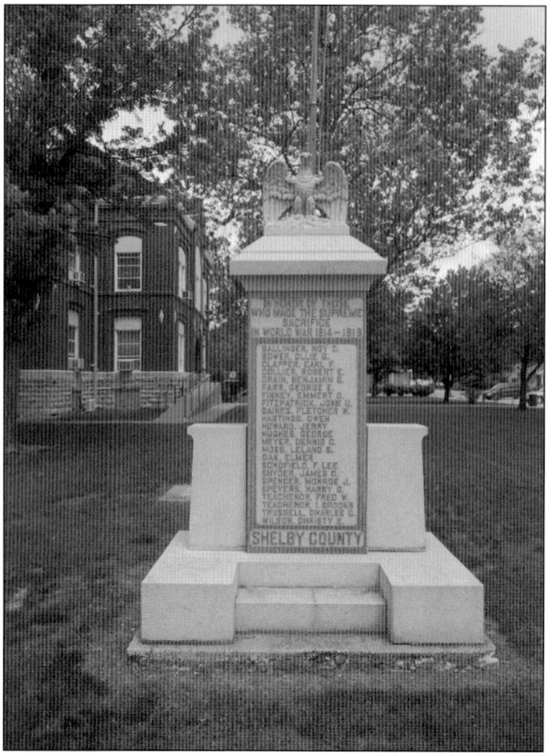

The Shelby County War Memorial was unveiled to the public on the lawn of the county courthouse in Shelbyville during a ceremony held on July 4, 1926. The memorial, which was constructed by the monuments manufacturers Bedwell and Sons from nearby Shelbina, lists the names of 23 local service members who lost their lives during the war.

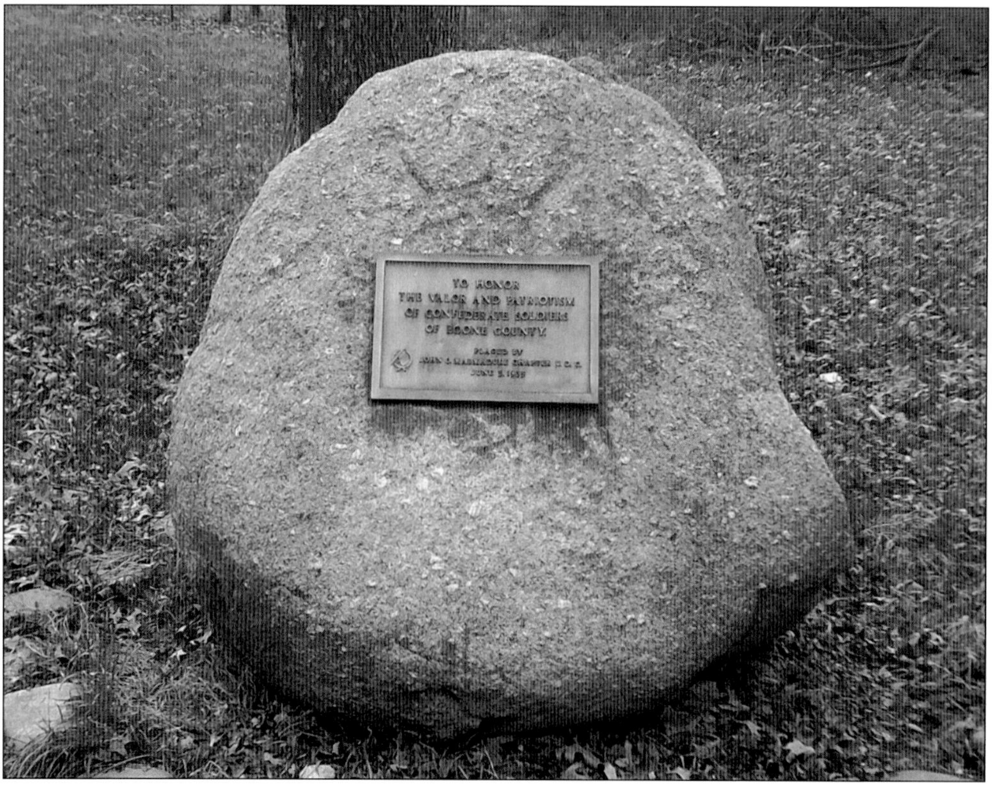

On June 3, 1935, members of the John S. Marmaduke Chapter of the United Daughters of the Confederacy dedicated a memorial in honor of the Boone County residents who served the Confederacy during the Civil War. The memorial consists of a plaque affixed to a red granite stone and for decades was situated in front of the Boone County Courthouse. In 2015, the county commission voted to relocate the memorial to the Centralia Battlefield. (Tina Amick.)

The Centralia Battlefield is located approximately three miles southeast of Centralia. On September 27, 1864, forces led by guerilla leader "Bloody Bill" Anderson stopped a train near Centralia that carried 23 recently discharged and furloughed Union soldiers. All but one of the Union soldiers were executed, and this event became known as the Centralia Massacre. In 2003, the Col. James S. Searcy Camp 1923 of the Sons of the Confederate Veterans dedicated this monument describing the day's horrific events. (Tina Amick.)

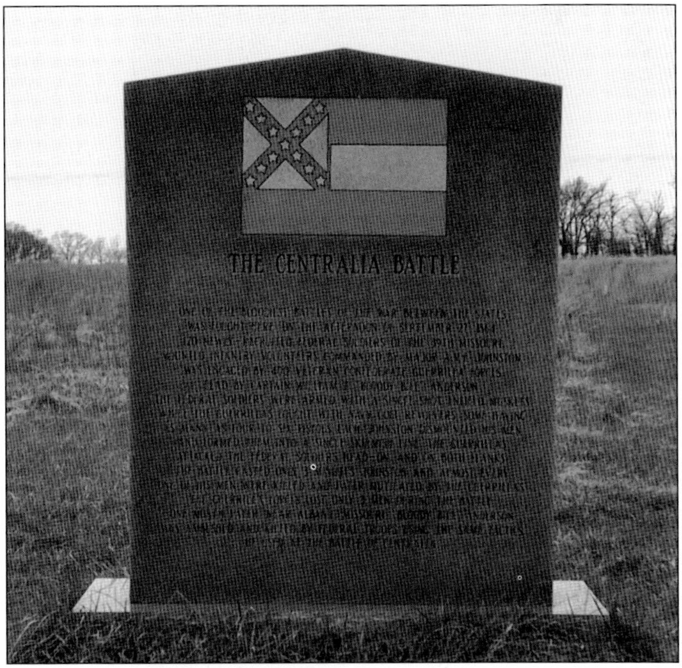

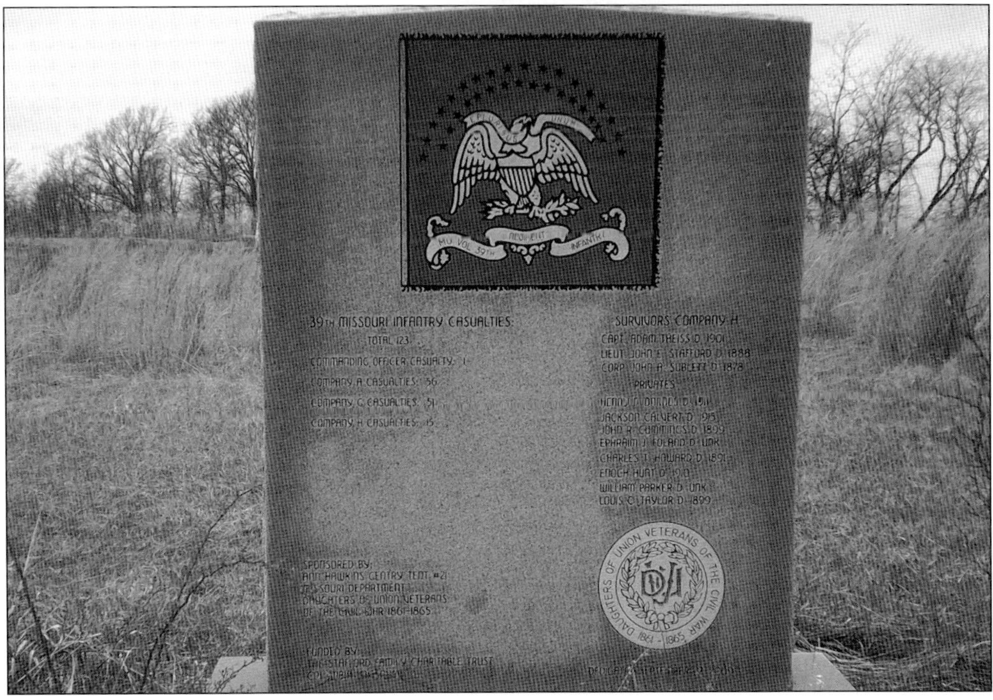

In the afternoon following the massacre that occurred on the morning of September 27, 1864, Union major A.V.E. Johnston led 155 soldiers of the 39th Missouri Mounted Infantry Volunteers to intercept and attack the forces of "Bloody Bill" Anderson. The guerrilla forces prevailed during the Battle of Centralia, killing 123 Union soldiers, including Major Johnston. The Daughters of Union Veterans of the Civil War dedicated this monument to the memory of the Union soldiers on September 27, 2009, at the Centralia Battlefield site. (Tina Amick.)

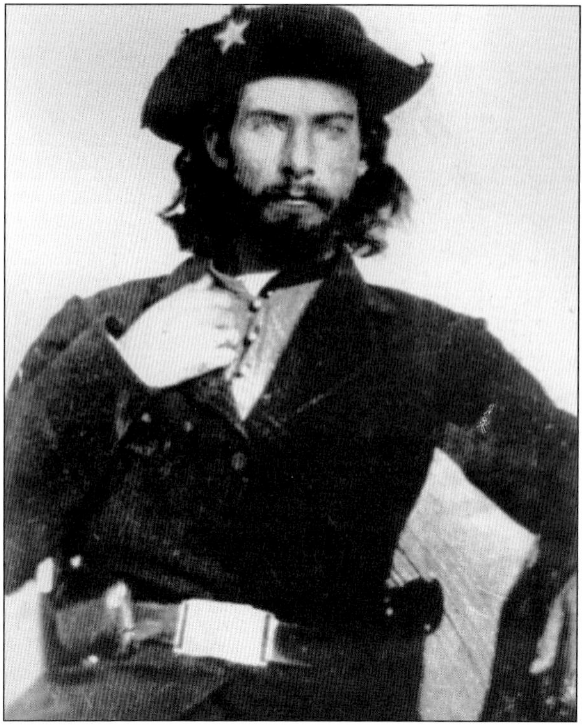

William "Bloody Bill" Anderson conducted many brutal raids during the Civil War in locations including Texas, Kansas, and Missouri. In addition to orchestrating the deadly attack against Union forces during the Centralia Massacre and the Battle of Centralia, the Confederate guerrilla also took part in Quantrill's raid on Lawrence, Kansas, in 1863. Anderson was killed by Missouri State Militia on October 24, 1864, when his camp was discovered near Albany, Missouri. (Museum of Missouri Military History.)

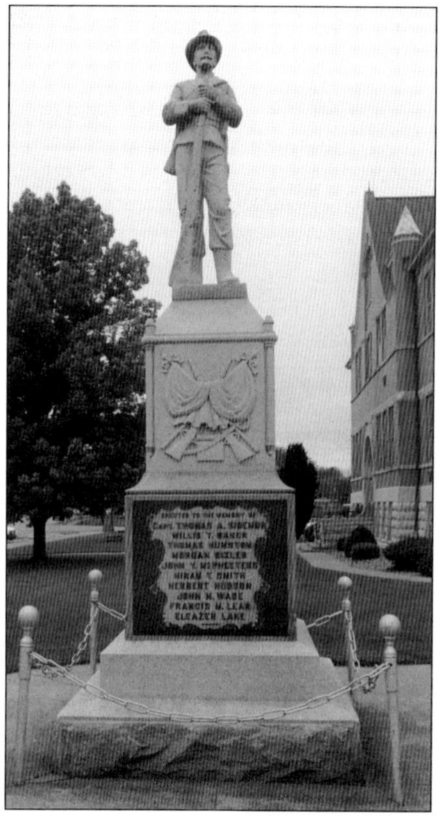

On October 18, 1862, ten Confederate prisoners were executed at Palmyra's fairgrounds in retaliation for the murder of a pro-Union citizen the previous month by Confederate forces under the command of Col. Joseph Porter. In 1907, a monument was erected on the grounds of the Marion County Courthouse to honor the memory of the executed Confederate prisoners. The monument features the figure of a Confederate soldier in addition to a bas-relief of Confederate flags draped over crossed rifles.

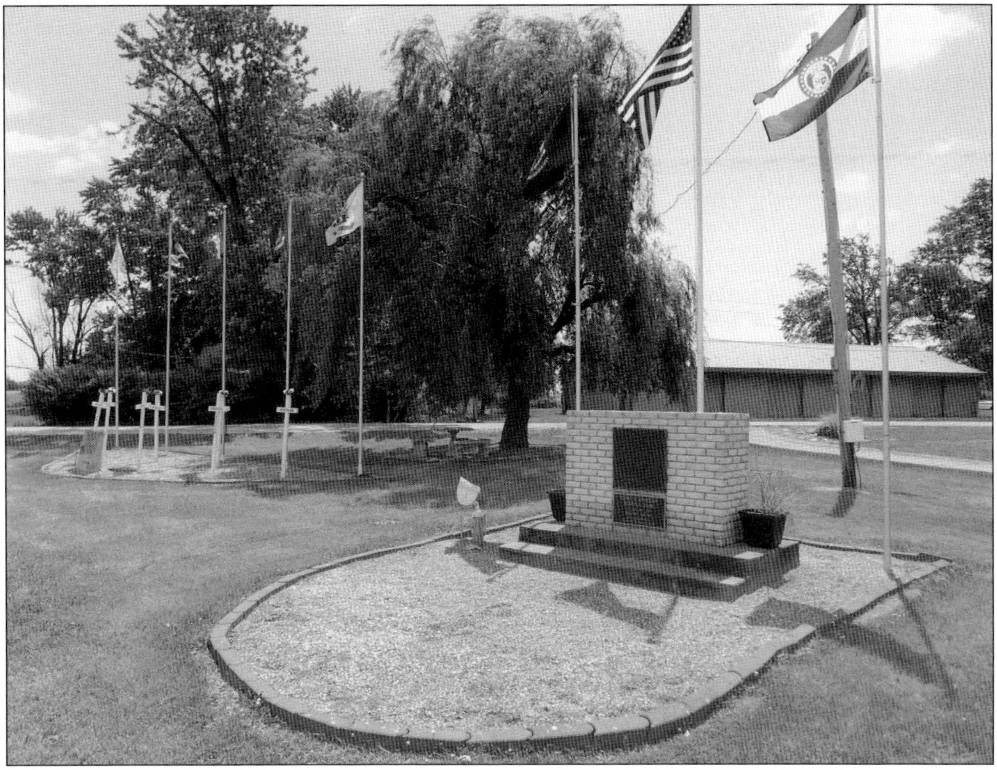

Along Highway 19 in the northwest Missouri community of Center is the half-acre Harry A. Anderson Memorial Park, named for a local World War I veteran who died in 1989. A brick and stone monument was dedicated by the local Veterans of Foreign Wars Post in 1973. The VFW post later disbanded, and the park was taken over by the city; however, since that time, a second memorial adjacent to the first has been added and is comprised of white crosses representing many of the wars in which the United States has been involved. (Tina Amick.)

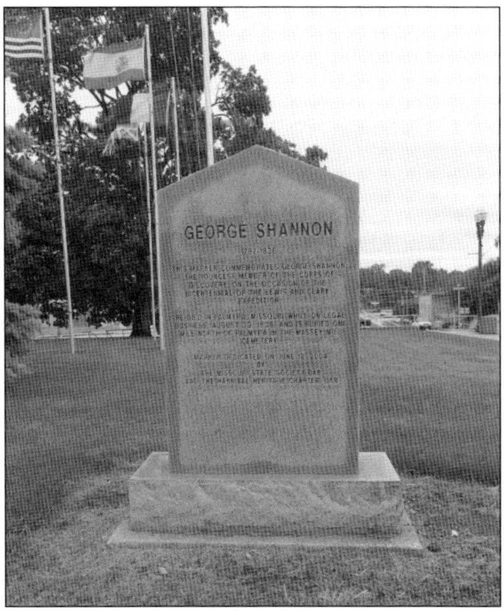

A memorial to the memory of Pvt. George Shannon was dedicated on the lawn of the Marion County Courthouse in Palmyra on June 13, 2004. Shannon acquired recognition as the youngest member of one of the most notable military missions to take place within the United States—the Corps of Discovery, otherwise known as the Lewis and Clark Expedition. He later became a lawyer and died while working a case in court in Palmyra in 1836; he is buried in a cemetery north of town.

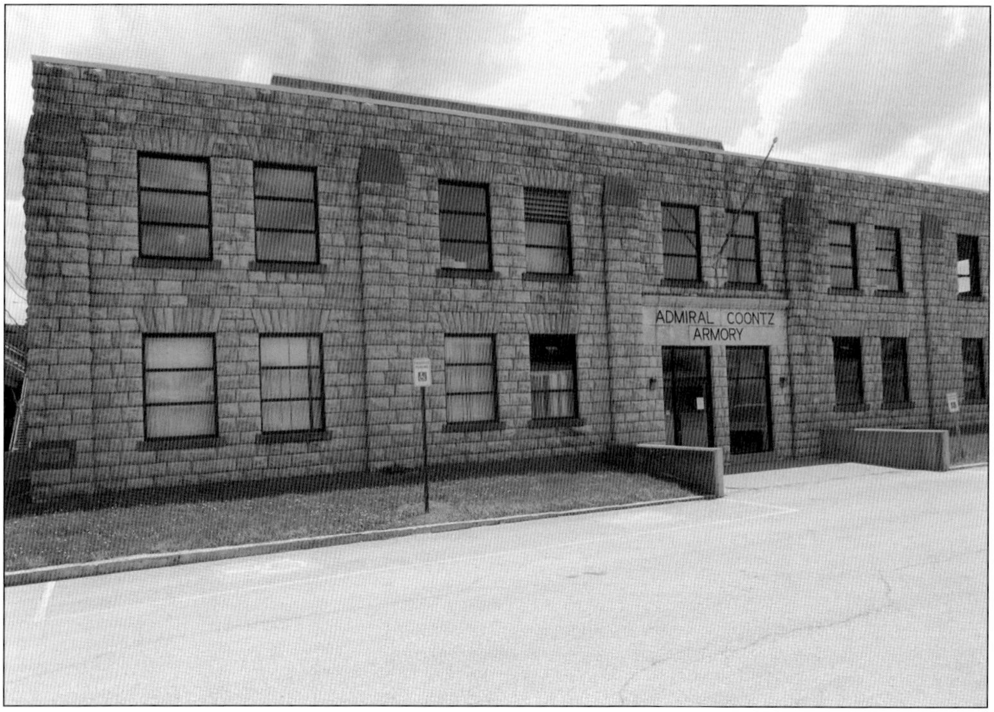

Construction on the Admiral Coontz Armory in Hannibal was completed in 1939 as a project primarily funded through a grant under the Great Depression program known as the Works Progress Administration. The armory was constructed using limestone from a local quarry and cost a total of $85,000 to build. The armory was used by the Missouri National Guard until 1977 and has since become a city-owned recreation center. (Tina Amick.)

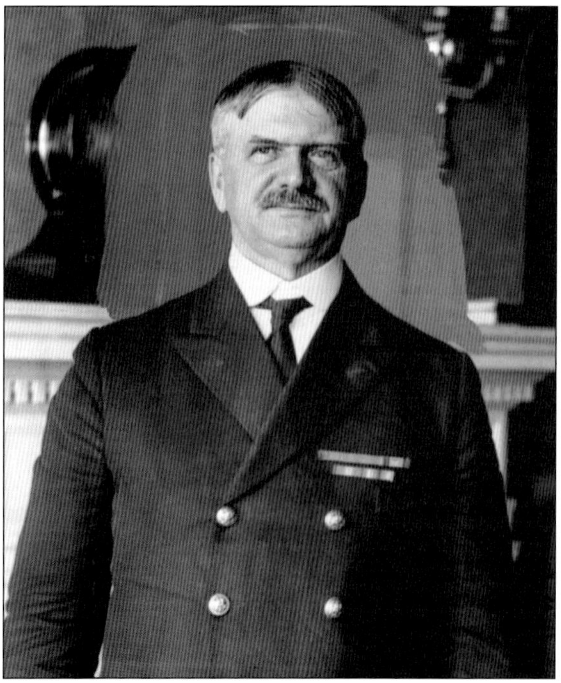

The Admiral Coontz Armory, now the Admiral Coontz Recreation Center, was named in honor of the late Robert E. Coontz, who was born and raised in Hannibal and later received appointment to the US Naval Academy. During his military career, he rose to the rank of four-star admiral and was selected to serve as chief of naval operations in 1919. Coontz passed away in 1935 and is buried in Mt. Olivet Cemetery in Hannibal.

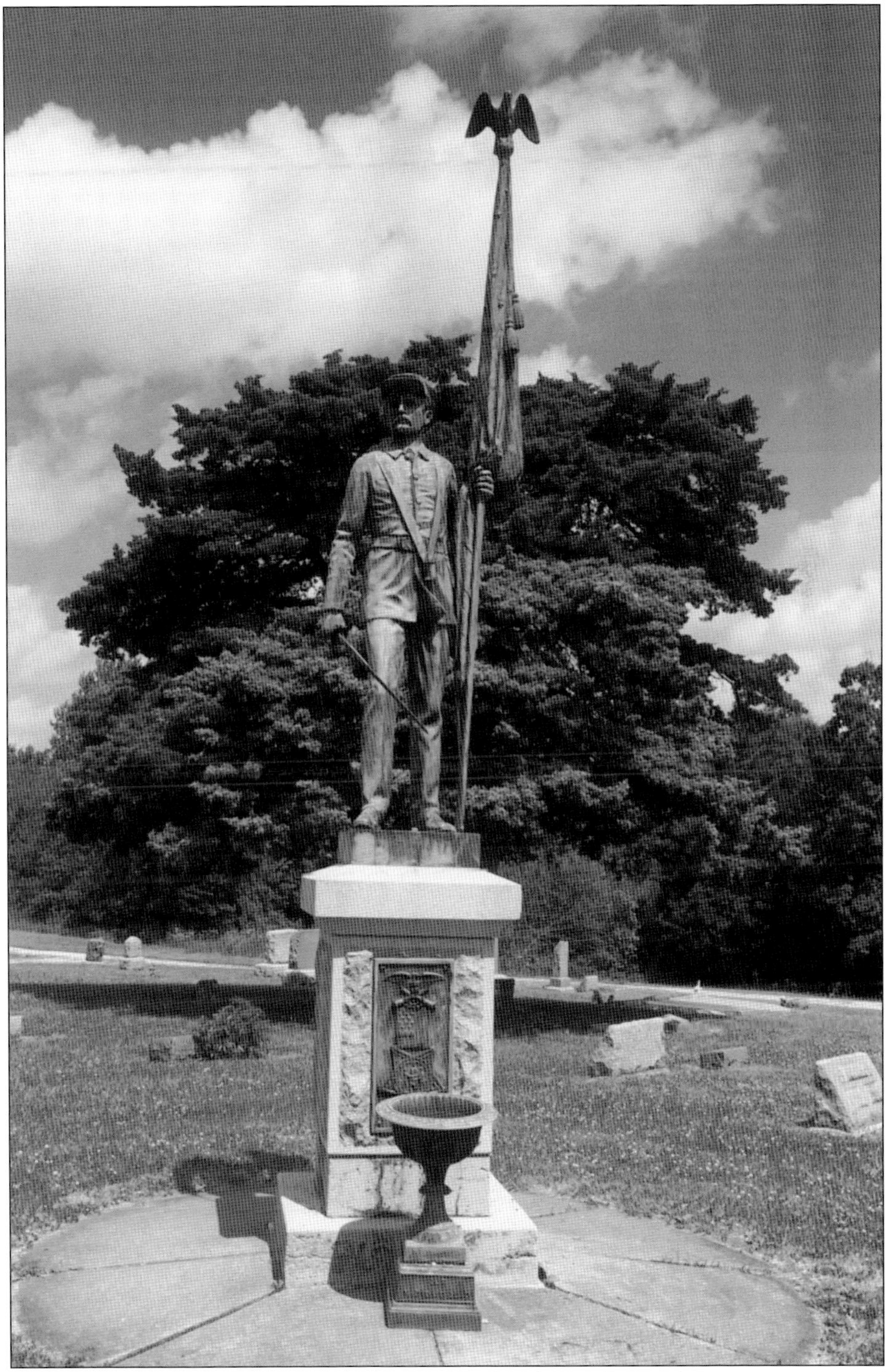

Erected in 1915 during the 50th anniversary of the end of the Civil War, this monument in Laclede City Cemetery features a Union soldier standing tall holding a flag in his left hand and a sword in his right. The project cost $625 and was sponsored by the Phil Kearney Post of the Grand Army of the Republic, Inc., which was mustered in Laclede in 1882. (Shawn C. Johnson.)

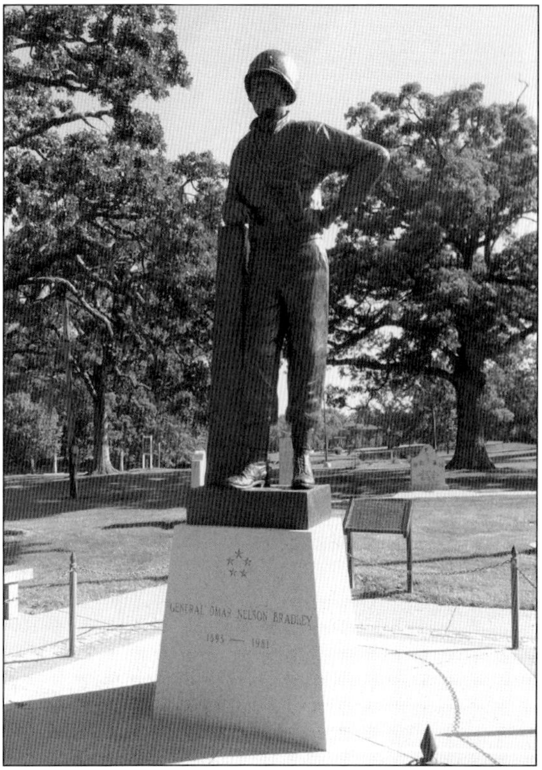

Situated in the War Memorial Plaza within Rothwell Park in Moberly stands an audacious tribute to Gen. Omar Bradley, which was funded entirely from donations received both locally and nationwide. The memorial was sculpted by the late Jim Brothers, who also created a centerpiece for the National D-day Memorial in Bedford, Virginia, and a likeness of Dwight D. Eisenhower that stands in the Capitol. Every couple of years, local Boy Scouts and volunteers wash down the Bradley statue and apply a coat of wax to prevent it from turning green.

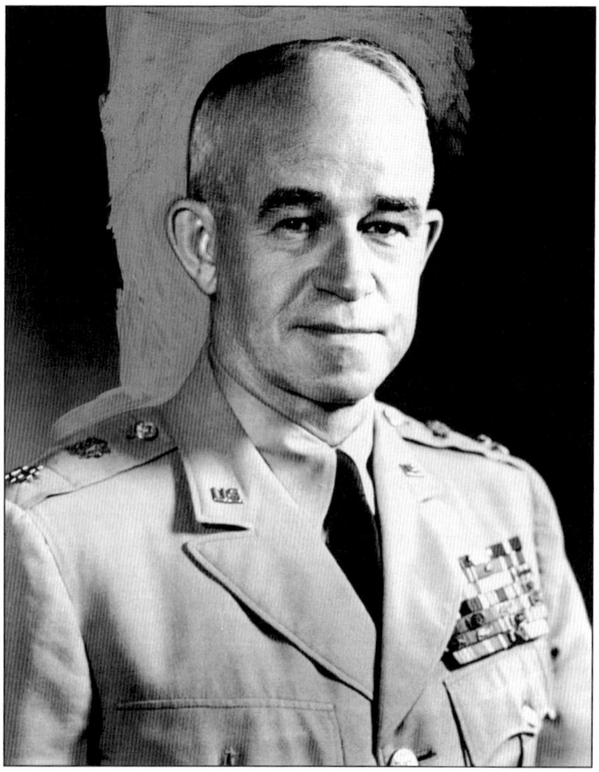

Omar Bradley was born near the Randolph County community of Clark on February 12, 1893, and later attended high school at nearby Moberly. Following his graduation from West Point in 1915, he rose through the ranks of the US Army and, during the latter part of World War II, became an army group commander with more than 1.3 million troops under his command. In 1949, he became the first chairman of the Joint Chiefs of Staff and, as of the publication of this book, was the last five-star general of the US military.

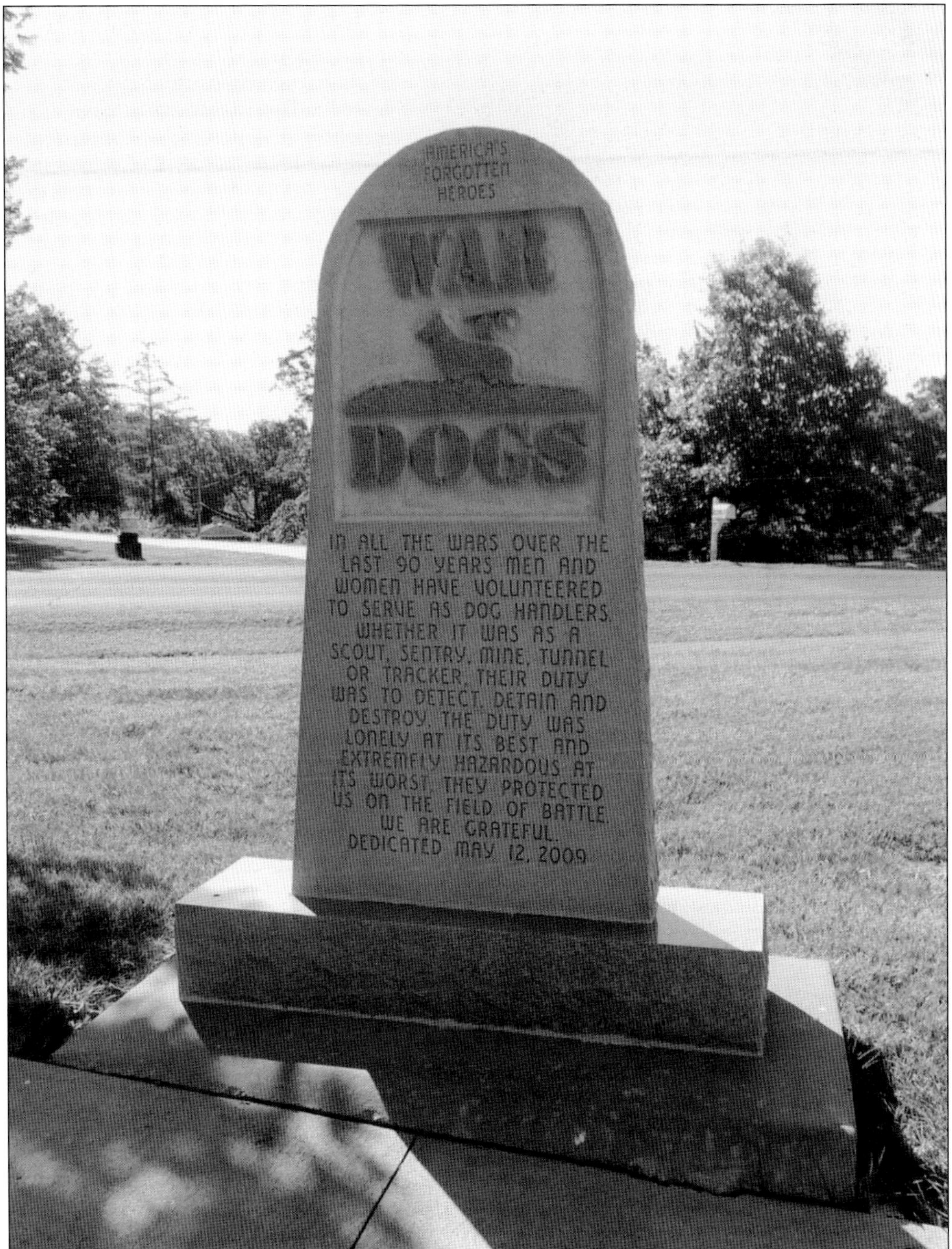

Also located in the 447-acre Rothwell Park in Moberly is a monument recognizing the contributions made by "War Dogs." The tribute to military canines was dedicated in 2009 and was the result of the efforts of the late John David Harris (1941–2013) of Moberly—a member of the National Vietnam Dog Handler association and an Air Force veteran who served as one of the earliest K-9 handler's in the Vietnam War.

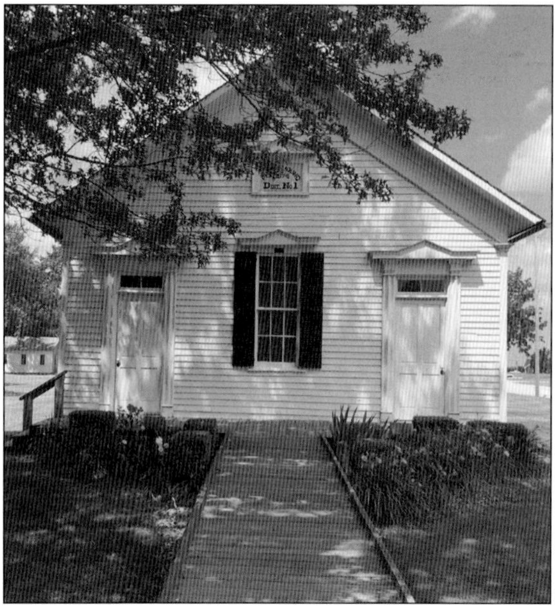

At the Gen. John J. Pershing Boyhood Home State Historic Site in the town of Laclede is the Prairie Mound School building where Pershing taught a couple of years prior to attending the US Military Academy at West Point. The schoolhouse was once located several miles outside of Laclede but has been moved to the historic site and is now used as a museum in honor of Pershing's life. (Shawn C. Johnson.)

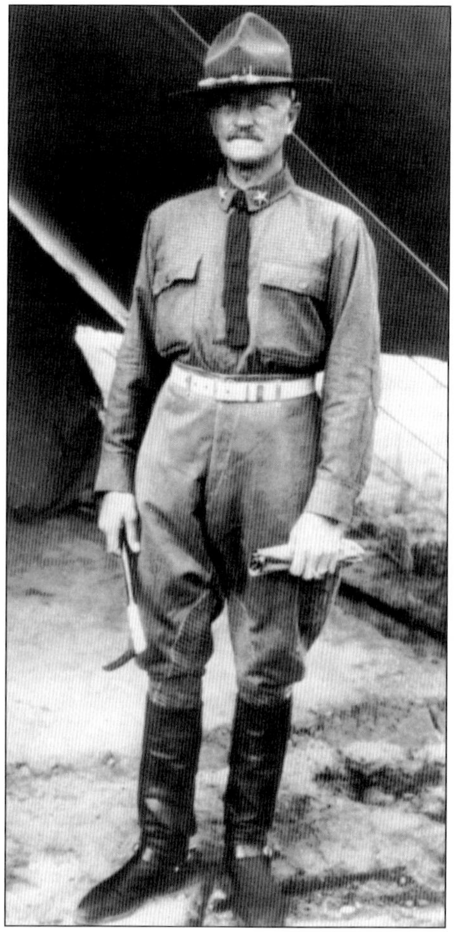

John J. Pershing, pictured here in 1916, is one of Missouri's best-known native sons, whose 38-year career included the command of cavalry troops during the latter part of the Indian Wars, the charging of San Juan Hill during the Spanish-American War, service in the Philippine-American War, and the pursuit of Pancho Villa during the Mexican Border Campaign. Pershing became a household name during World War I when he served as commander of the American Expeditionary Forces.

A monument honoring the 49 county citizens who lost their lives during World War I was dedicated during a ceremony held on November 13, 1921, on the south lawn of the Macon County Courthouse in the community of Macon. The memorial was funded in part by a $1,000 appropriation made by the state legislature to counties that raised at minimum an equal amount for the erection of such a monument.

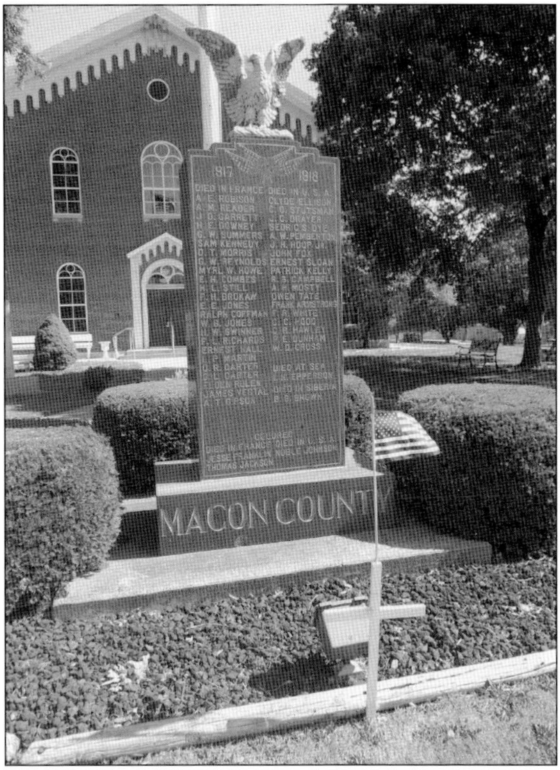

Situated near the World War I memorial at the Macon County Courthouse in Macon is a memorial that was dedicated to the county residents who lost their lives during World War II. Excavation work for the memorial began in September 1946 through a contract awarded to the Stevenson Monument Works of Macon. The monument was constructed from pink granite and cost $2,683.

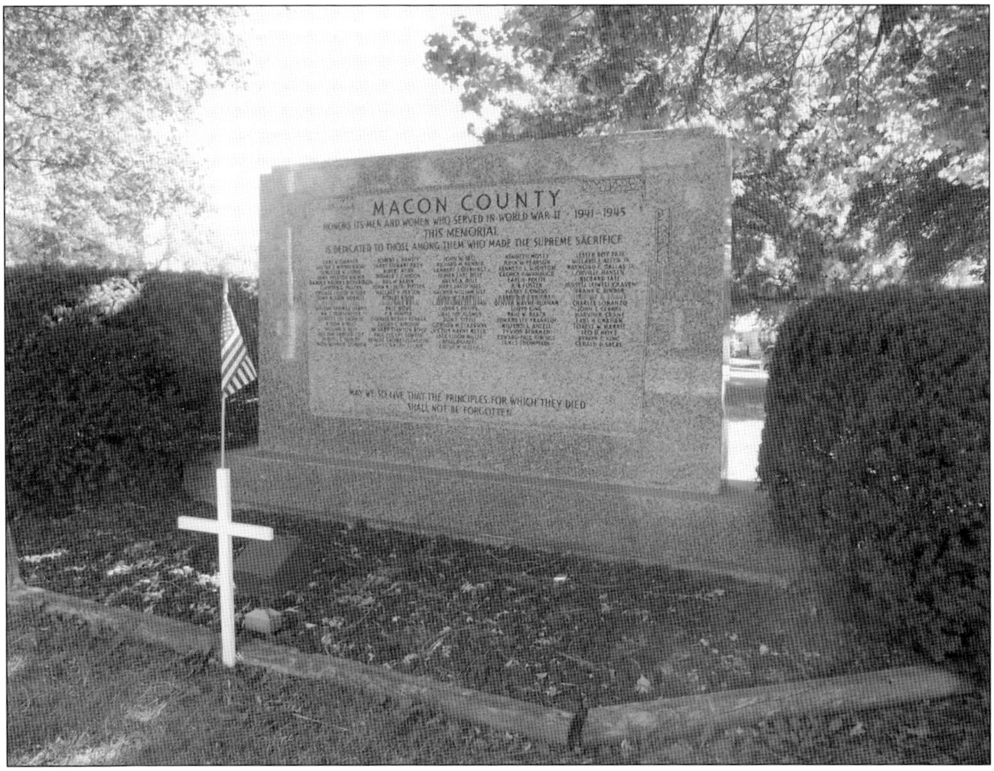

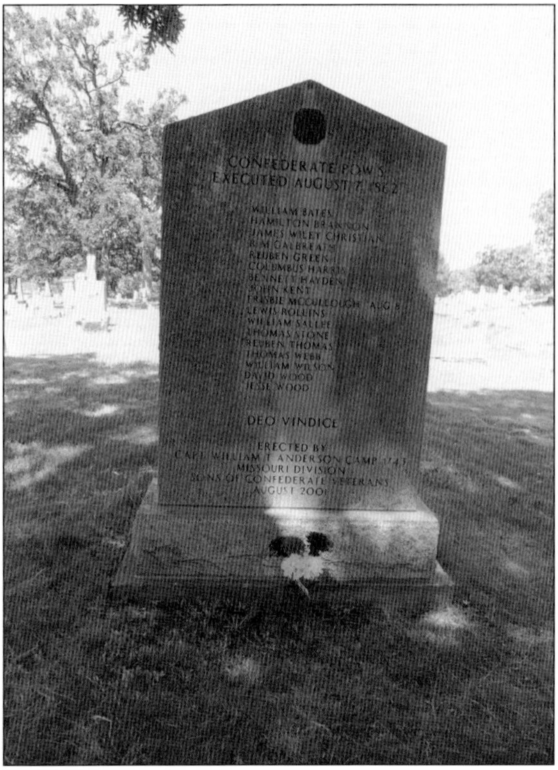

This monument was erected in August 2001 in the Forest-Llewellyn Cemetery in Kirkville in remembrance of 17 Confederate POWs who were executed the day after the Battle of Kirksville. According to Col. John McNeil, who commanded the Union forces, the battle lasted three hours and resulted in an estimated 150 Confederates killed, between 300 and 400 wounded, and 47 taken prisoner, many of whom were summarily tried and executed for violations of parole.

This memorial plaque on the lawn of the Adair County Courthouse in Kirksville explains much of the background regarding the Civil War engagement known as the Battle of Kirksville. Reports indicate that the focal point of the August 6, 1862, battle was the area in and around the courthouse square, resulting in a Union victory that helped consolidate Union control in Missouri.

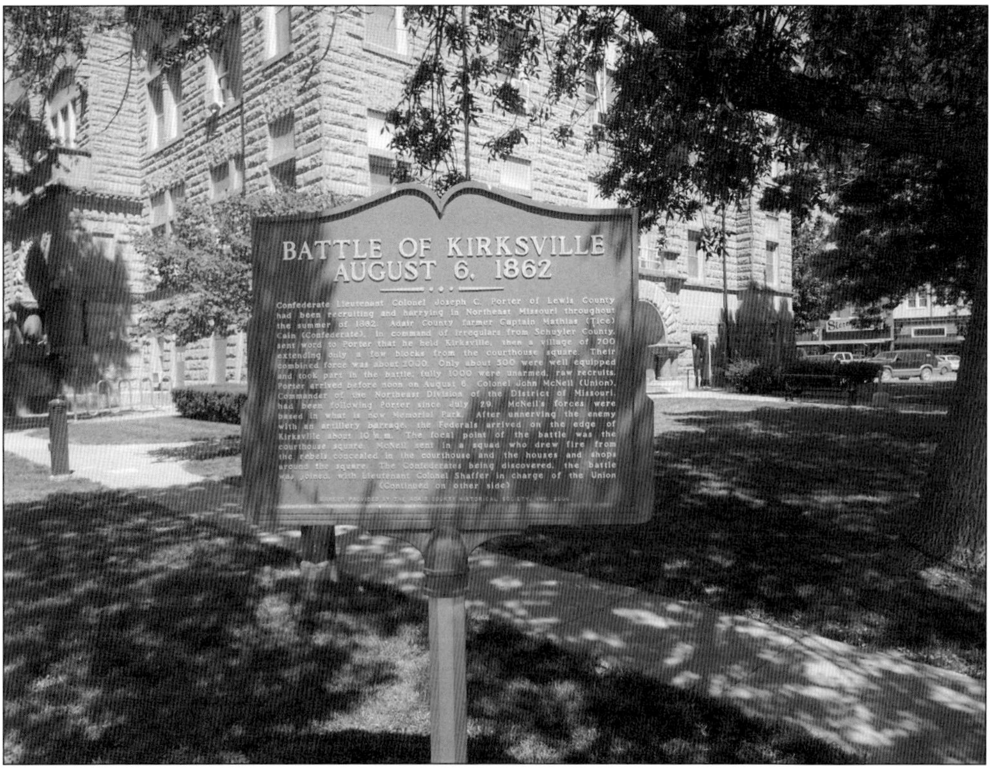

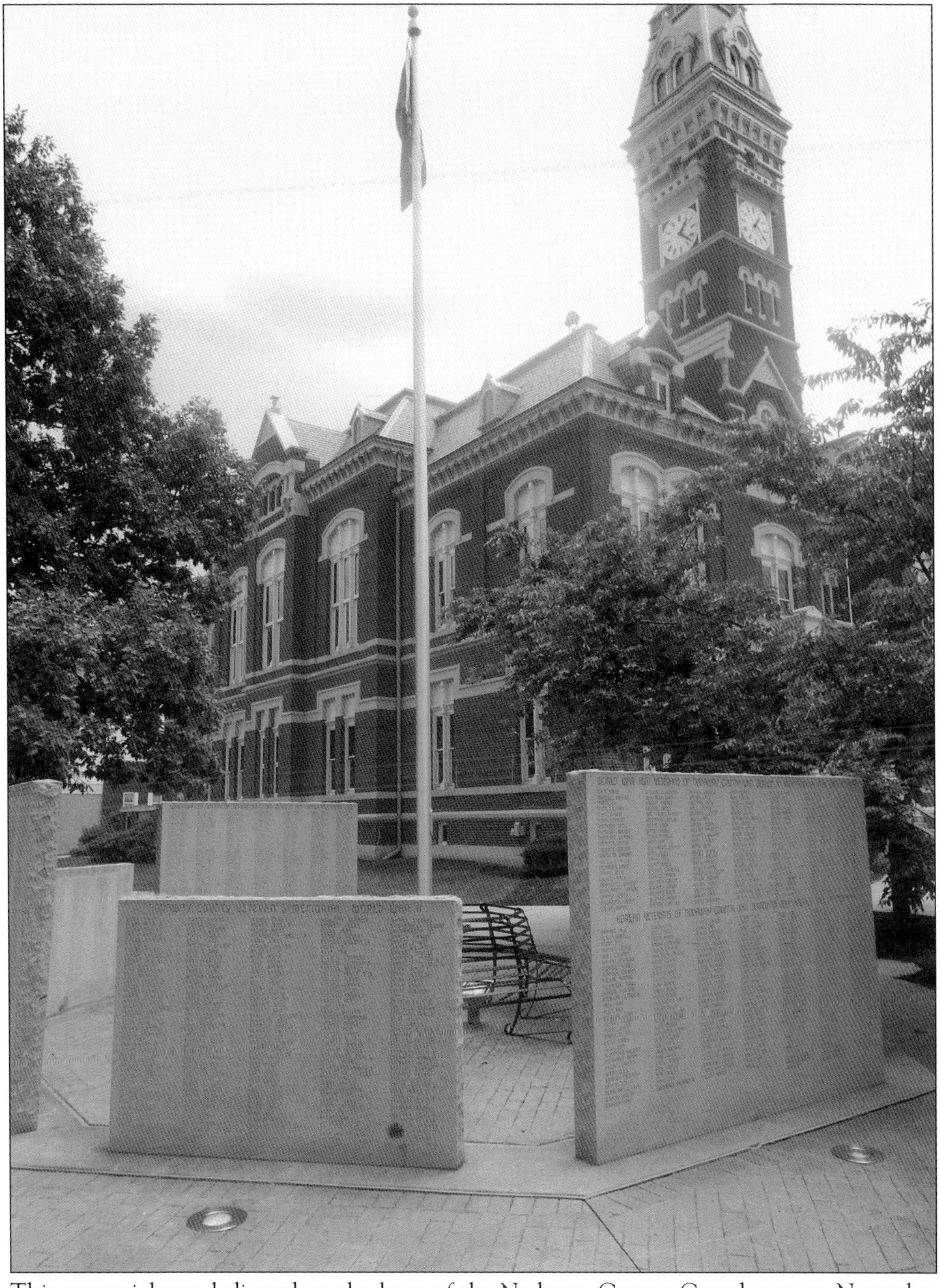

This memorial was dedicated on the lawn of the Nodaway County Courthouse on November 11, 1979, and honors the memory of local veterans who lost their lives in the conflicts beginning with the Civil War and up to and including the Vietnam War. Nearby this memorial is another monument that was dedicated in 1983 and is comprised of marble slabs that list the names of Nodaway County veterans who served in the nation's wars. (Tina Amick.)

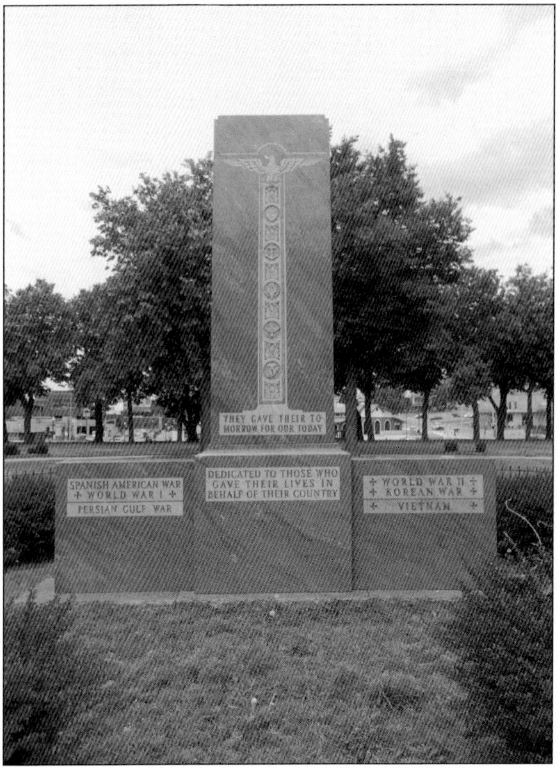

The St. Joseph War Memorial is located in Civic Center Park behind city hall and was built in 1953. The memorial was originally erected in honor of veterans from the Spanish-American War through the Vietnam War, but was subsequently updated to include veterans of the Persian Gulf War. The marble monument measures more than 15 feet in height was funded through local donations.

Also located in Civic Center Park in St. Joseph are memorials dedicated to the memory of James "Josh" Munger, Edward "Eddie" Lee Myers, and Brian Jay Bradbury—three local veterans who lost their lives in the conflicts in Iraq and Afghanistan. Each individual memorial displays a photograph of the veteran along with a description of his military service under the bronze cast of a "battlefield cross," which is a symbolic cross made from boots, rifle, and helmet to honor a fallen service member.

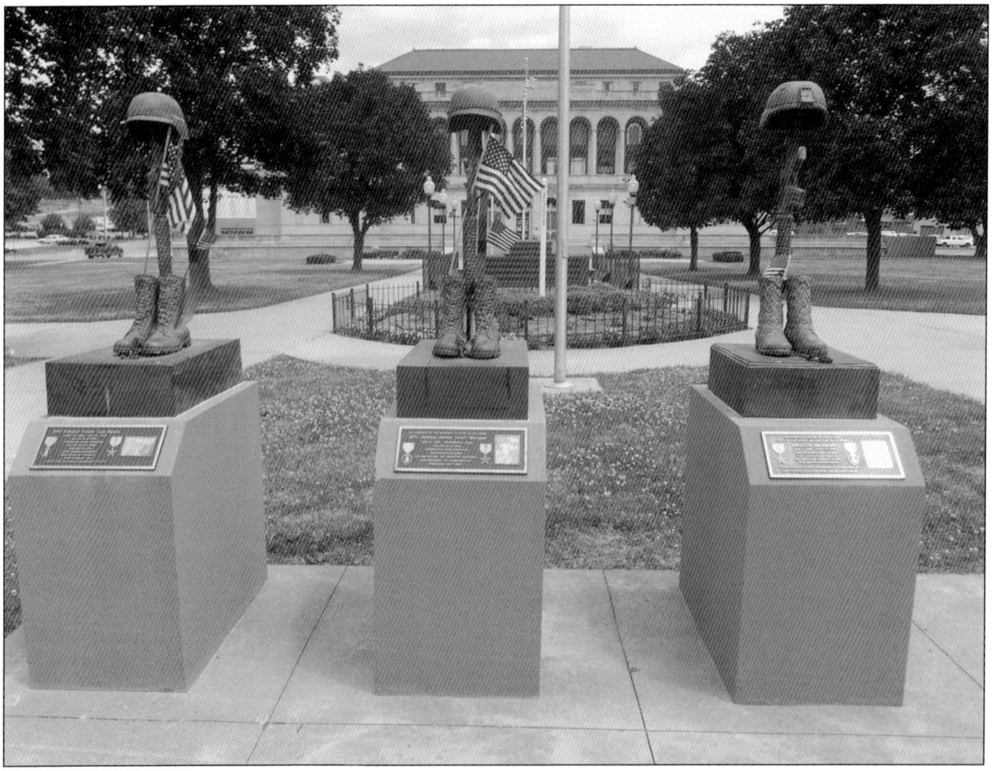

Born in Kirksville in 1870, Arthur Lee Willard went on to graduate from the US Naval Academy in 1891. He later served in the Navy during the Spanish-American War and World War I, eventually achieving the rank of vice admiral. The Missouri native passed away on April 7, 1935, and was laid to rest in Arlington National Cemetery.

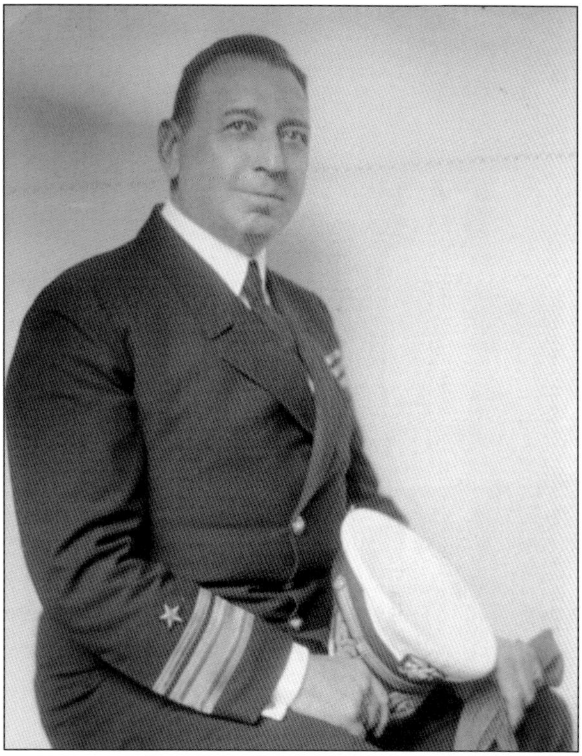

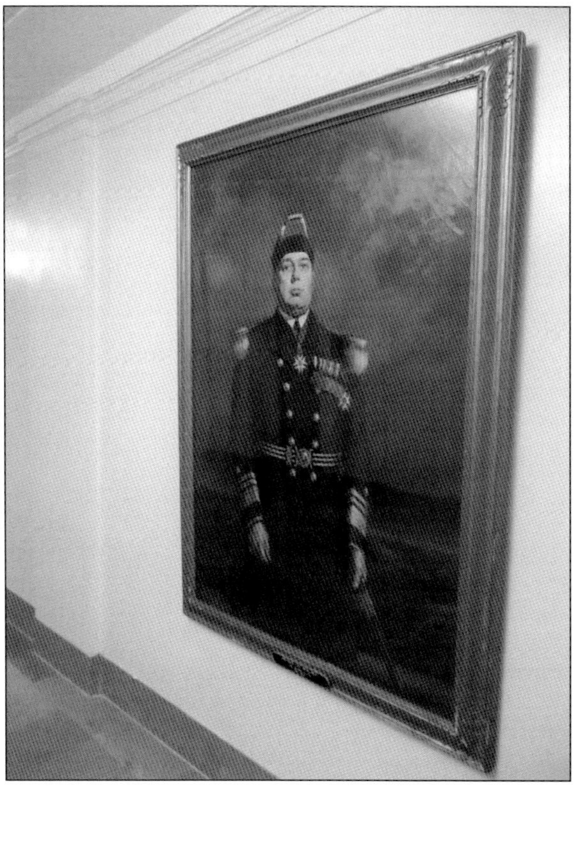

The State of Missouri has chosen to honor many of its military leaders who have made significant contributions during times of war through portraits that hang in the state capitol. In addition to paintings of Gen. John J. Pershing and Gen. Enoch H. Crowder, this painting of Admiral Willard was commissioned by the state in the late 1930s. The painting hangs on the third floor of the capitol in Jefferson City as a memorial to the late Admiral Willard's naval service.

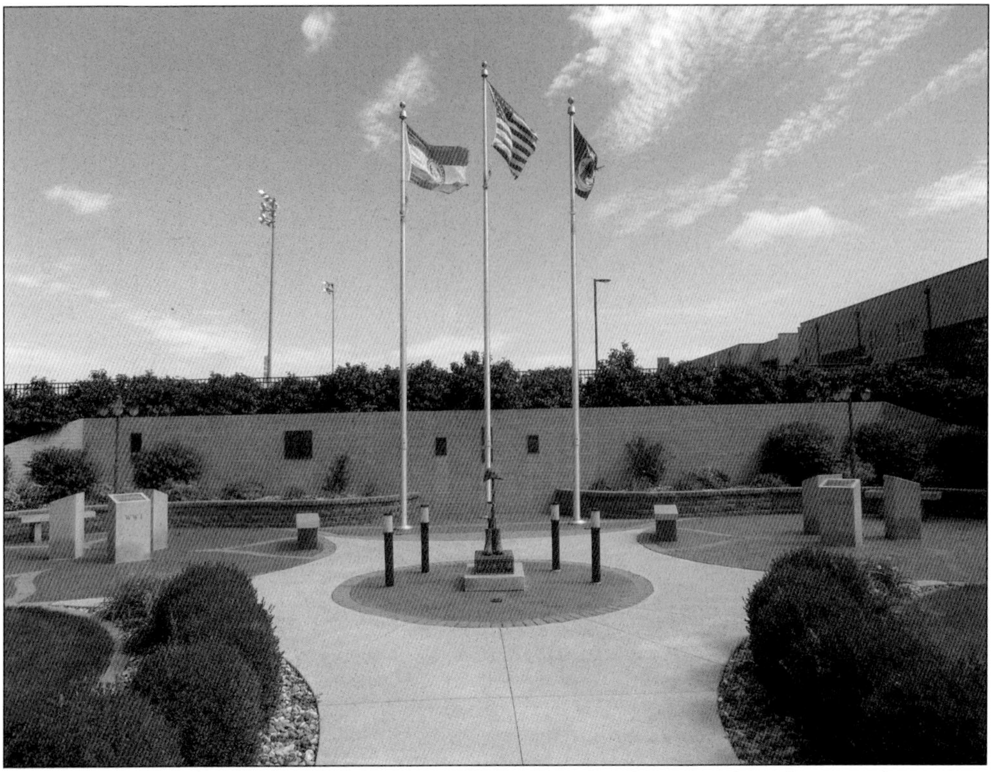

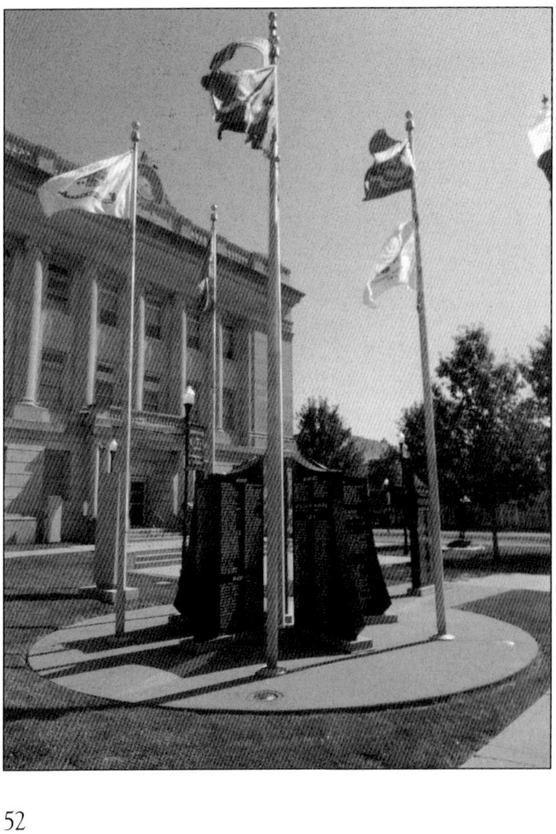

Land was purchased in 1946 by a veterans group in the city of Cameron for the purpose of building a veterans' memorial. It the ensuing years, recreational facilities and schools were built, but it was not until 1990 that the memorial finally began to take shape. The memorial consists of a wall and tablets honoring local veterans and is the site used by the community to host Memorial Day and Veterans Day ceremonies. (Tina Amick)

The Livingston County Veterans Memorial located on the grounds of the courthouse in Chillicothe was dedicated on November 11, 2002. The memorial consists of several dark granite markers that list the names of local residents who fought for the country in the various branches of service in addition to listing those who were killed in action.

Three

Southern Missouri

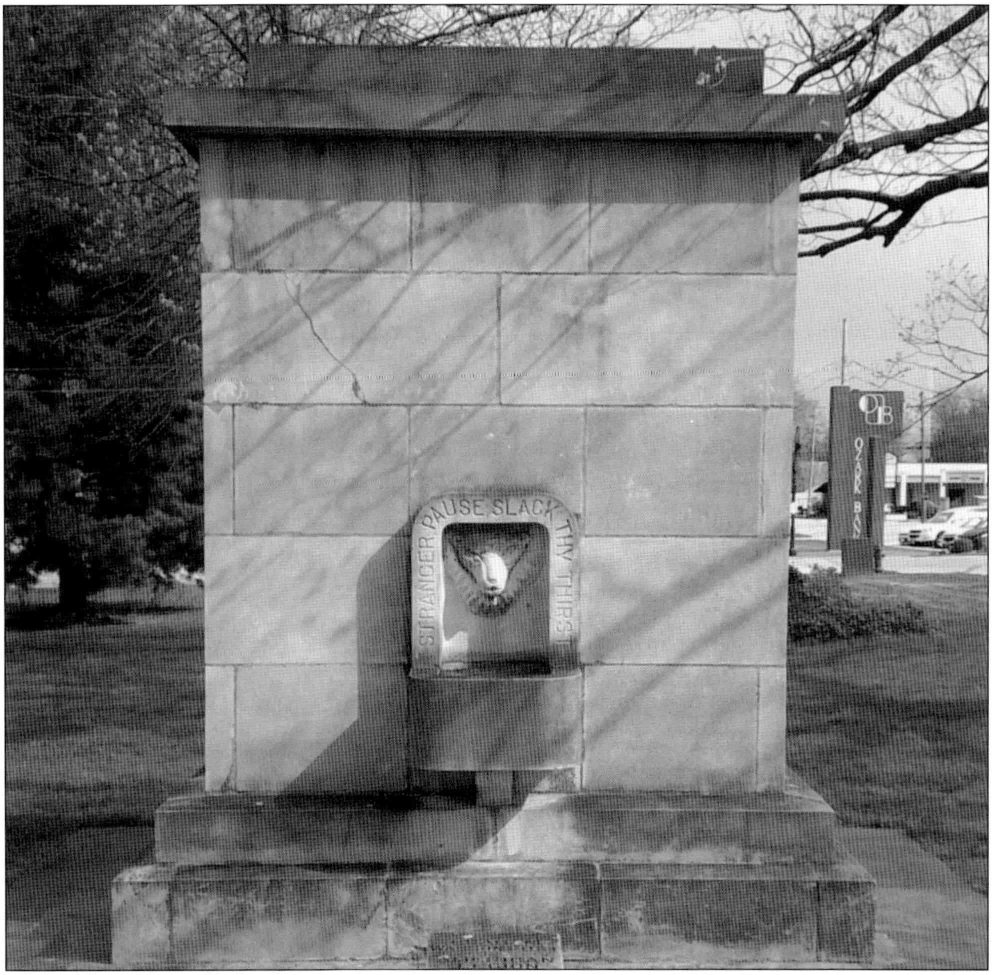

In 1931, the Graham-Wasson American Legion Post 327 erected this impressive memorial drinking fountain along the sidewalk leading to the Christian County Courthouse in the southwest Missouri community of Ozark. The spout is a lion's head with the phrase "Stranger, Pause, Slack Thy Thirst" inscribed around the fountain. The American Legion Post 327 was chartered in 1920 and is co-named for two local servicemen killed in World War I.

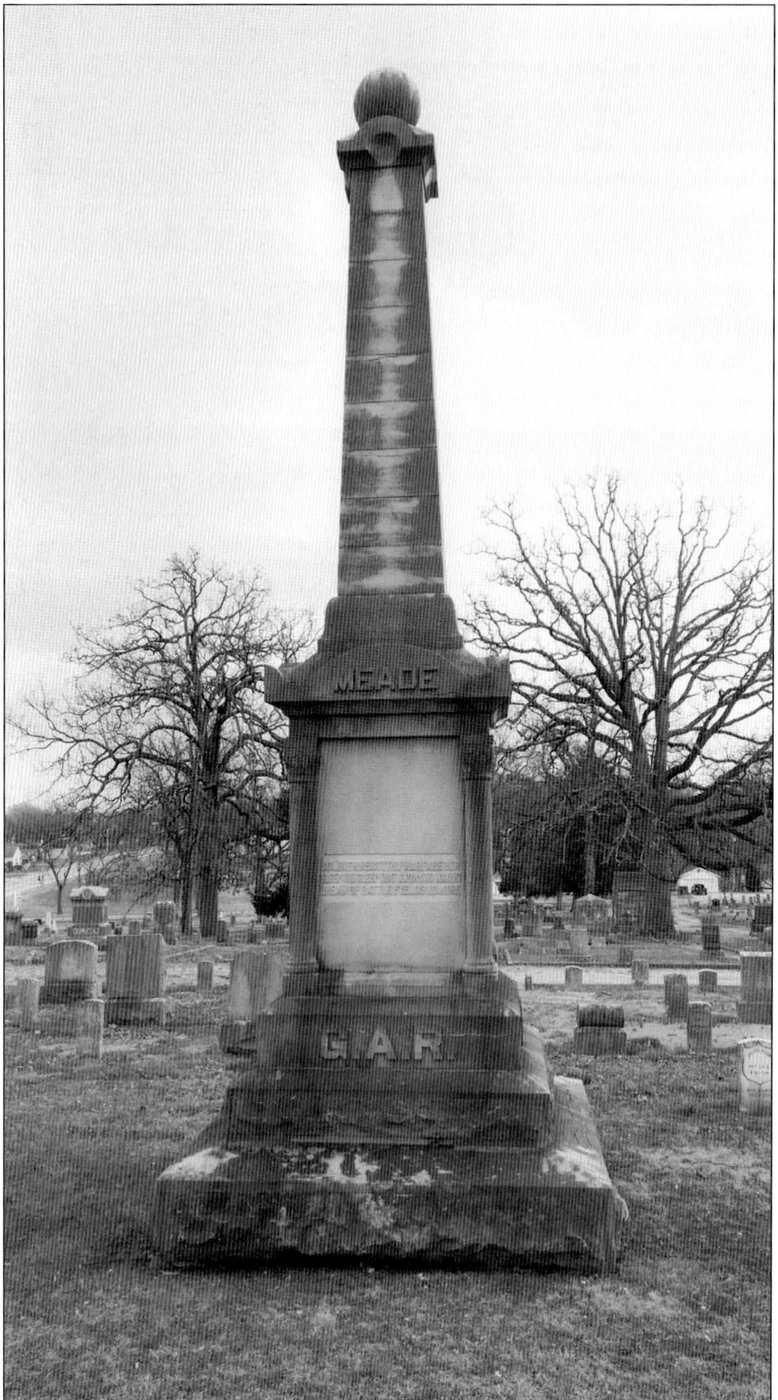

The Stanton Post 16 of the Grand Army of the Republic in 1906 erected this monument in the Park Cemetery in Carthage as a tribute to Union soldiers and sailors who served in the Civil War. Each side of the monument serves as a tribute to a specific Union general, which includes the names Ulysses S. Grant, William T. Sherman, Philip H. Sheridan, and George G. Meade.

A World War II memorial honoring the 164 Joplin residents who lost their lives during World War II was dedicated on the east grounds of Memorial Hall in Joplin on June 29, 1947. Sponsored by the Joplin Army Mothers and Wives Club, the initial cost of the memorial was $9,000 and consists of a granite shaft measuring 18 feet in height and 10 feet in width.

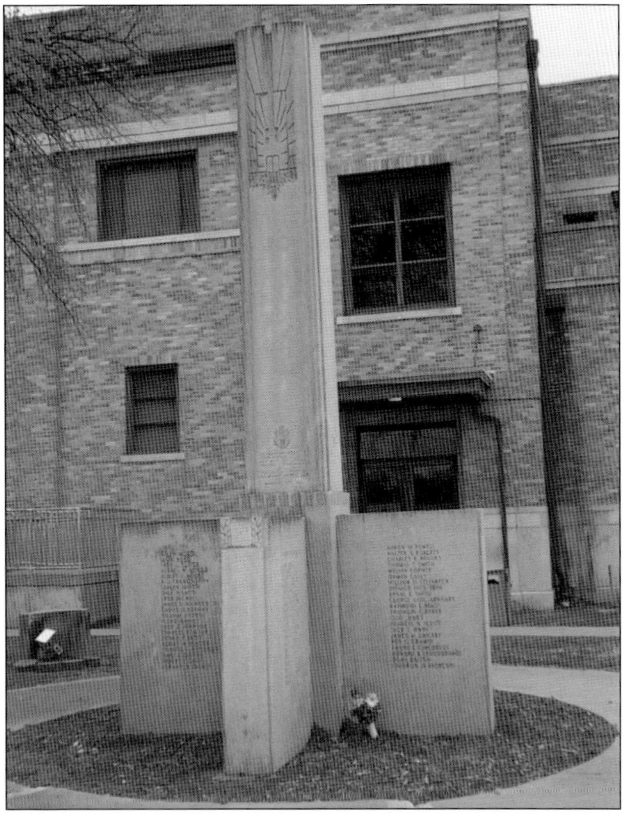

Static artillery displays have been used by many communities as a memorial to the local men and women who served in the military. In this spirit, the lawn of the Christian County Courthouse in Ozark, Missouri, features a three-inch M5 anti-tank gun that was built at Rock Island Arsenal in 1943. In 2014, the gun was repainted by county employees and placed on a new concrete pad on the northeast corner of the courthouse lawn.

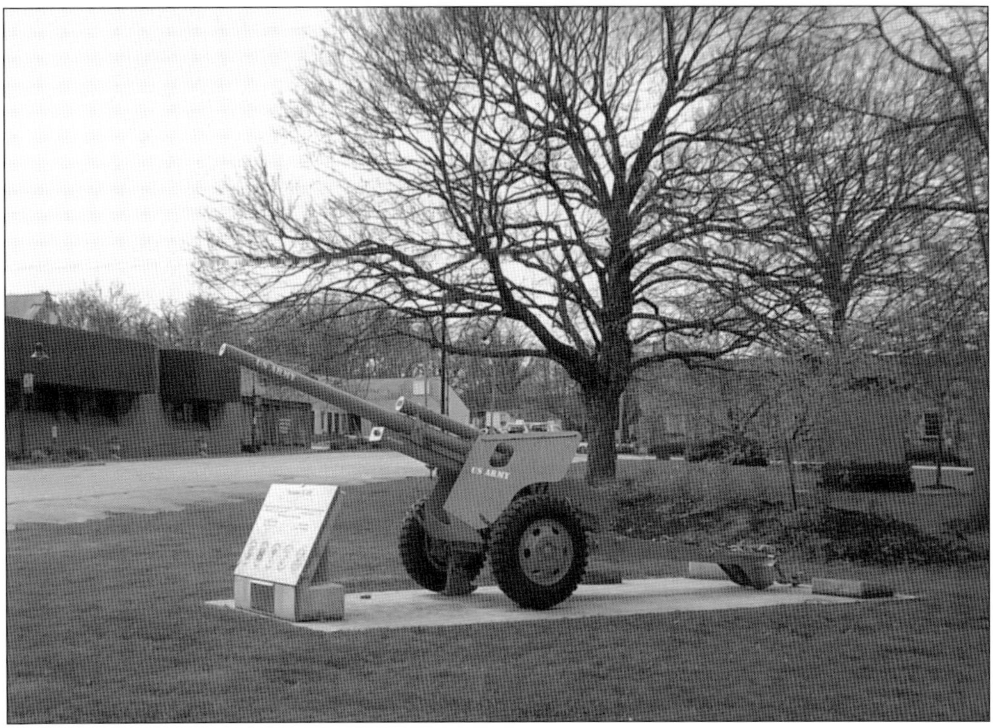

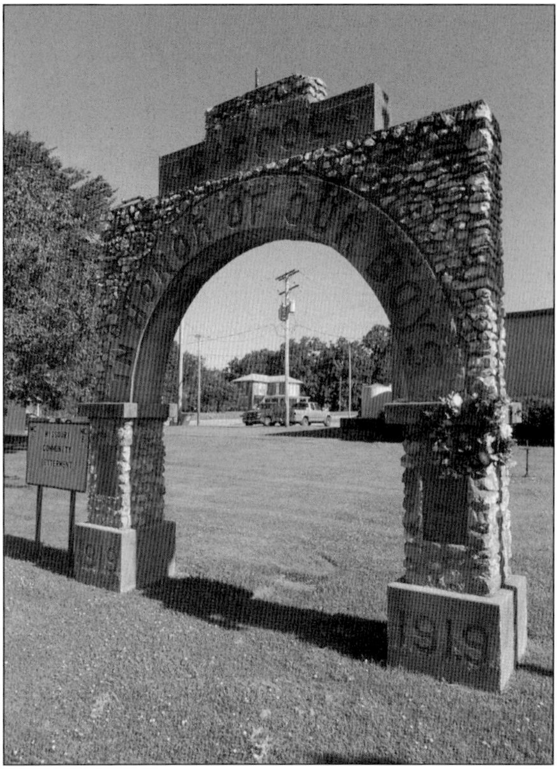

The Victory Arch Memorial made of native stone and concrete was dedicated in the Texas County community of Cabool in September 1919 to honor local casualties of World War I. Several months after it was built, bronze plates were added to the arch, which listed the names of local men who were killed in the war.

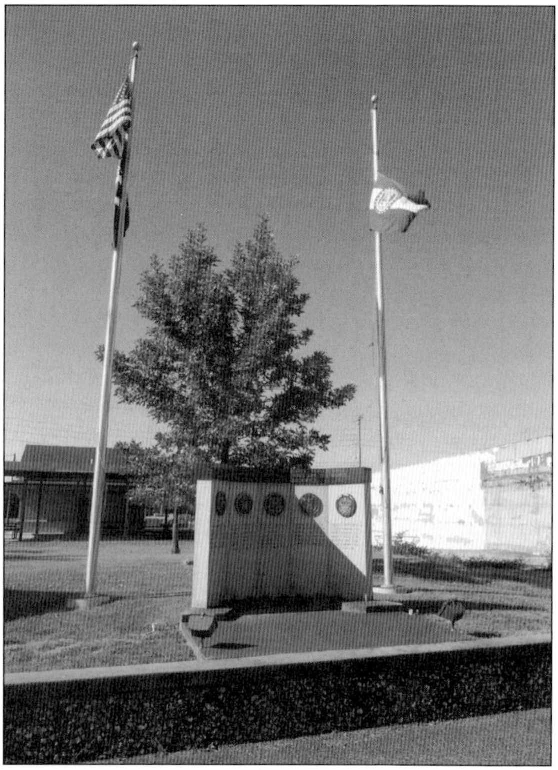

Across the street from Victory Memorial Arch and located within Gateway Memorial Park in Cabool stands an exceptional memorial dedicated on July 4, 1992, to honor veterans of all wars and eras. Money for the memorial came from both private donations and monies received from local businesses.

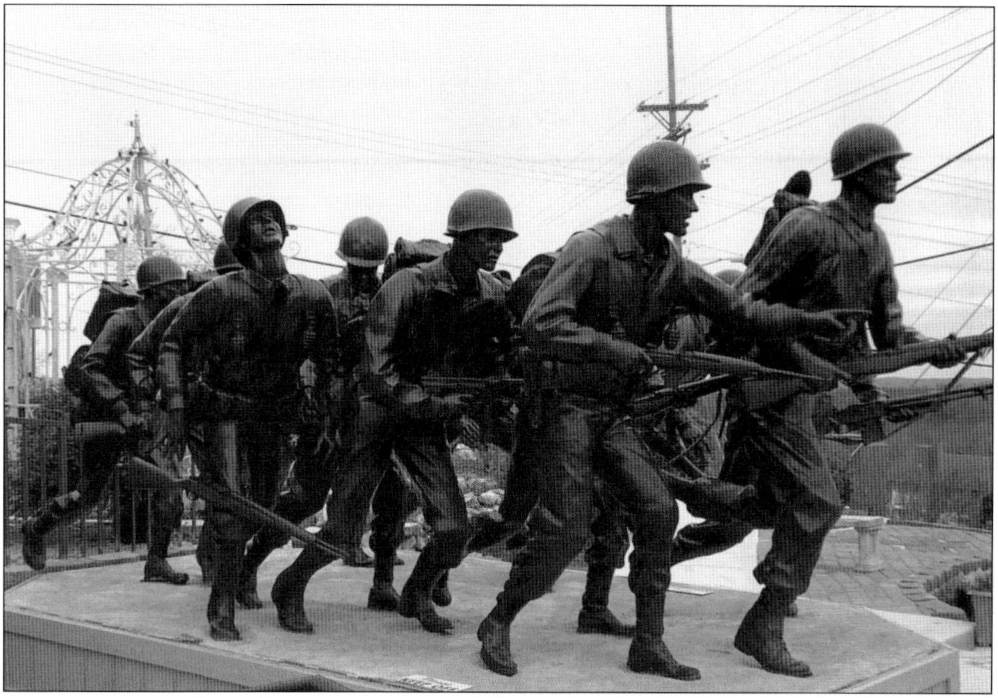

Veterans Memorial Garden was established in 2008 by a nonprofit group in Branson and is located at the intersection of Highway 76 and Roark Valley Road. In addition to a landscaped hillside full of various types of trees, flowers, and bushes, the focal point is a 12-soldier sculpture called "Stay Low," which was purchased by the city of Branson in December 2015 and authorized by the board of aldermen for placement in the memorial garden. (Tina Amick.)

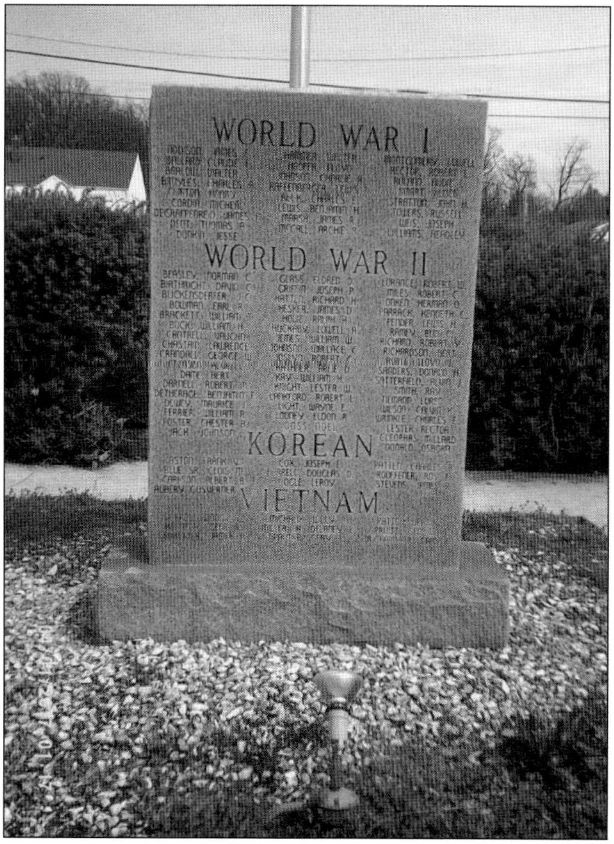

Discreetly situated along Highway 5 in front VFW Post 4107 in Lebanon is a memorial marker dedicated to the men from Laclede County who made the ultimate sacrifice while in service to the nation. This marker has engraved upon it the names of those from the area who died in World War I, World War II, Vietnam, Korea, Iraq, and Afghanistan.

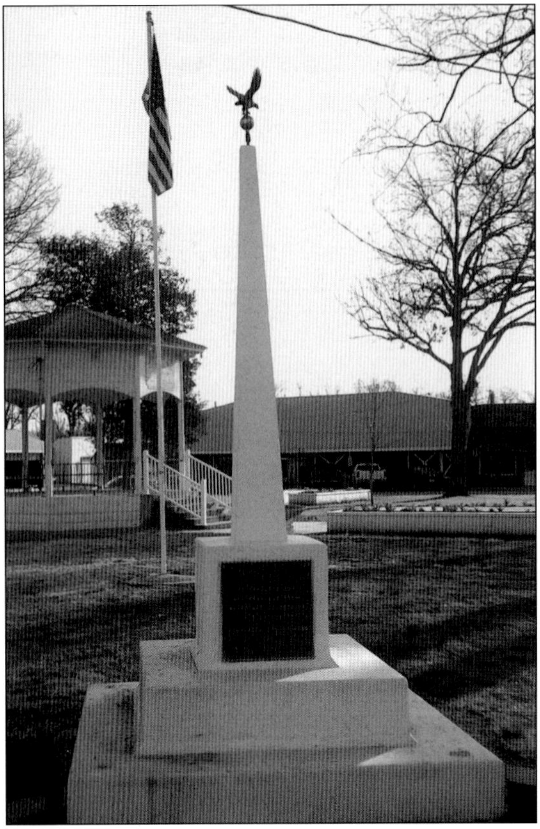

In the southwest corner of a small park in the historic town square of Sarcoxie, Missouri—the oldest town in Jasper County—stands a simple, white memorial capped with a bronze eagle that was dedicated to all US veterans on September 6, 1997. A very patriotic community and active during World War II, the May 20, 1944, edition of the *Joplin Globe* reported that local school in Sarcoxie used their auditorium to provide entertainment for soldiers and WACs (Women's Army Corps) stationed at nearby Camp Crowder.

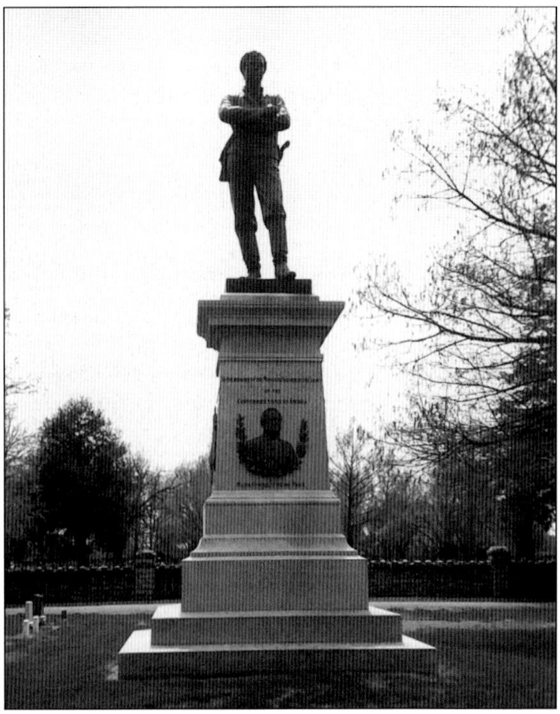

Towering above thousands of white marble tombstones in the Springfield National Cemetery is a monument in the form of a bronze figure that was dedicated on August 10, 1901—the 40th anniversary of the clash between more than 5,000 Union troops and 12,000 Confederate troops during the Battle of Wilson's Creek. Designed as a tribute to Gen. Sterling Price and Missouri soldiers who served in the Confederacy, the monument was sponsored by the United Confederate Veterans of Missouri and the Daughters of the Confederacy of Missouri and, at the time, cost $10,000. (Tina Amick.)

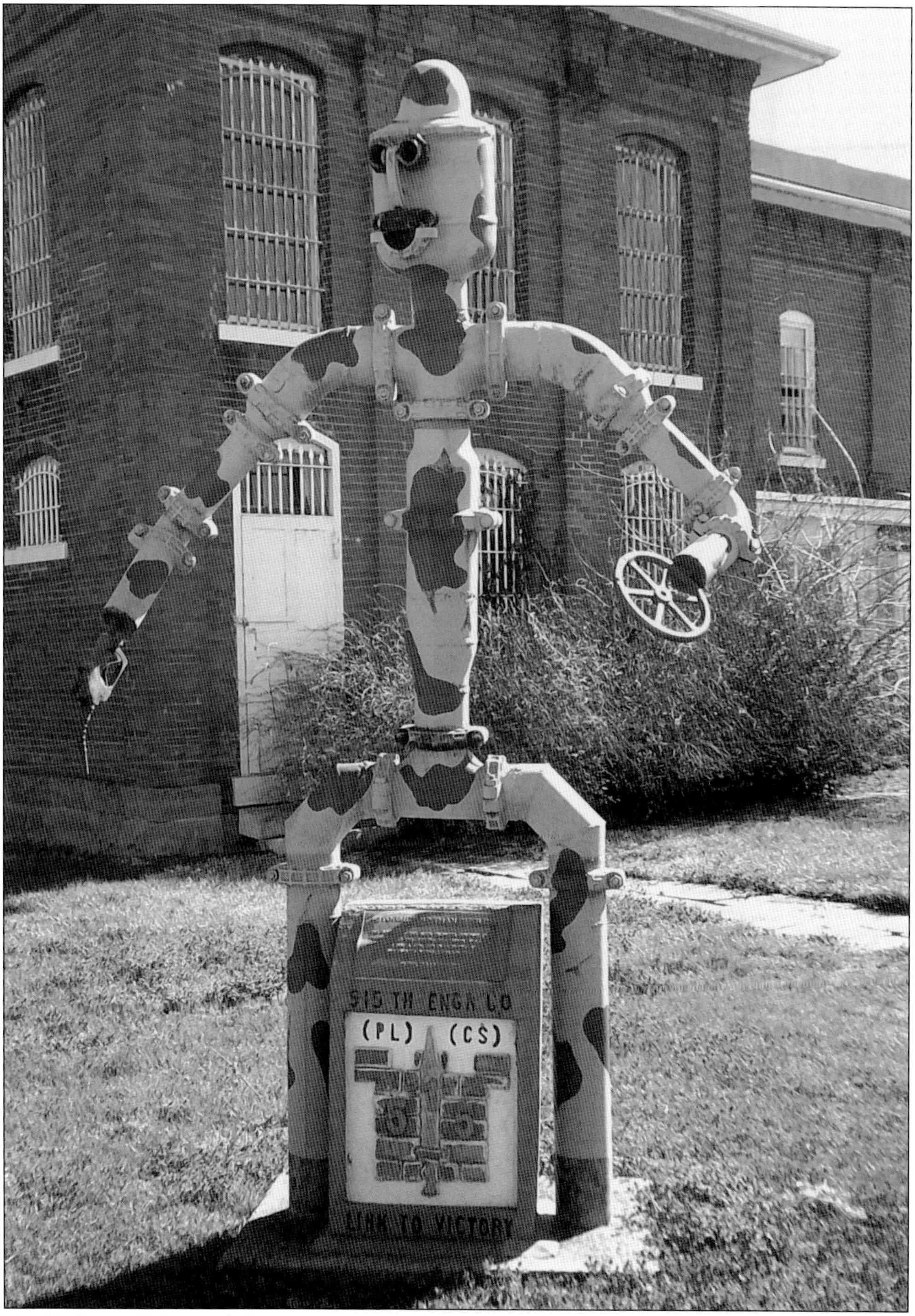

On the lawn of the Laclede County Courthouse in the city of Lebanon is a memorial that was a gift from the 515th Engineer Company from nearby Fort Leonard Wood to the citizens of Lebanon. The "pipeman" was presented on May 4, 1991, in recognition of the support the community provided to the soldiers and their families during Operation Desert Storm.

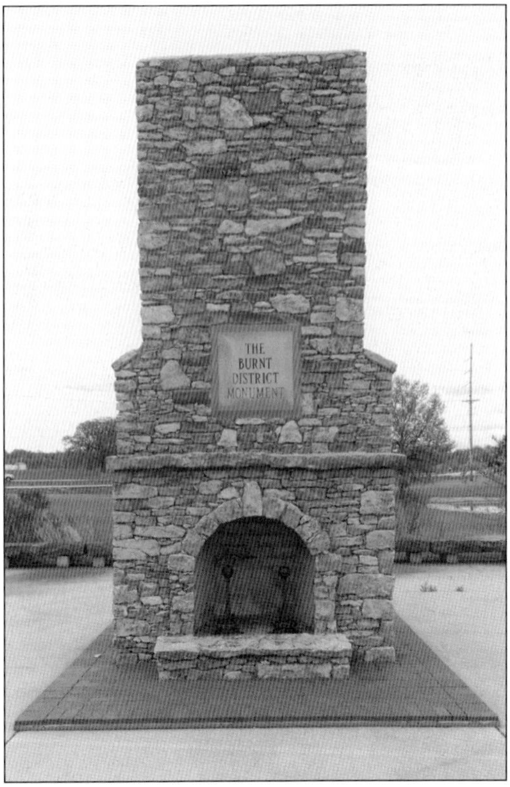

The Burnt District Monument was dedicated in April 2009 on the grounds of the Cass County Justice Center. During the Civil War, the homes of thousands of families living in Harrisonville and the surrounding counties were burned to the ground in a Union army attempt to control guerrilla activity. Once the homes were torched, oftentimes all that would remain was a chimney, which was otherwise known as "Jennison's tombstone," so named for Jayhawker Col. Charles Jennision.

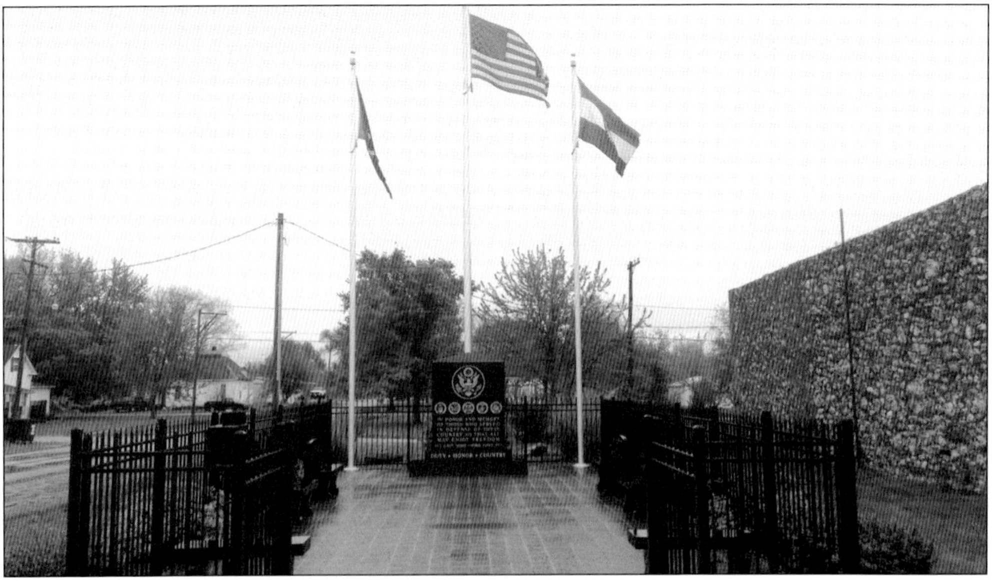

The small community of Weaubleau in Hickory County gathered on November 11, 2006, to officially dedicate an impressive memorial in honor of all veterans located at the intersection of Highway 54 and Gentry Street. The funds used in the construction of the memorial were generated by the Weaubleau Merchants Community Association through the sale of imprinted pavers and benches. The marker, which is the centerpiece of the memorial, reads, "In honor and memory of those who served in defense of their country so that all may enjoy freedom."

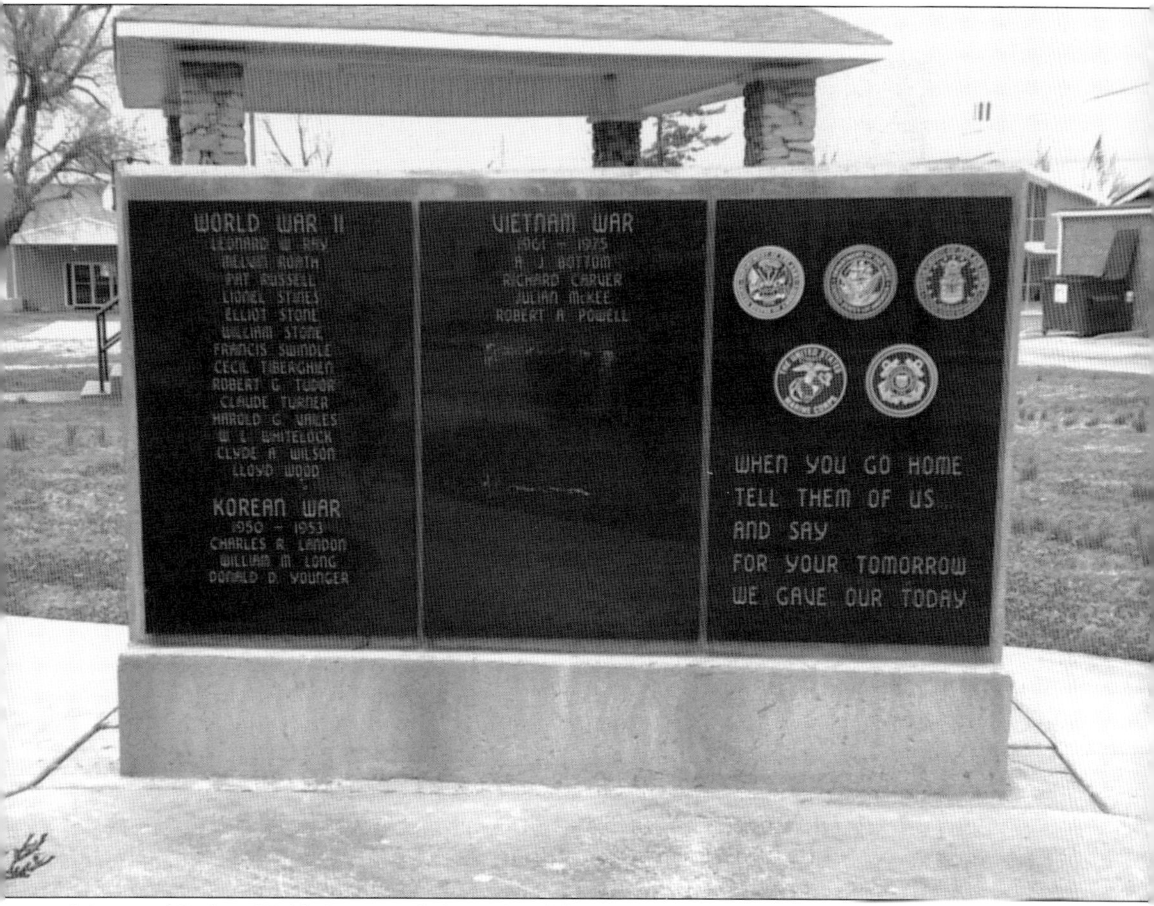

Memorial Park in Webb City was dedicated on Flag Day, June 14, 1921. Initially, a memorial board was erected in honor of local citizens who served during World War I but was replaced in 1956 with a granite veteran's memorial marker. Fifty-one years later, in 2007, the Veterans Memorial was remodeled to include the names of the 77 Webb City veterans who died in the Spanish-American War, World War I, World War II, Korea, and Vietnam.

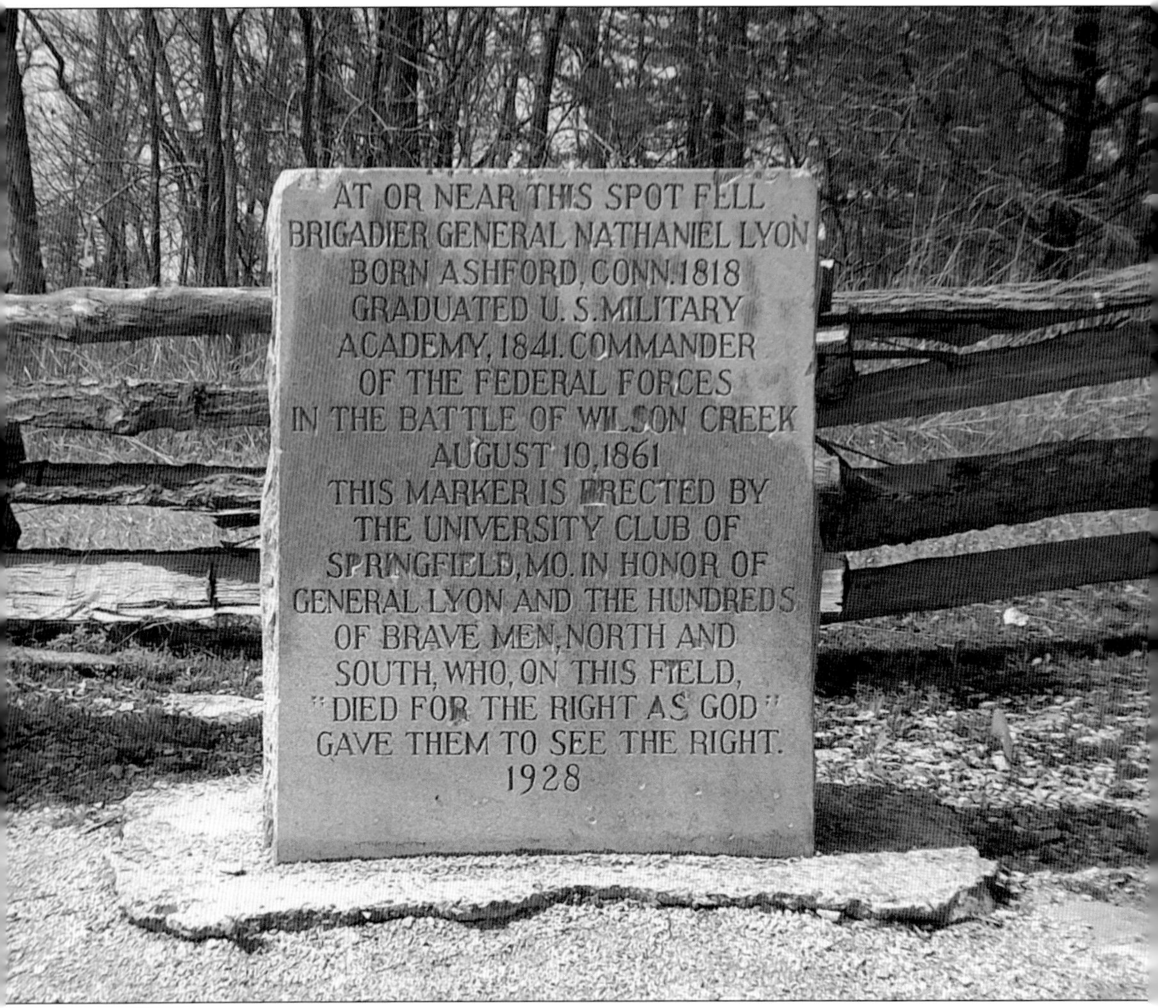

A monument dedicated to the memory of Brig. Gen. Nathaniel Lyon, who was killed on August 10, 1861, and other soldiers who lost their lives during the Battle of Wilson's Creek near Springfield, was unveiled on May 26, 1928. The simple marker is made of white Georgia marble, is situated in the location near where it is believed General Lyon fell during the battle and is now located on the National Park Service site known as Wilson's Creek National Battlefield. (Tina Amick.)

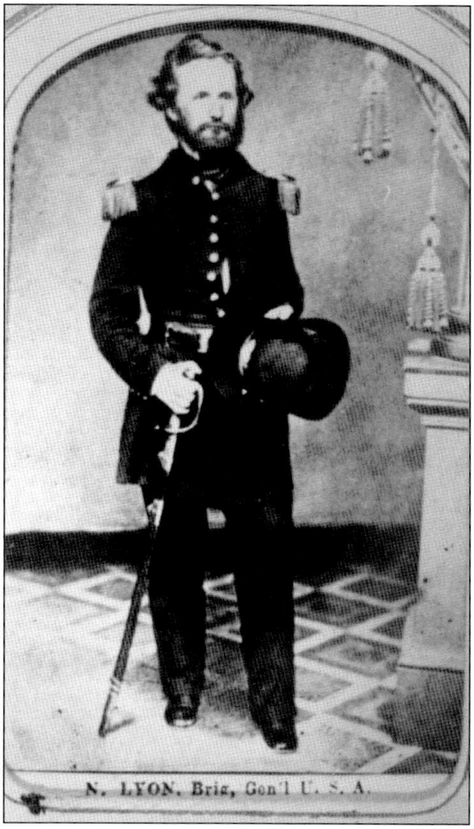

Brig. Gen. Nathaniel Lyon was born in Connecticut in 1818 and went on to graduate from the US Military Academy in 1841. He was a veteran of the Seminole Wars and the Mexican-American War but was killed during the Civil War in the Battle of Wilson's Creek, becoming the first Union general to lose his life in the conflict. The fallen general was initially buried on a farm near Springfield, Missouri; however, his remains were later reinterred in his native Connecticut. (Museum of Missouri Military History.)

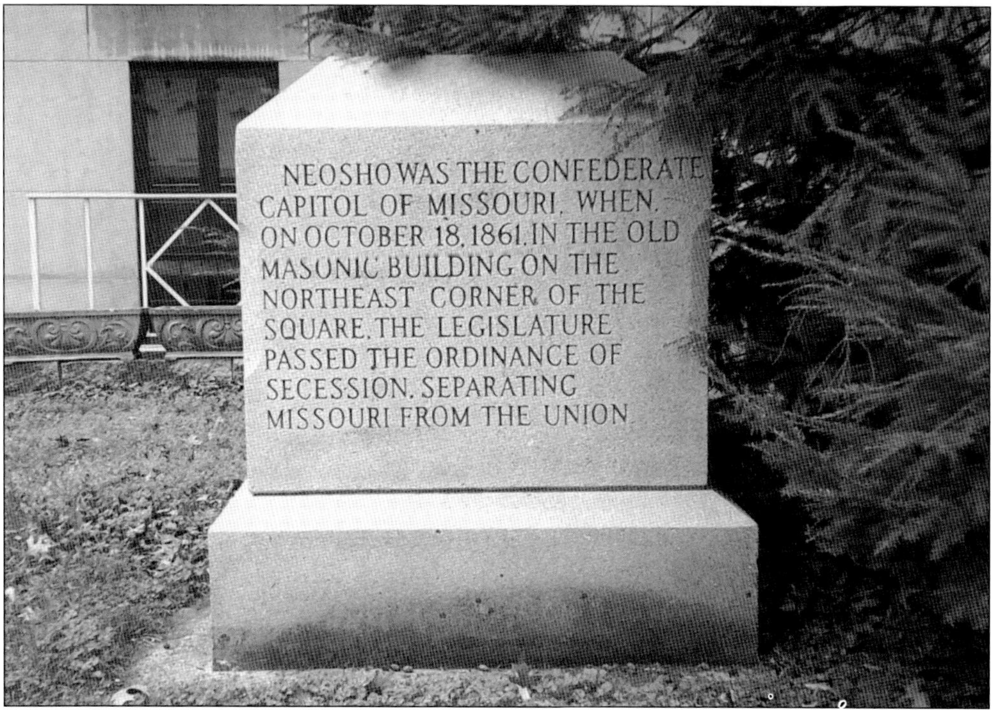

On the north lawn of the Newton County Courthouse in Neosho is a small marker that stresses the prominent role the community played during the Civil War. Neosho was the site of several surprise attacks against Union troops by Confederate forces, served briefly as the provisional capital of Missouri's secessionist government and is where, in October 1861, the Confederate Legislature convened to pass the Ordinance of Secession in an effort to establish Missouri as a member of the Confederacy.

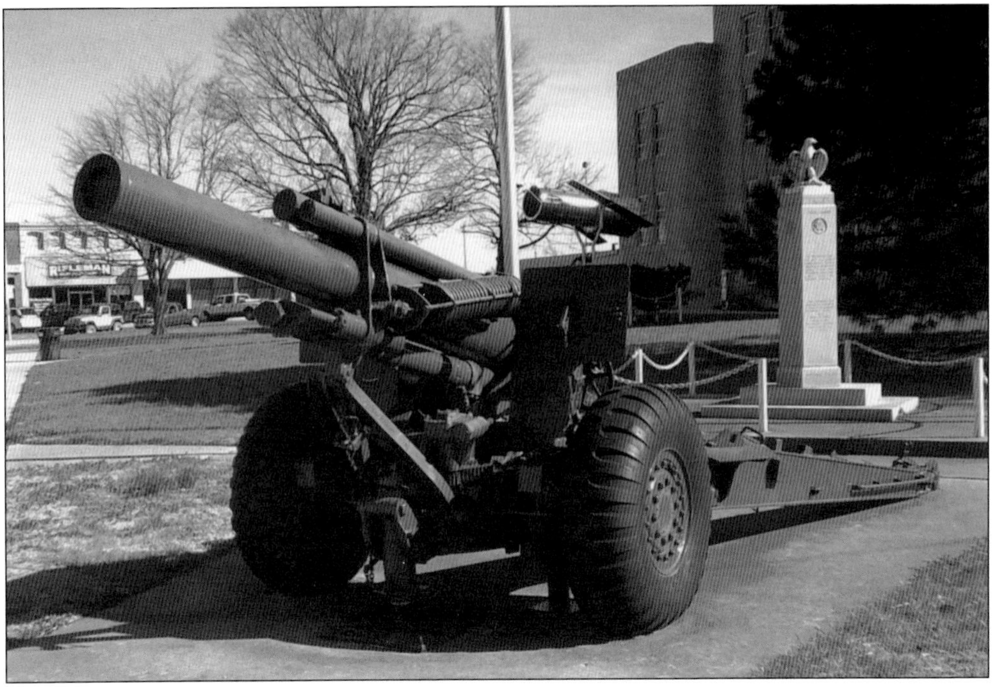

On the grounds of the Webster County Courthouse in Marshfield is beautifully restored M114A2 155mm towed howitzer that was used by the Army from World War II through the Vietnam War. Behind the howitzer is a granite shaft that was dedicated in 1972 as a memorial to Webster County citizens who lost their lives during World War I, World War II, Korea, and Vietnam.

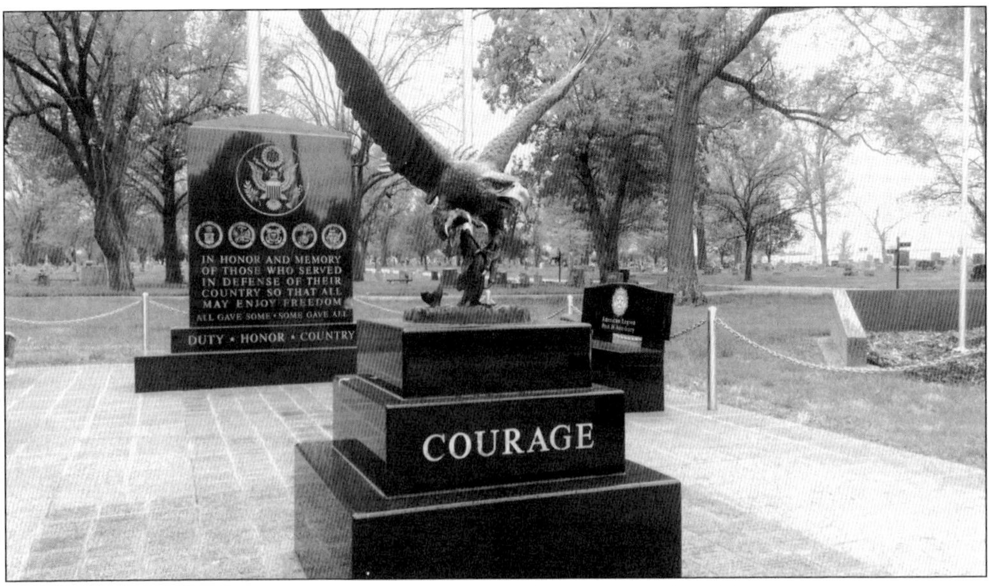

Located inside the historic Englewood Cemetery on the east end of the Henry County community of Clinton is this stunning tribute to veterans. The memorial consists of a bronze bald eagle on a pedestal of "courage" that is situated in front of a black marble marker inscribed with the seals of the five military branches and is flanked by benches donated by the local American Legion, Veteran of Foreign Wars, and their auxiliaries.

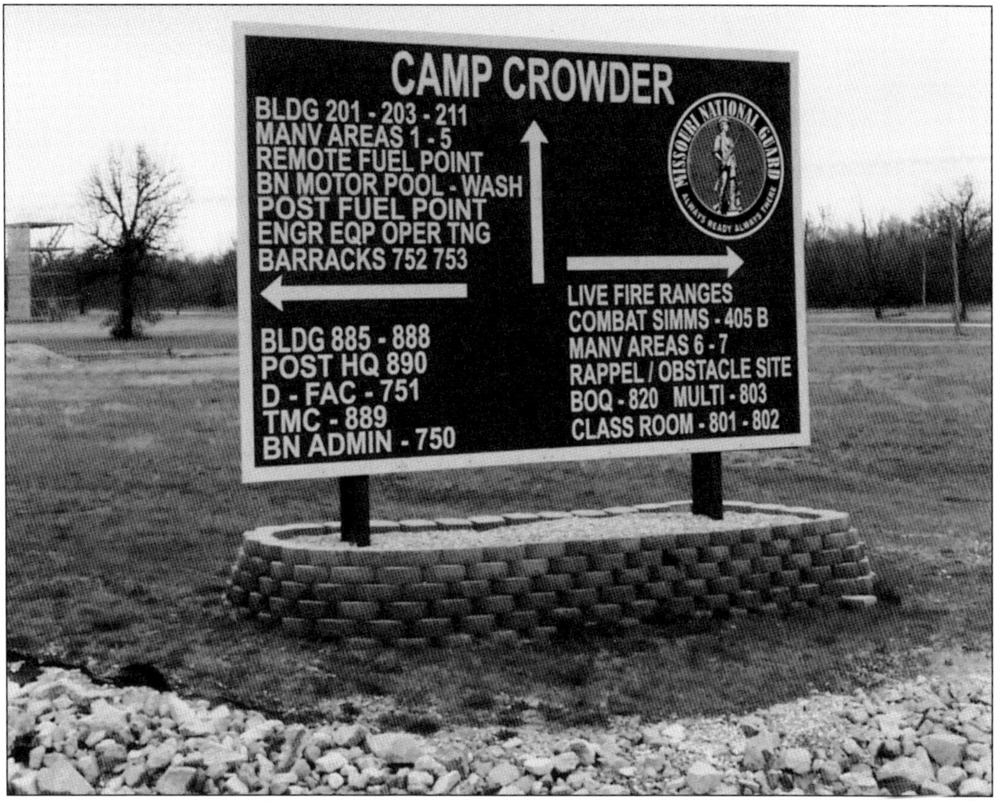

This prominent sign on the site of Camp Crowder serves as a memorial to the memory of the late Maj. Gen. Enoch H. Crowder. On August 30, 1941, ground was broken for the US Army camp and during World War II it became a major training site for the Signal Corps. In the years after the Korean War, much of the land was sold off; what remained became property of the Missouri National Guard and is now used as a training site.

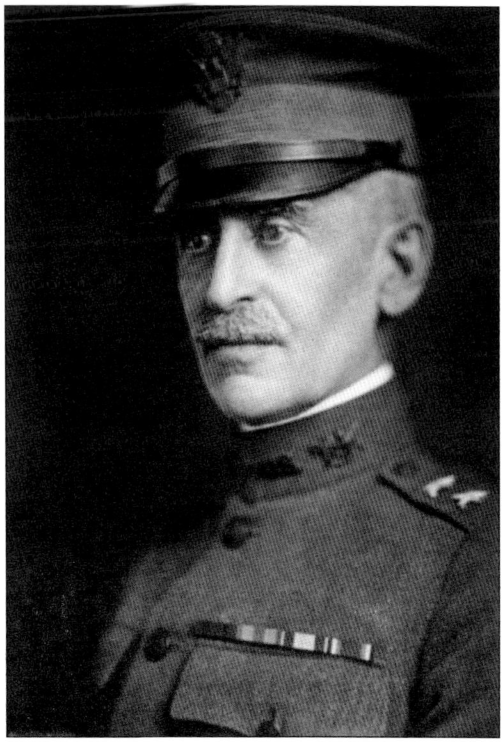

Camp Crowder received its name from Maj. Gen. Enoch Crowder—a Missouri native who rose to the national scene by drafting the Selective Service Act during World War I, which established the system of local draft boards. Born near the historic community of Trenton in Grundy County, Crowder graduated from West Point in 1881 and served in several prominent capacities during his 50 years of public service, including an ambassadorship to Cuba following his World War I service.

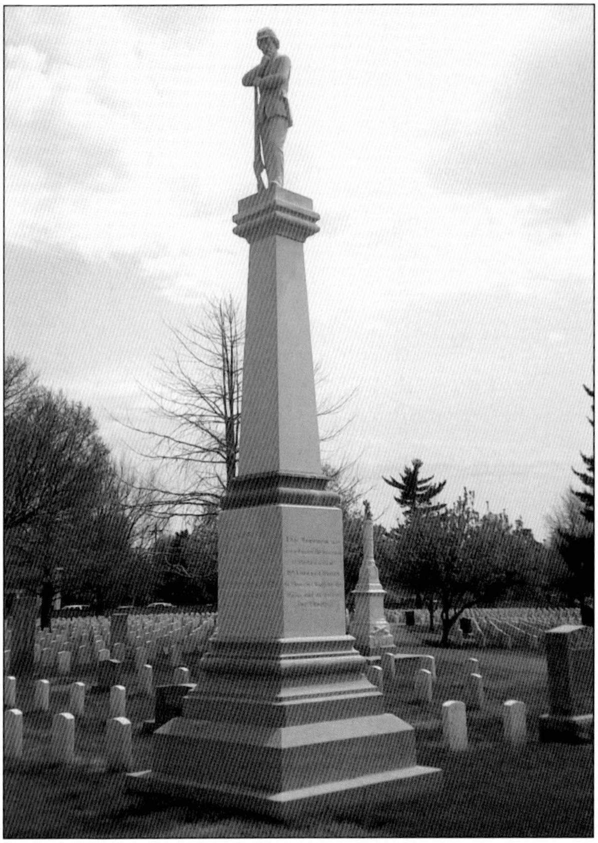

Per the provisions of the will of Dr. Thomas J. Bailey, a monument was placed near the entrance of Springfield National Cemetery in 1907 "to show his love for the Union and its defenders," as the inscription reads. The Bailey Monument is topped by a six-foot, two-inch soldier with his left hand resting on the muzzle of a Springfield rifle and is constructed from white marble. The monument was erected to memorialize the Union soldiers killed at the Battle of Springfield on January 8, 1863. (Tina Amick.)

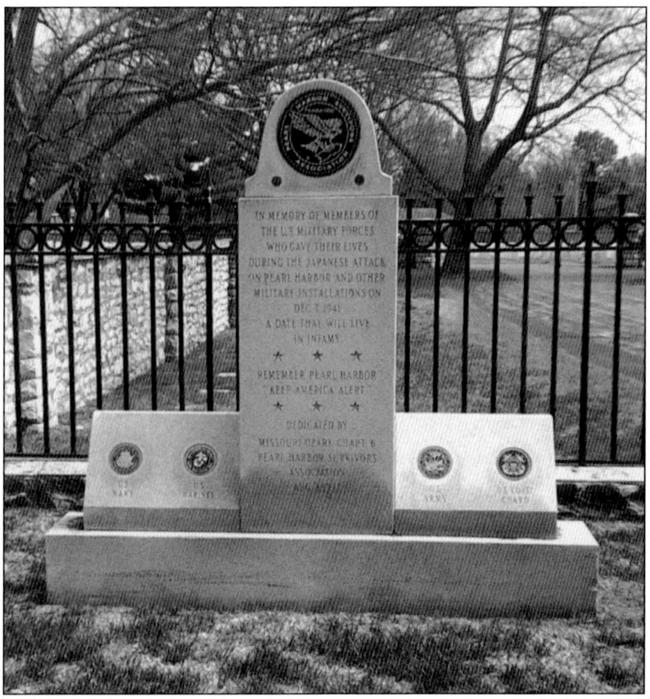

The Missouri Ozarks Chapter 6 of the Pearl Harbor Survivors Association dedicated this granite and bronze memorial to those who died during the attack on Pearl Harbor in 1941 in the Springfield National Cemetery on August 8, 1992. The taller section of the monument contains a large bronze medallion of the Pearl Harbor Survivors Association in addition to an inscription in honor of the fallen, while the shorter side panels contain the bronze seals of four branches of the armed forces. (Tina Amick.)

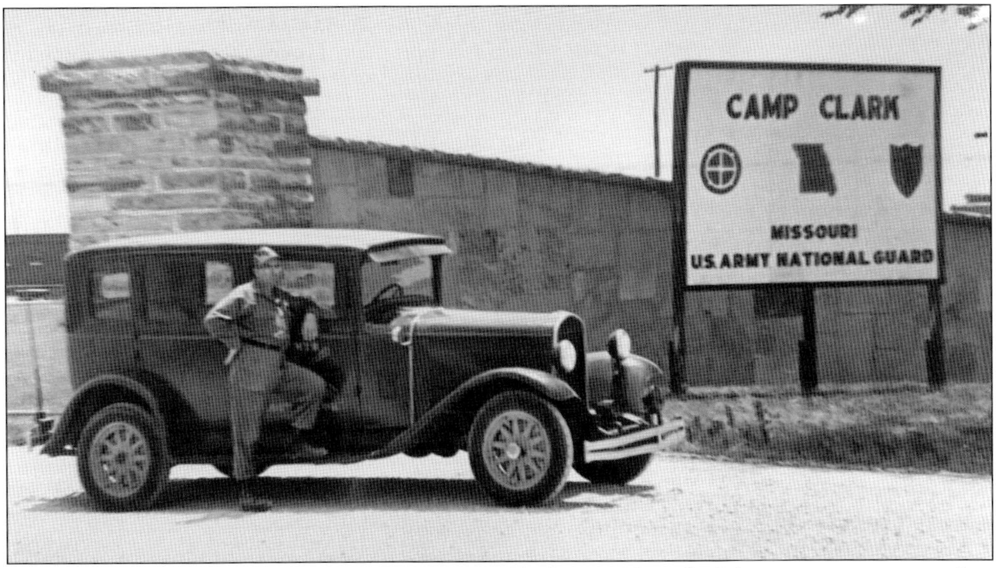

This photograph shows the entrance to Camp Clark near Nevada, Missouri, as it appeared in the 1960s. Also pictured is a 1927 Chrysler Staff Car that was found in 1947 buried under hay in one of the old barns that once stood on Camp Clark. The car was the property of the US Army but was left behind when Camp Clark was turned over to the Missouri National Guard following the end of World War II. The car was brought to Jefferson City several years ago, restored and is now on display in the Museum of Missouri Military History on the grounds of the Missouri National Guard Headquarters.

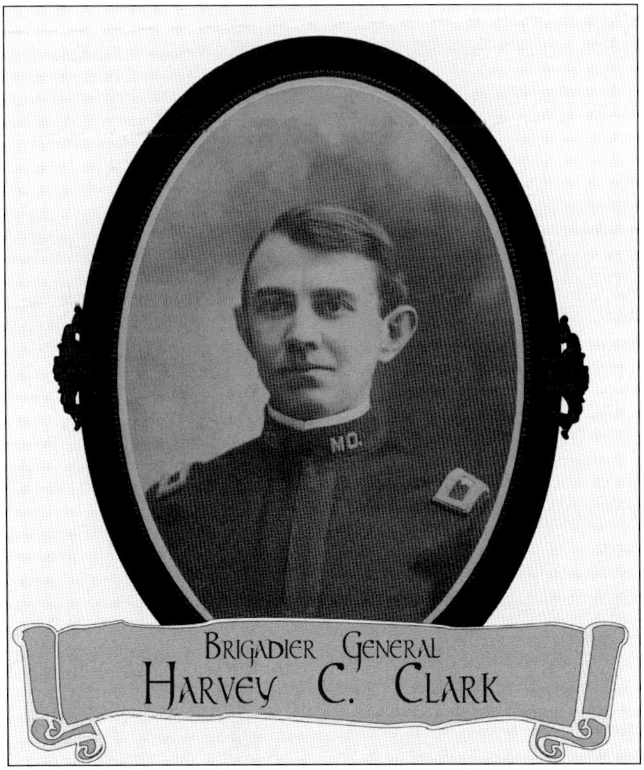

Camp Clark was first established in 1908 as the State Rifle Range but was renamed on April 21, 1921, in honor of Brig. Gen. Harvey Clark. A native of Bates County, Clark was a cadet at the former Wentworth Military Academy in Lexington and a veteran of the Spanish-American War. In 1899, Clark became a brigadier general and was appointed adjutant general of the Missouri National Guard on January 1, 1918. He passed away when only 52 years old from meningitis on April 11, 1921. (Museum of Missouri Military History.)

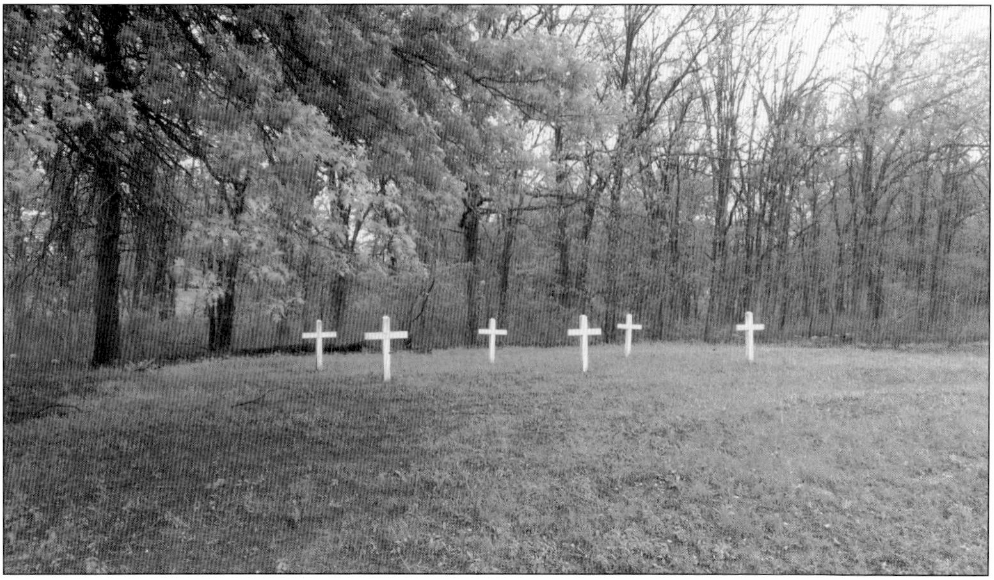

During World War II, as many as 5,000 German and Italian prisoners of war (POWs) were held at Camp Clark. A small plot of land on the post was used as a cemetery for POWs who died while imprisoned at Camp Clark during the war; however, their remains were returned to their respective homes at the end of the war. Camp Clark continues to honor the memory of those who died as POWs at the camp by maintaining white crosses in the former area that served as the POW cemetery.

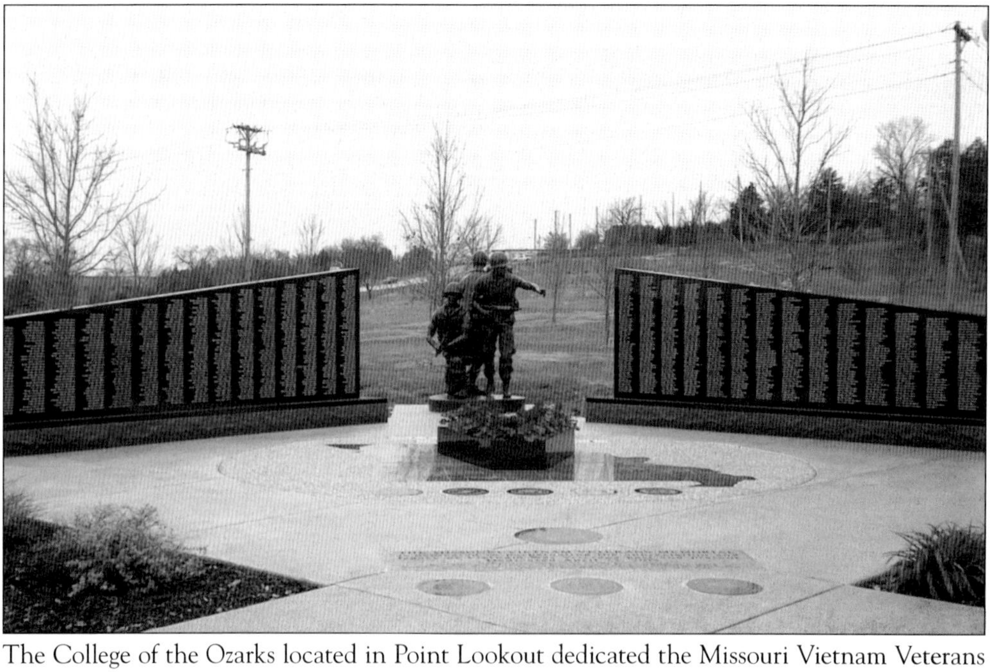

The College of the Ozarks located in Point Lookout dedicated the Missouri Vietnam Veterans Memorial on their campus on April 22, 2015, before a crowd of more than 3,500 attendees. In addition to a bronze statue featuring Vietnam veterans, the memorial is comprised of two walls of granite upon which are inscribed the names of the 1,410 Missourians who lost their life during the war. (Tina Amick.)

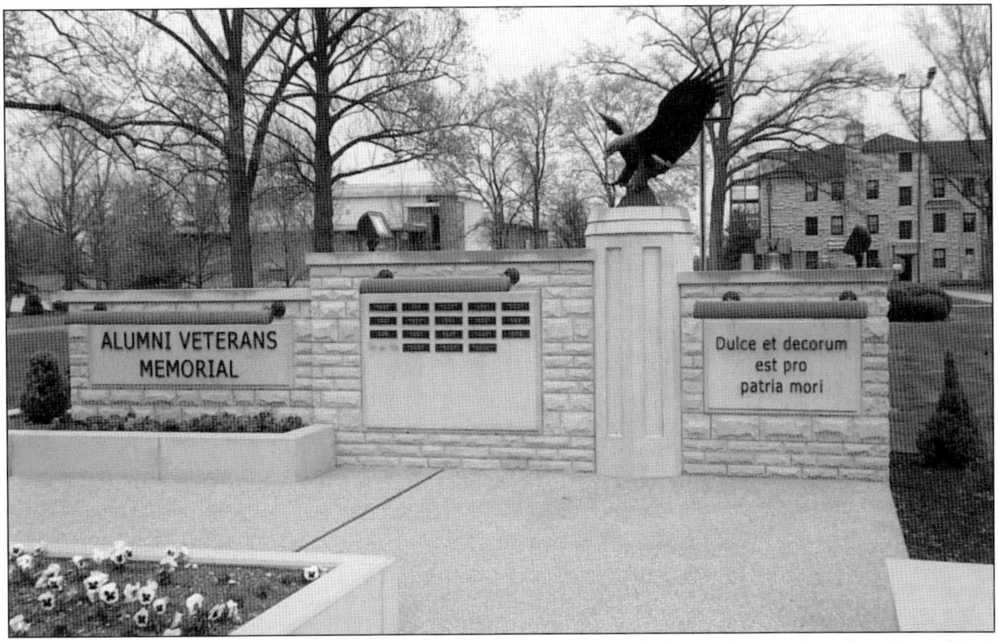

The Alumni Veterans Memorial was erected on the campus of the College of the Ozarks in 2013 to replace a previous memorial that was built in 1983 but had become weathered and could not accommodate additional names. The memorial contains a listing of the school's alumni who lost their lives while serving in the armed forces. (Tina Amick.)

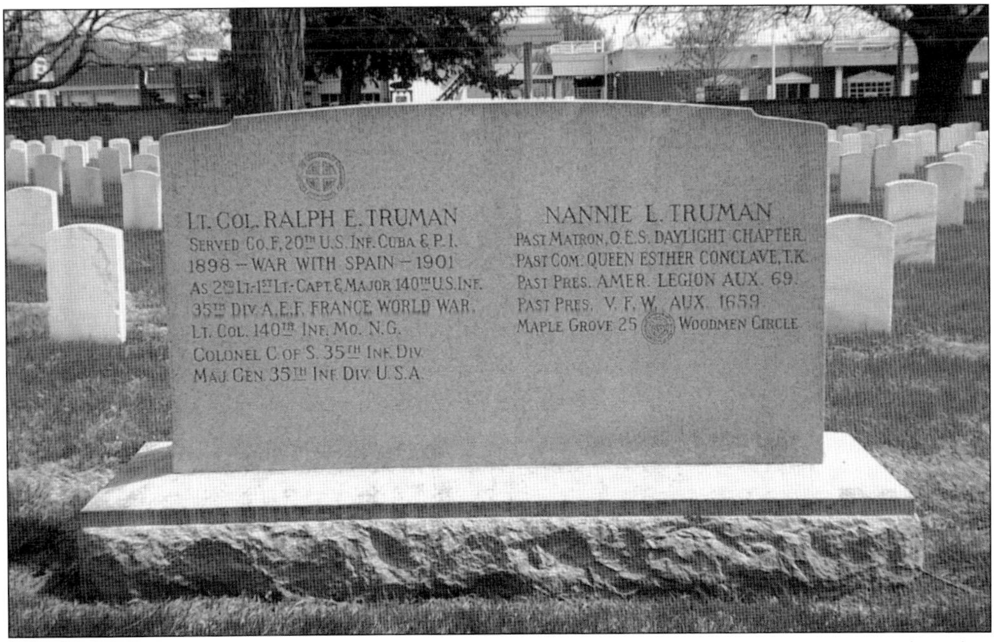

This memorial tombstone tucked with the confines of the Springfield National Cemetery describes the numerous contributions made by Maj. Gen. Ralph E. Truman and his first wife, the former Nannie Watson. Truman was laid to rest on May 3, 1962, during a ceremony under the charge of the American Legion Goad-Ballinger Post 69 of Springfield, of which Gen. Truman was a charter member.

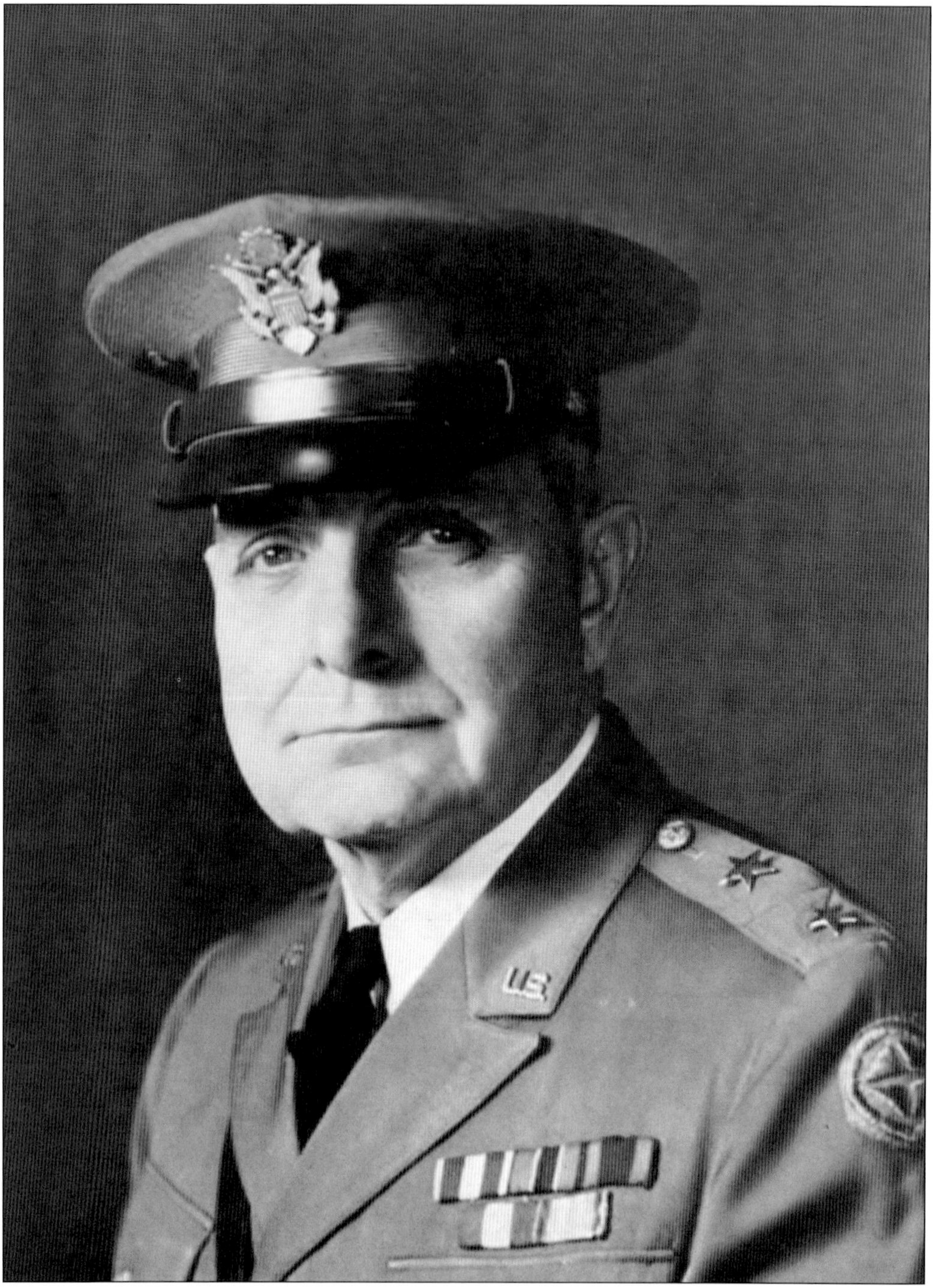

Maj. Gen. Ralph Truman was a veteran of four wars and first cousin and close friend of Pres. Harry S. Truman. Born in Kansas City, Missouri, Ralph Truman was perhaps best known for his command of the 35th Division from 1938 to 1941. The Missouri veteran retired from the Missouri National Guard in 1944 after 28 years of military service. He moved to Springfield in 1951, where he resided when he passed away from a heart attack on April 30, 1962. (Museum of Missouri Military History.)

Near the Reynolds County community of Ellington is a veterans' memorial that was erected inside the Ellington Memorial Cemetery. The cemetery, which was the first perpetual care cemetery in the area, was established by the late Charles "Bud" Pewitt, a Reynolds County resident who served in the Army during the Korean War, was the county coroner for 20 years, and operated an insurance agency and ambulance service.

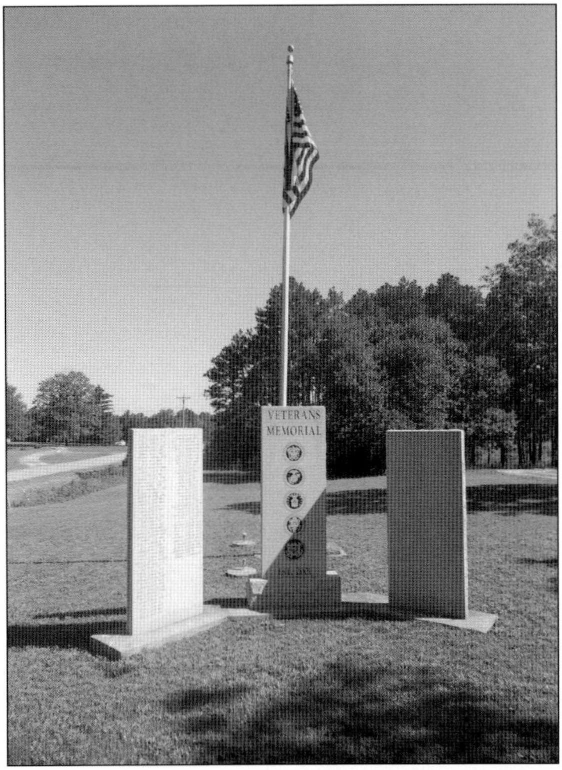

The Reynolds County Courthouse in Centerville has on its lawn a memorial constructed from pink granite that honors the men and women of the county who served in the nation's wars. Dedicated in 1984, this memorial is comprised of obelisks and walls listing the names of the county residents who died in World War I, World War II, Korea, and Vietnam.

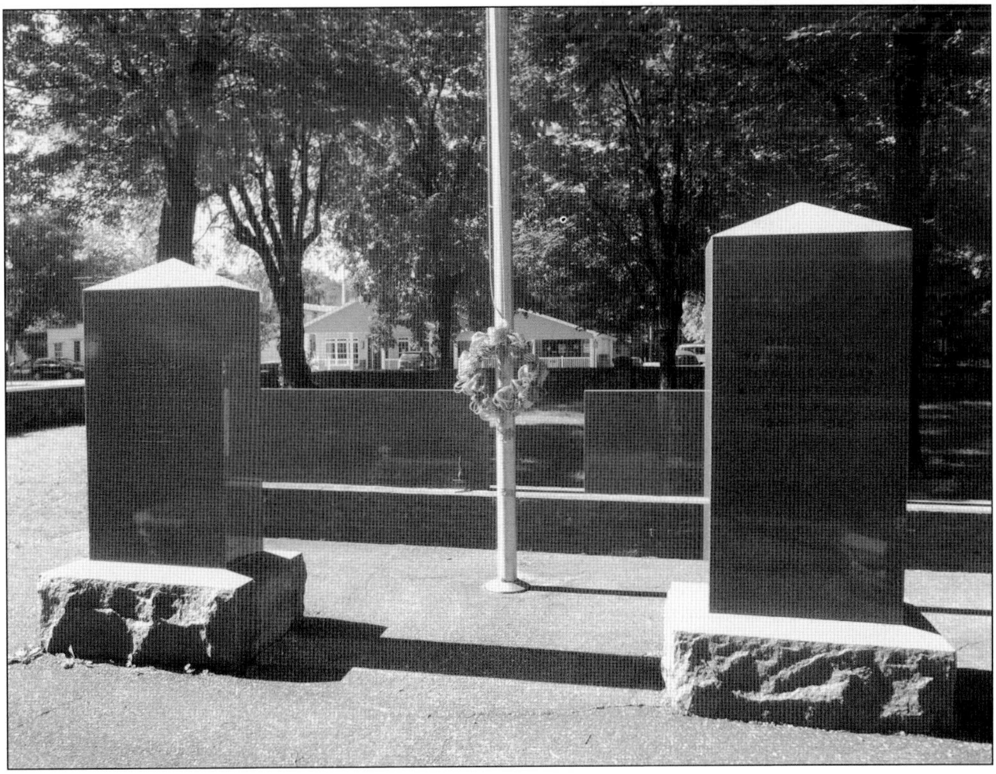

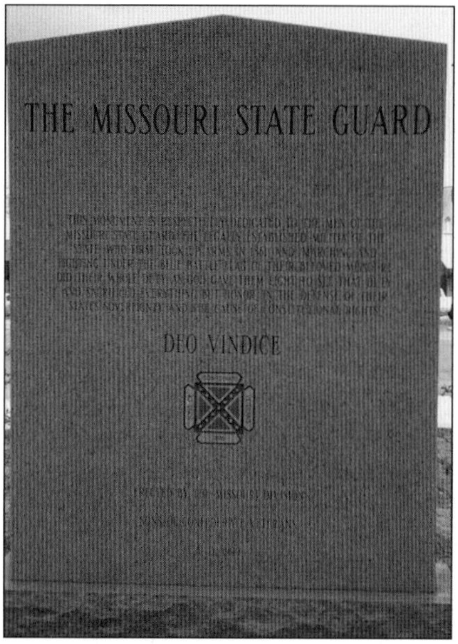

A memorial to the soldiers of the Missouri State Guard was placed on the grounds of the Jasper County Courthouse in Carthage in 1999 by the Missouri Division of the Sons of Confederate Veterans. The Missouri State Guard flag and a brief account of the Battle of Carthage, which occurred on July 5, 1861, and resulted in a Confederate victory over Union forces, is inscribed upon the opposite side of the memorial.

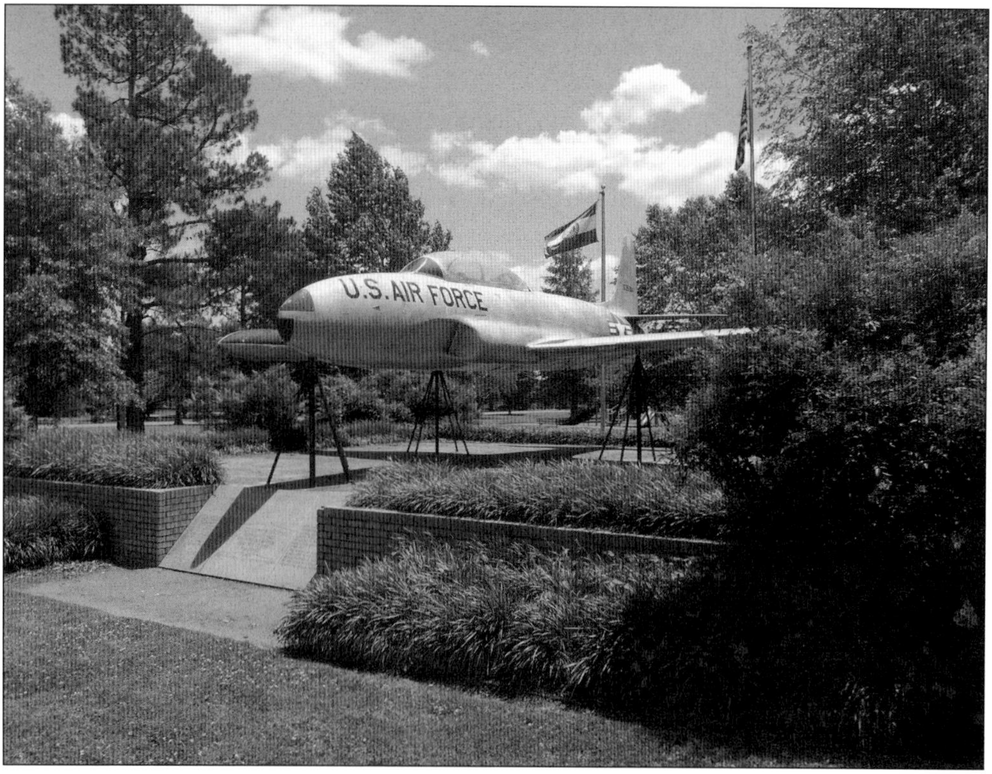

A memorial to the late Lt. Col. John England, who died in 1954, was dedicated on June 17, 1967, in England City Park in the southeastern Missouri community of Caruthersville. England was Missouri's leading flying ace in Europe and participated in 108 combat missions during World War II. His memorial consists of a plaque citing his military service record in addition to a T-33 jet trainer donated by the Air Force. Barry Goldwater, Republican candidate for president in 1964, was the featured speaker at the dedication and a friend of England's.

A native of Caruthersville, John England entered the US Army in 1942 and went on to complete flight training and become a commissioned officer and pilot in the US Army Air Forces in 1943. During World War II, he distinguished himself with 17.5 enemy aircraft destroyed and earned a Silver Star medal for gallantry. England was killed on November 17, 1954, when he grounded his F-86 Sabrejet at an air base in France while veering to avoid hitting barracks that housed fellow airmen. (Museum of Missouri Military History.)

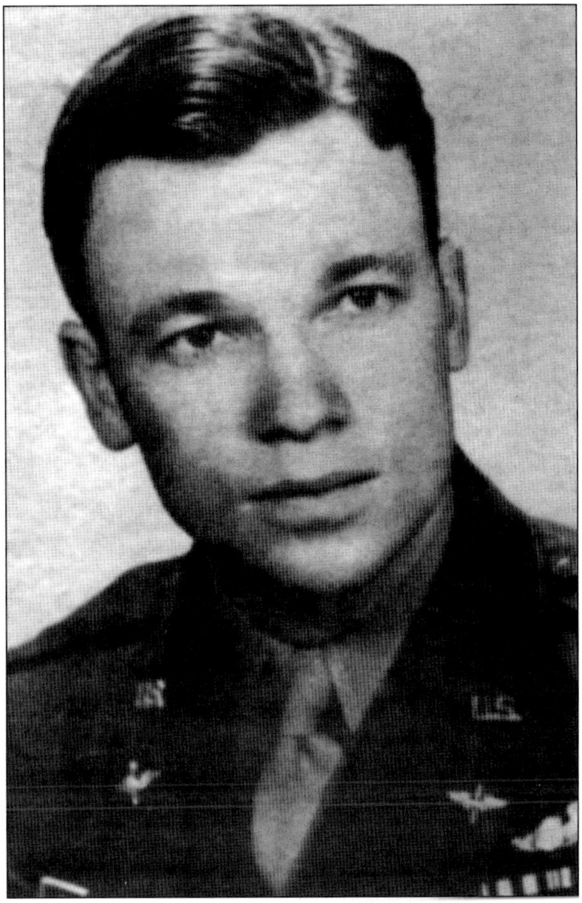

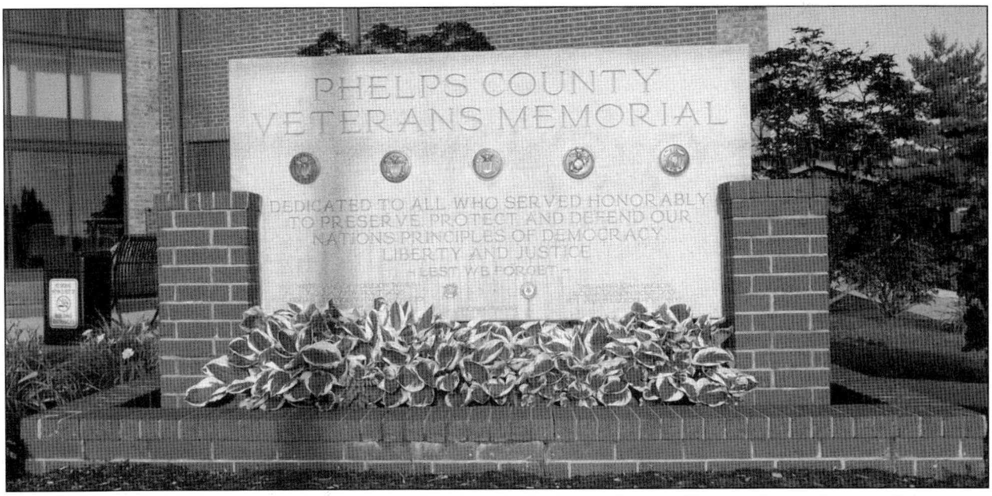

The Phelps County Veterans Memorial is located along the traffic circle in front of the new courthouse in Rolla. This is a multi-war monument that was dedicated on June 2, 2007, while Rolla celebrated its sesquicentennial. The memorial was sponsored by local American Legion and Veterans of Foreign Wars posts and "dedicated to the men and women of Phelps County who have defended the cause of freedom."

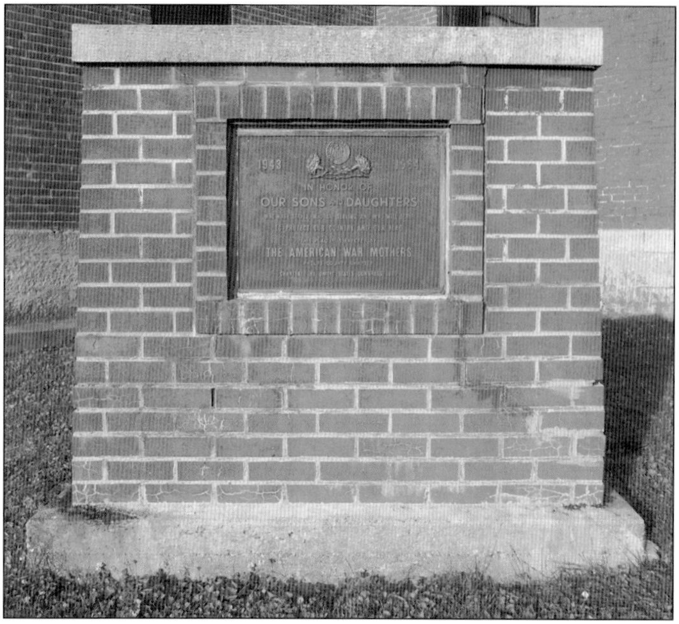

An unadorned, brick monument with an inset bronze plaque was dedicated by the American War Mothers in front of the old Phelps County Courthouse in Rolla, which is now owned by the county's historical society. The monument was dedicated in 1964 in memory of all who have served the nation in uniform.

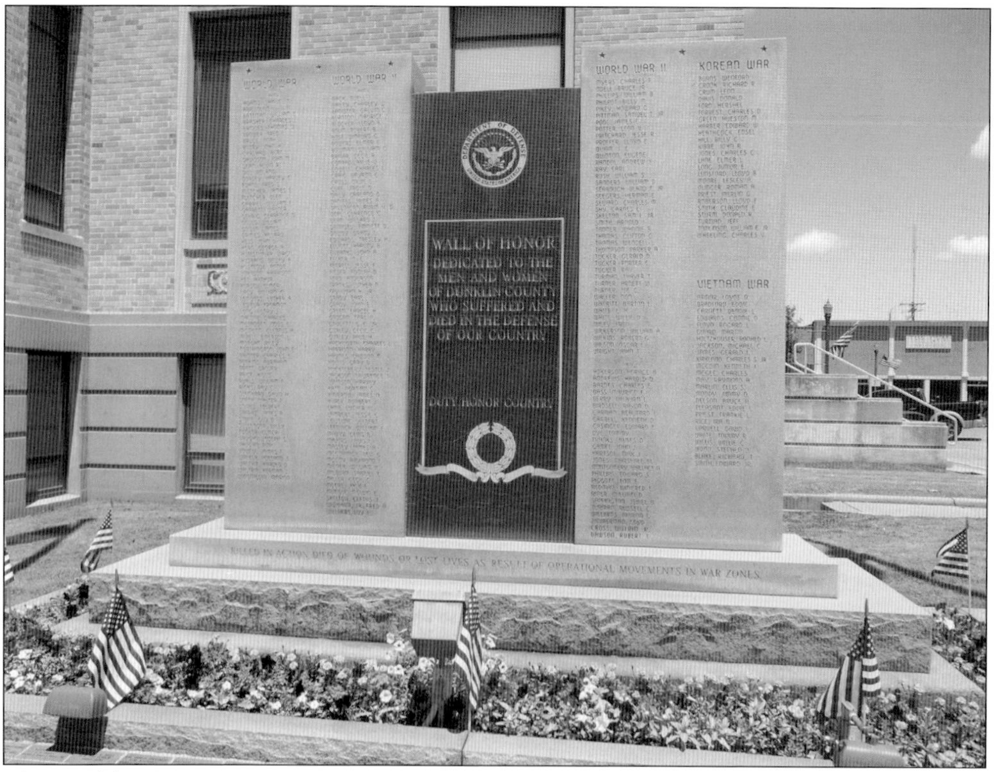

The Dunklin County Veterans Memorial is located on the grounds of the county courthouse in Kennett. The monument consists of three panels—of which the center is "dedicated to the men and women of Dunklin County who suffered and died in the defense of our country," while the outer columns list the names of county residents who lost their lives during the various wars in which the nation has been involved.

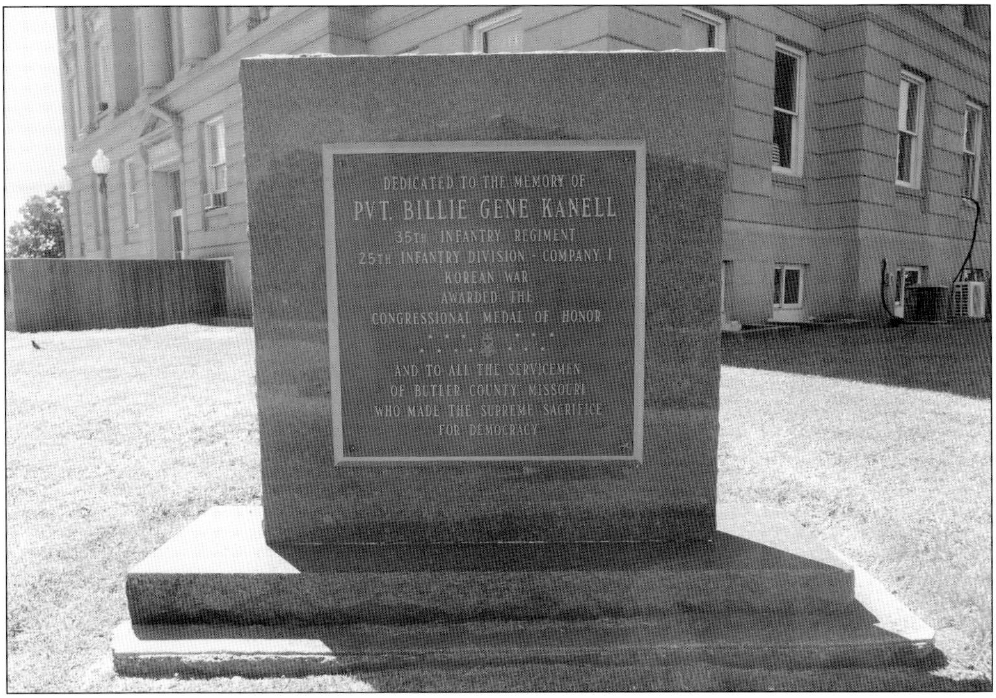

The service of Congressional Medal of Honor recipient Pvt. Billie Gene Kanell is commemorated through a memorial on the lawn of the Butler County Courthouse in Poplar Bluff. The 19-year-old Kanell was serving with the Army's 25th Infantry Division in Korea when he was killed on September 7, 1951, using his body to shield his fellow soldiers from an enemy grenade.

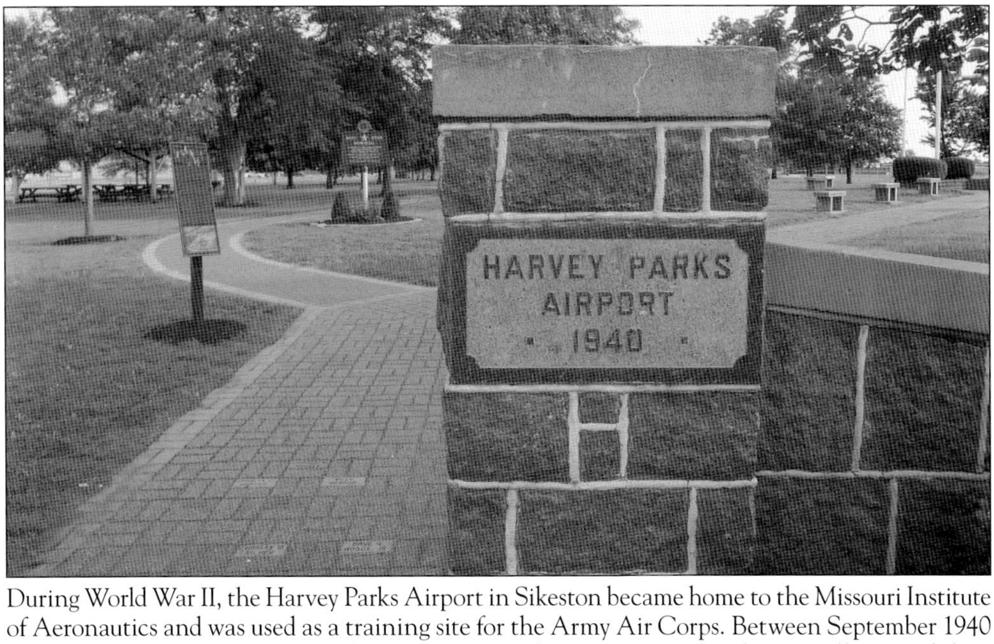

During World War II, the Harvey Parks Airport in Sikeston became home to the Missouri Institute of Aeronautics and was used as a training site for the Army Air Corps. Between September 1940 and November 1944, an estimated 5,000 aspiring pilots were trained and eventually earned their aviation wings. In 1992, on the grounds of the former aviation site, the community established the Sikeston Veterans Park, which has various military vehicles and aviation pieces on display.

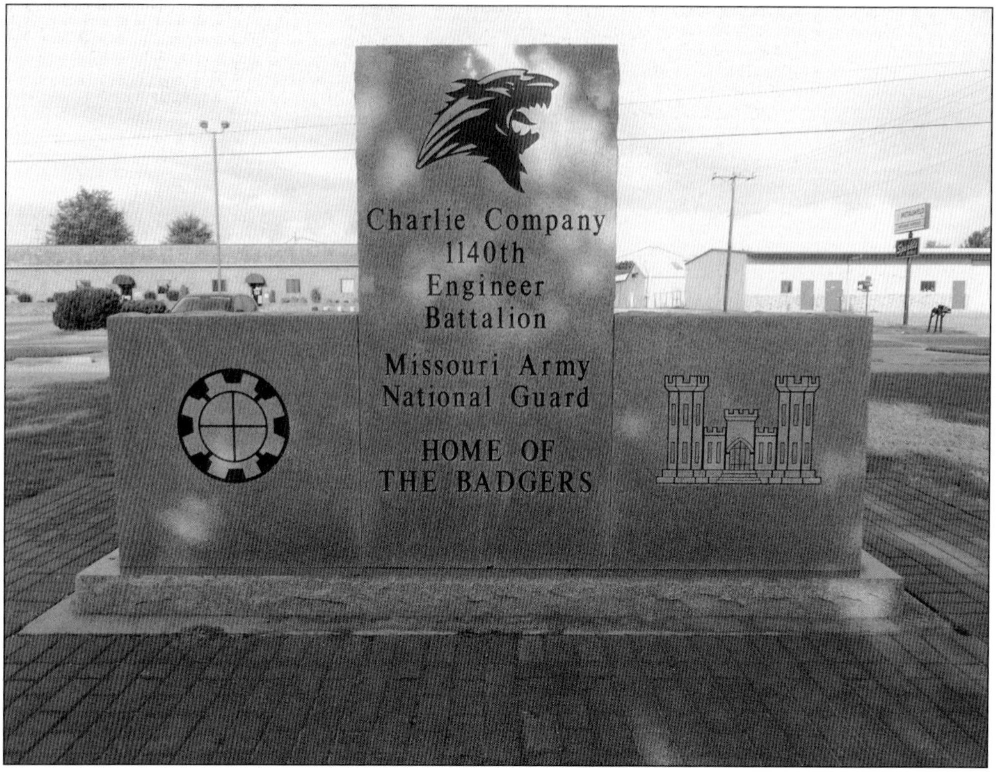

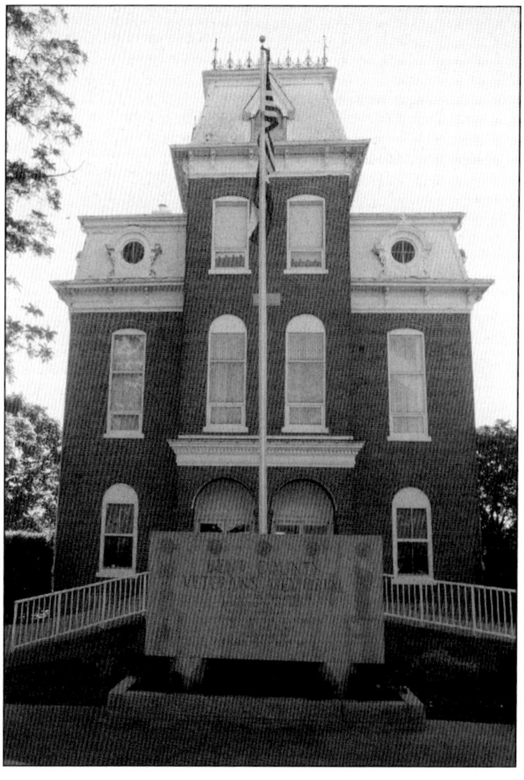

In addition to displaying an anchor from a World War II destroyer, F4J Phantom Fighter, M101A1 Light Howitzer, HUL-1 Sioux Helicopter, and an M60 Patton Tank, the Sikeston Memorial Park also houses a monument dedicated to the men and women of the Missouri National Guard's Charlie Company, 1140th Engineer Company who served in Operation Iraqi Freedom between 2004 and 2005.

The Dent County Veterans Memorial is located on the lawn of the Dent County Courthouse in the county seat of Salem. The monument was sponsored by the local Walker-Roney Post 99 of the American Legion and was dedicated on July 4, 1992, to "all who served honorably in defense of our country."

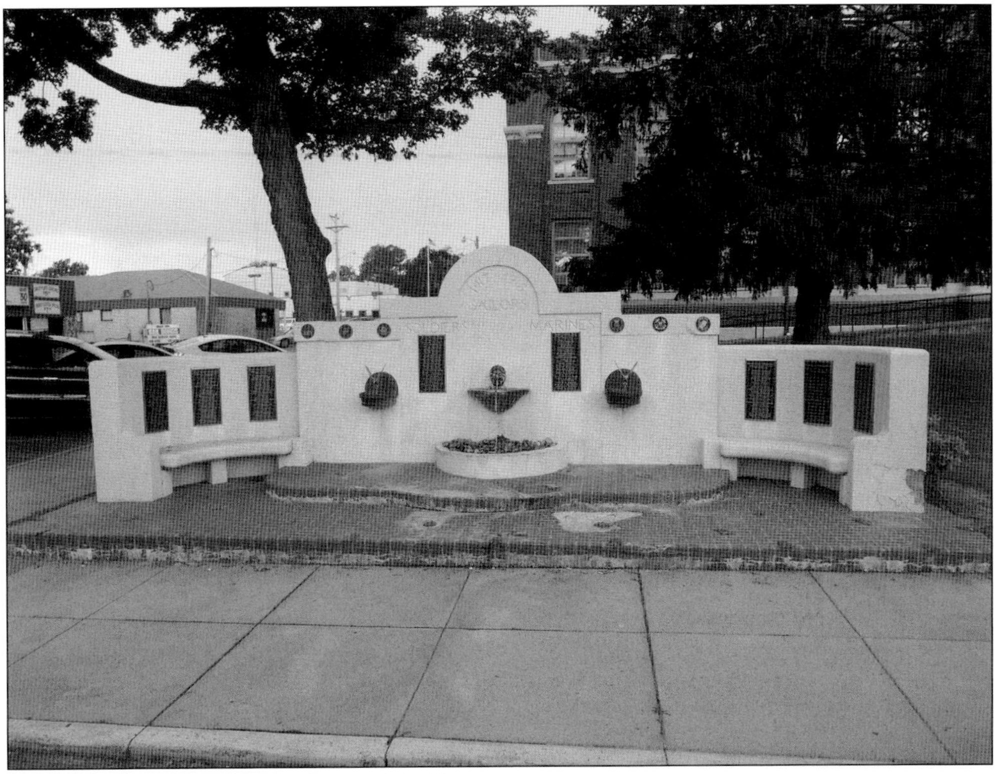

A memorial fountain on the lawn of the Scott County Courthouse in Benton was initially constructed to honor veterans of World War I. Although the fountain was once adorned with plaques that listed the names of county citizens killed in World War I, in recent years, the memorial has been updated to include the names of county residents who have lost their lives in military engagements since World War I.

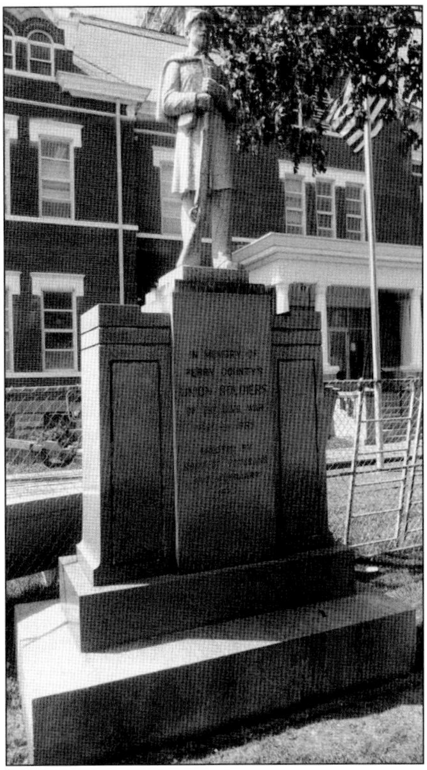

This monument was dedicated in 1923 "in Memory of Perry County's Union Soldiers in the Civil War" at north entrance of the Perry County Courthouse in the county seat of Perryville. The impressive, 10-foot-tall monument features a sculpted Union soldier made from granite and was placed by Sons of Veterans and Auxiliaries.

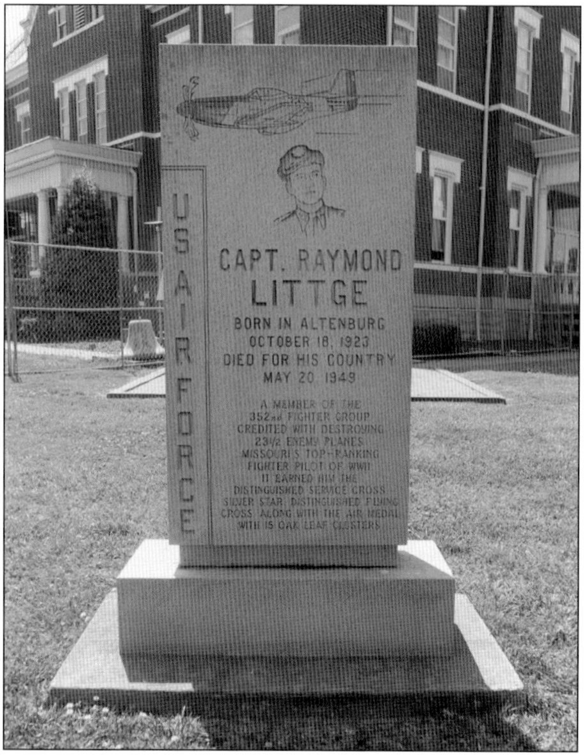

The World War II service of Capt. Raymond H. Littge is memorialized through this monument on the lawn of the Perry County Courthouse in Perryville. Born in Altenburg, Missouri, in 1923, Littge was a 1942 graduate of Perryville High School and enlisted in the Aviation Cadet Program later the same year. In December 1943, he earned his pilot wings and was commissioned a second lieutenant.

During World War II, Capt. Raymond Littge flew the P-51 Mustang with the 352nd Fighter Group in Europe. When the war ended, he was credited with 10.5 aerial victories and 13 aircraft destroyed on the ground. Sadly, on May 20, 1949, Littge lost his life when the F-84 Thunderjet he was piloting crashed in Oregon due to what is suspected to have been a faulty oxygen system. (Museum of Missouri Military History.)

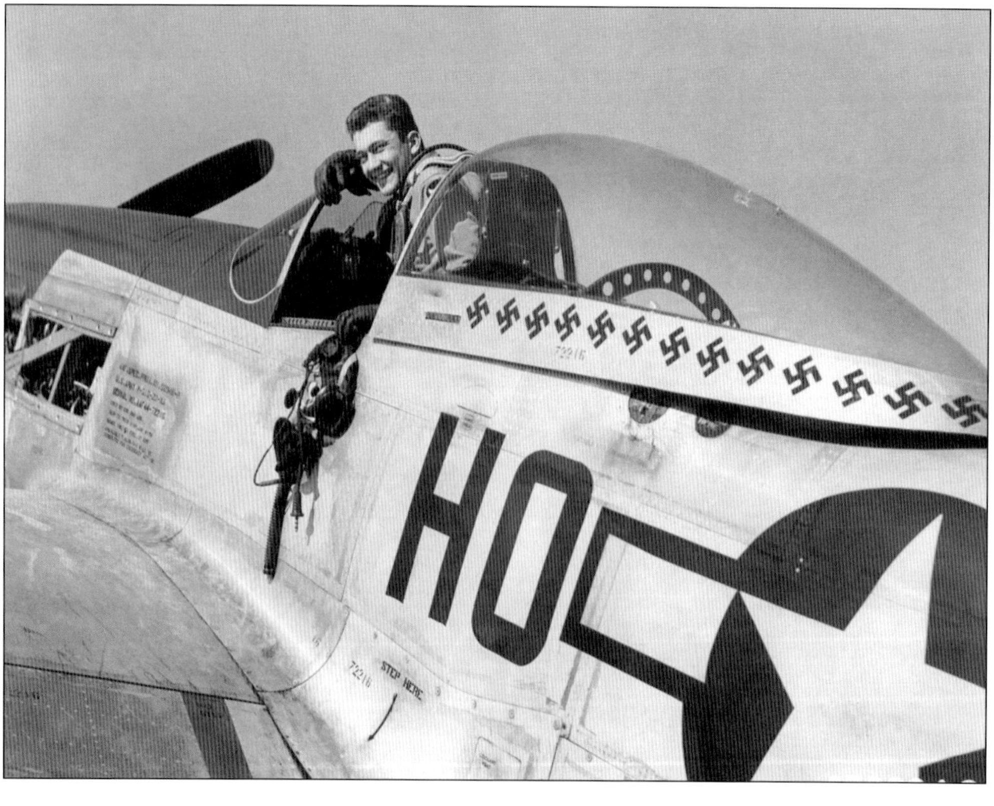

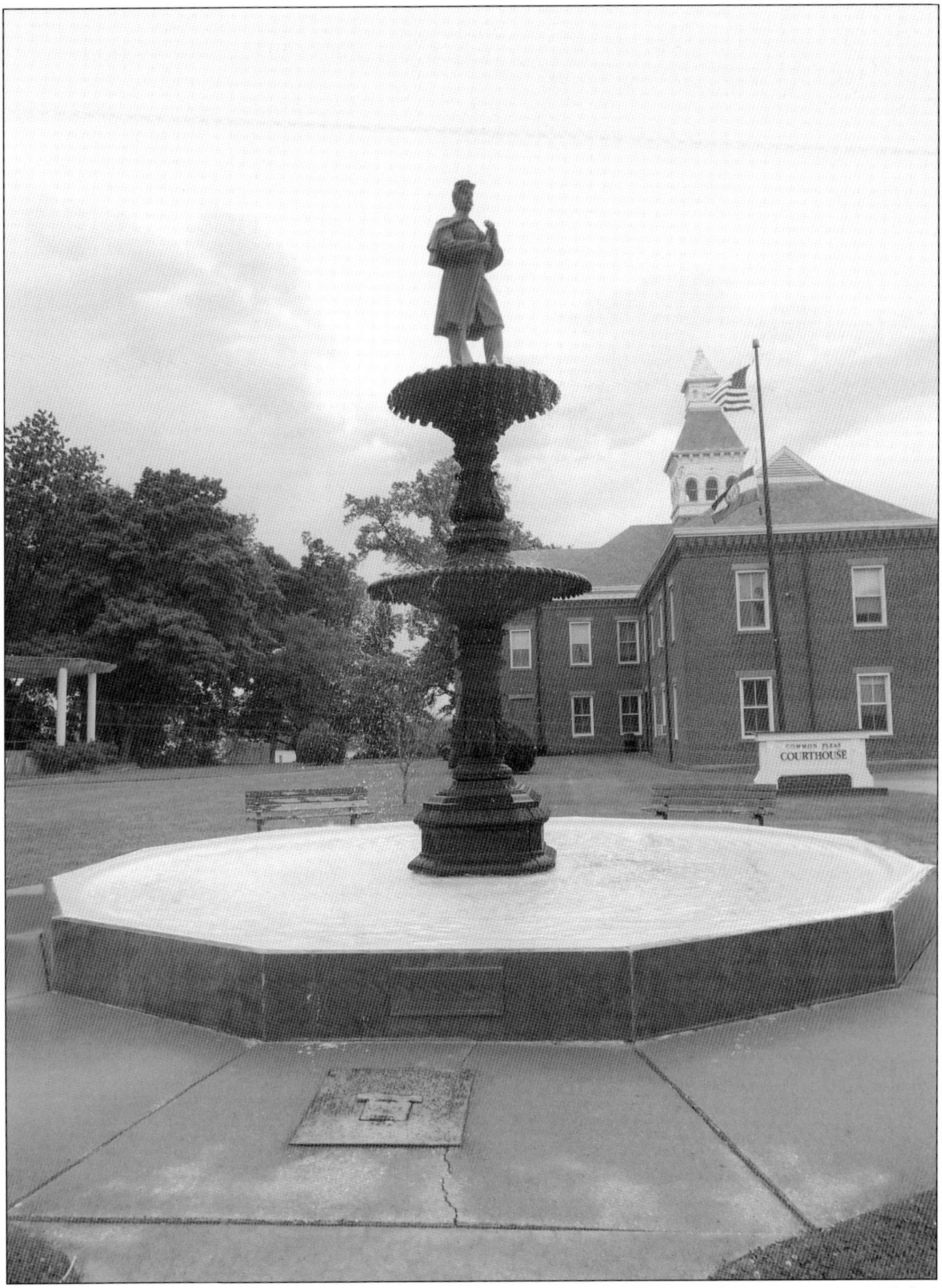

The Woman's Relief Corps—an auxiliary of the Grand Army of the Republic, Inc.—erected this fountain in 1911 at the Common Pleas Courthouse in Cape Girardeau in memory of the Union soldiers who served in the Civil War. The original cast iron statue was destroyed by a limb that fell from a nearby tree on May 12, 2003, but was restored several months later through the efforts of Dexter, Missouri, sculptor Alan Gibson.

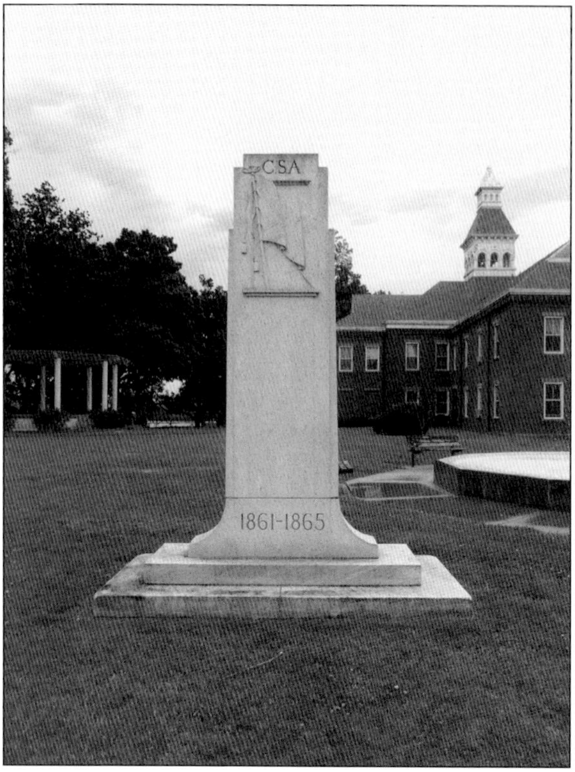

An upright marble slab on the lawn of the Common Pleas Courthouse in Cape Girardeau was dedicated to the memory of Confederate soldiers from southeast Missouri by the United Daughters of the Confederacy in 1931. During the Civil War, the basement of the nearby courthouse was used by the Union as a prison for Confederate soldiers and Southern sympathizers.

Situated within City Park in the southeast Missouri community of Scott City is the Scott City Area Veterans Memorial. The memorial is dedicated to citizens from the communities of Kelso, Commerce, and Scott City who have or will serve in the armed forces of the United States. The memorial was constructed through the efforts of the Scott City Kiwanis Club and Boy Scout Troop 29.

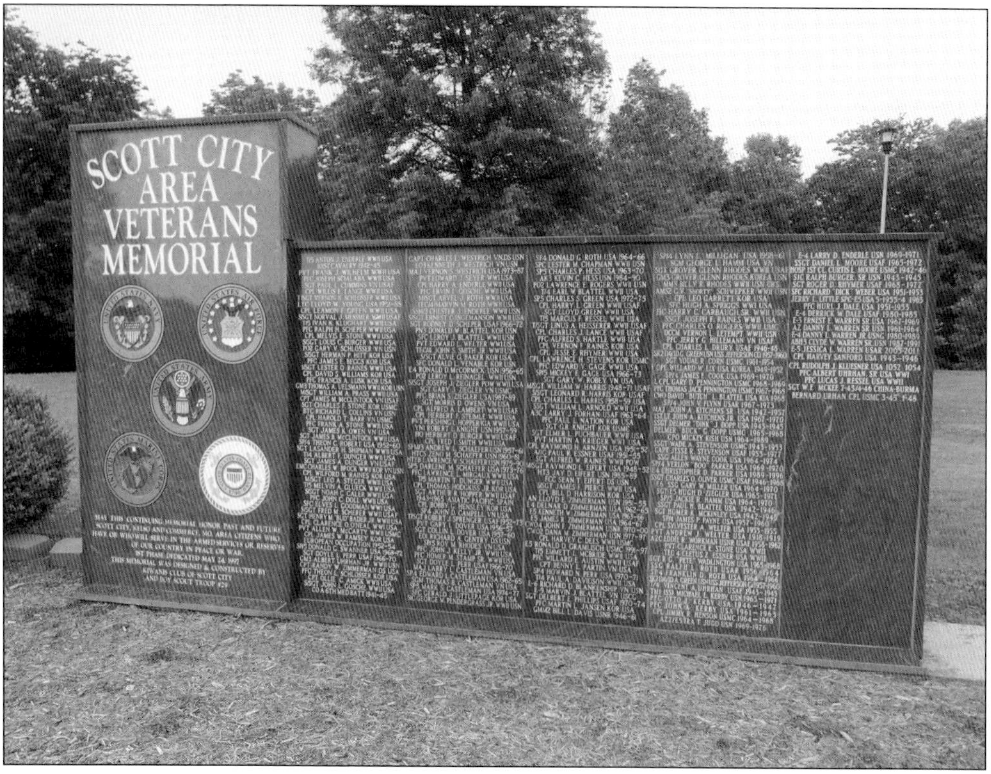

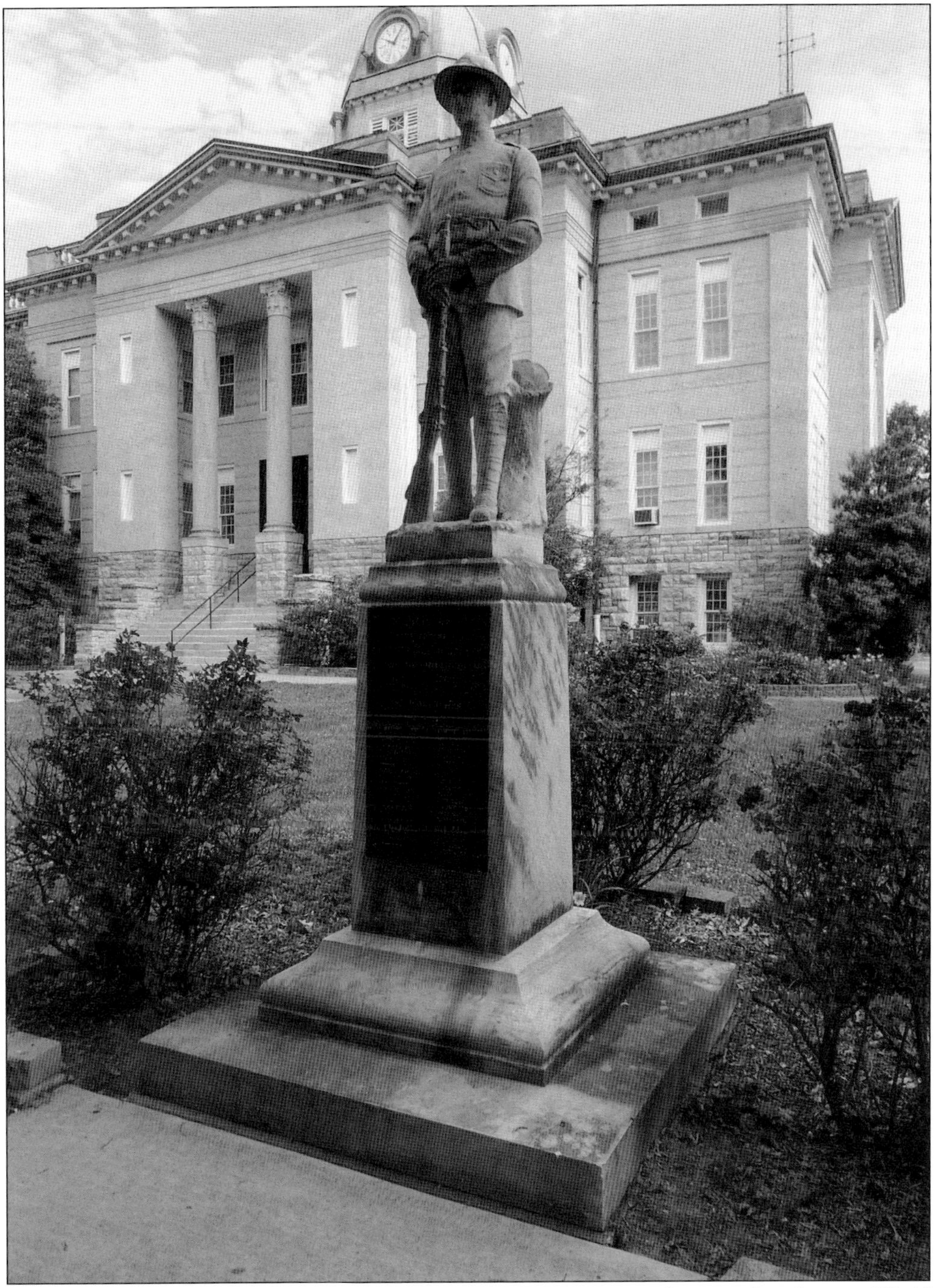

A time-worn memorial honoring Cape Girardeau County citizens who gave their lives in World War I was dedicated on Decoration Day, May 30, 1925, on the south lawn of the county courthouse in the community of Jackson. The memorial features a World War I soldier standing at parade rest and holding the barrel of a rifle in his hands. The base of the memorial features a brass plate listing the names of the county's war casualties.

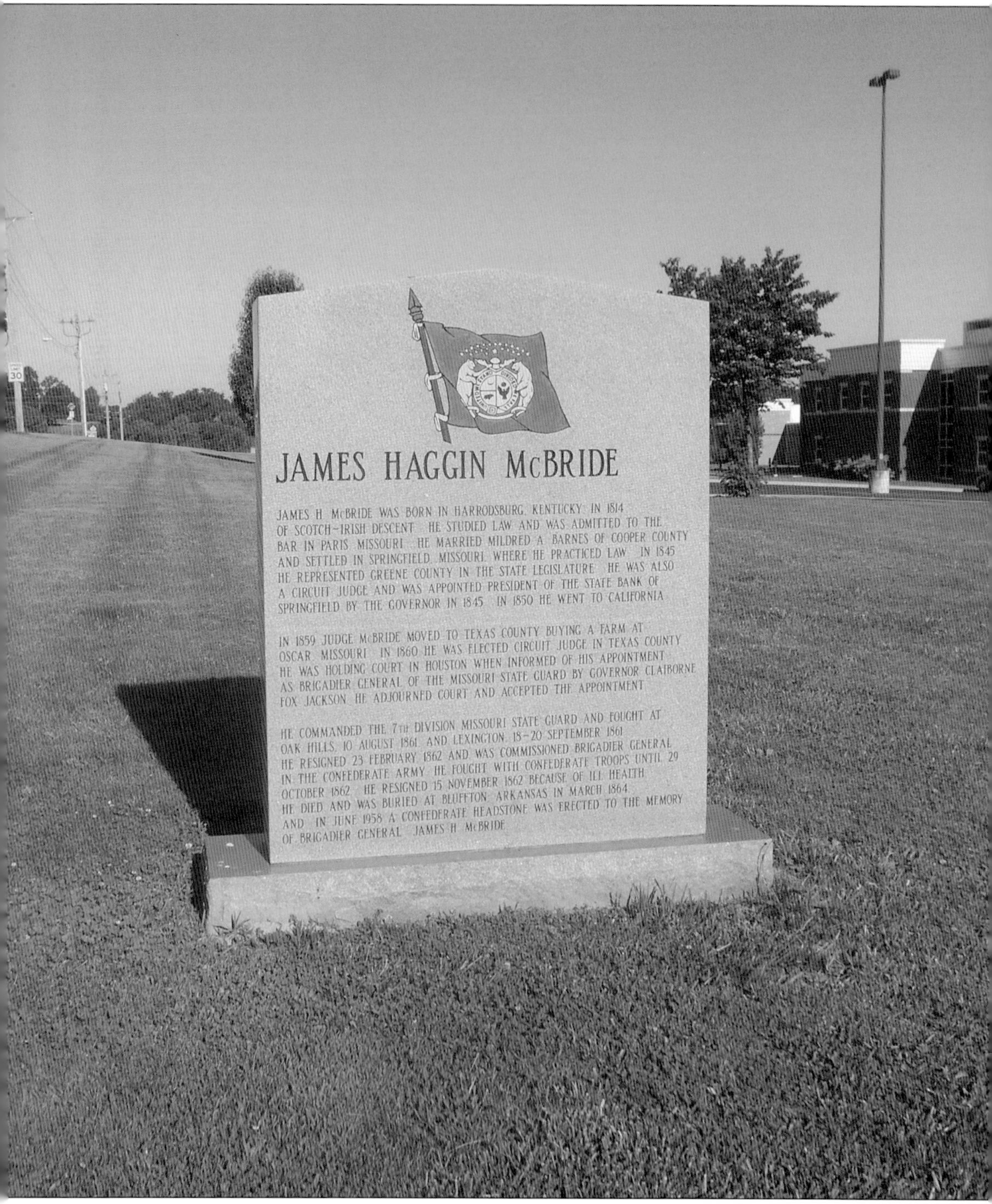

A memorial to James Haggin McBride was dedicated on the lawn of the Texas County Justice Center in Houston in 2009 by the Gen. J.H. McBride Camp 632 of the Sons of Confederate Veterans. A native of Kentucky, McBride later moved to Missouri, where he became a merchant and went on to study law and work as an attorney. He moved to Texas County, Missouri, in 1859 and was elected county circuit court judge—a position he held at the beginning of the Civil War.

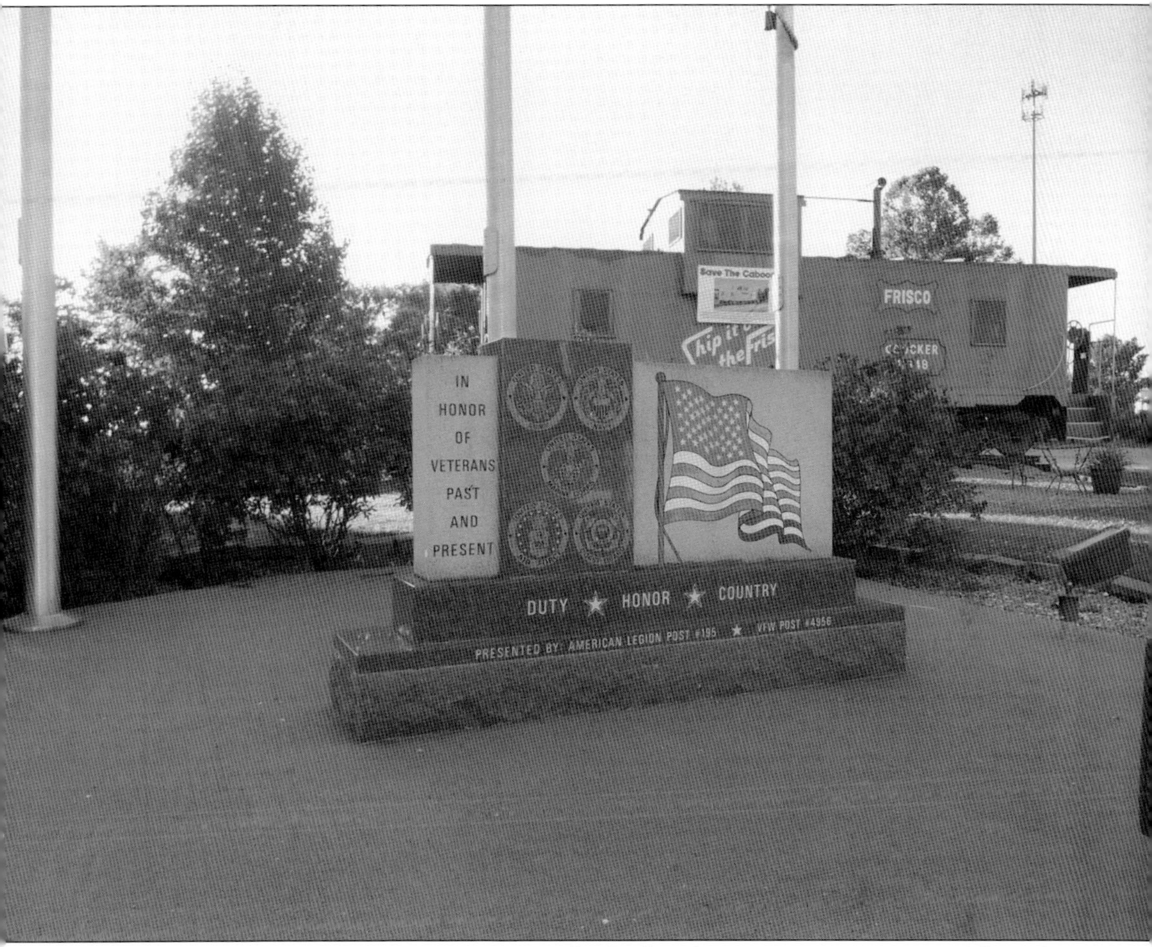

A memorial dedicated to all veterans is proudly displayed in Norma Lea's Frisco Park in the Pulaski County community of Crocker. The park was named in honor of Norma Lea Mihalevich, who served as the town mayor for 24 years, and also recognizes the area's rich railroad history. In 2013, Crocker became a Purple Heart City through a program of the Military Order of the Purple Heart.

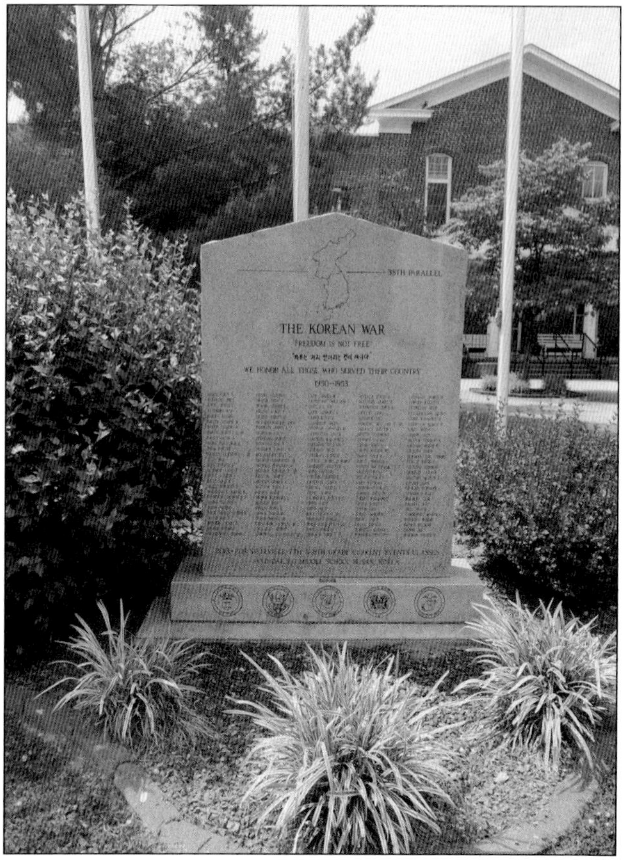

Local students at the Steelville Middle School worked together to erect this monument on the lawn of the Crawford County Courthouse in Steelville that lists the names of local residents who served in the Korean War. Dedicated on May 30, 2011, the monument became a reality through bake sales and fundraisers sponsored by the seventh- and eighth-grade students.

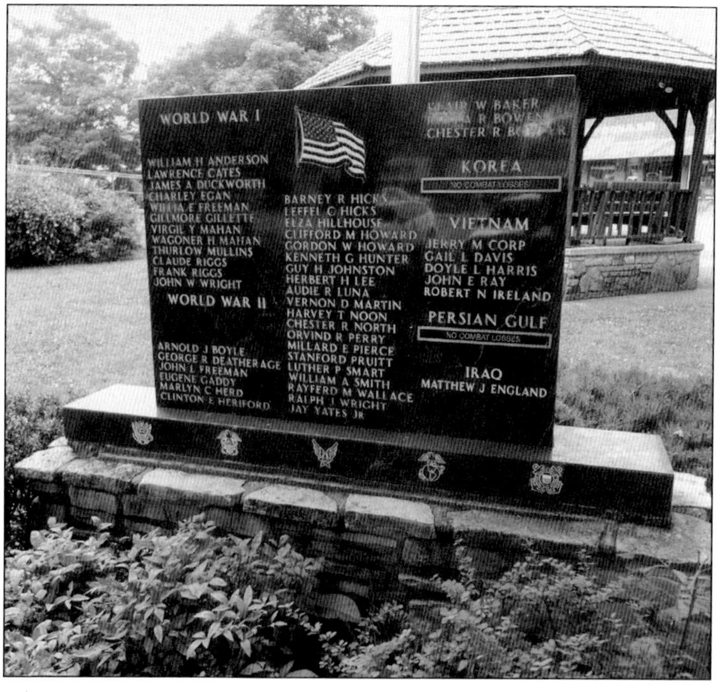

The Ozark County War Memorial in Gainesville is located on the lawn of the county courthouse. Constructed from black granite and dedicated in 1991, the memorial lists the names of county residents who have been killed in the conflicts beginning with World War I and has been updated to include the name of a local resident killed in Iraq in 2011.

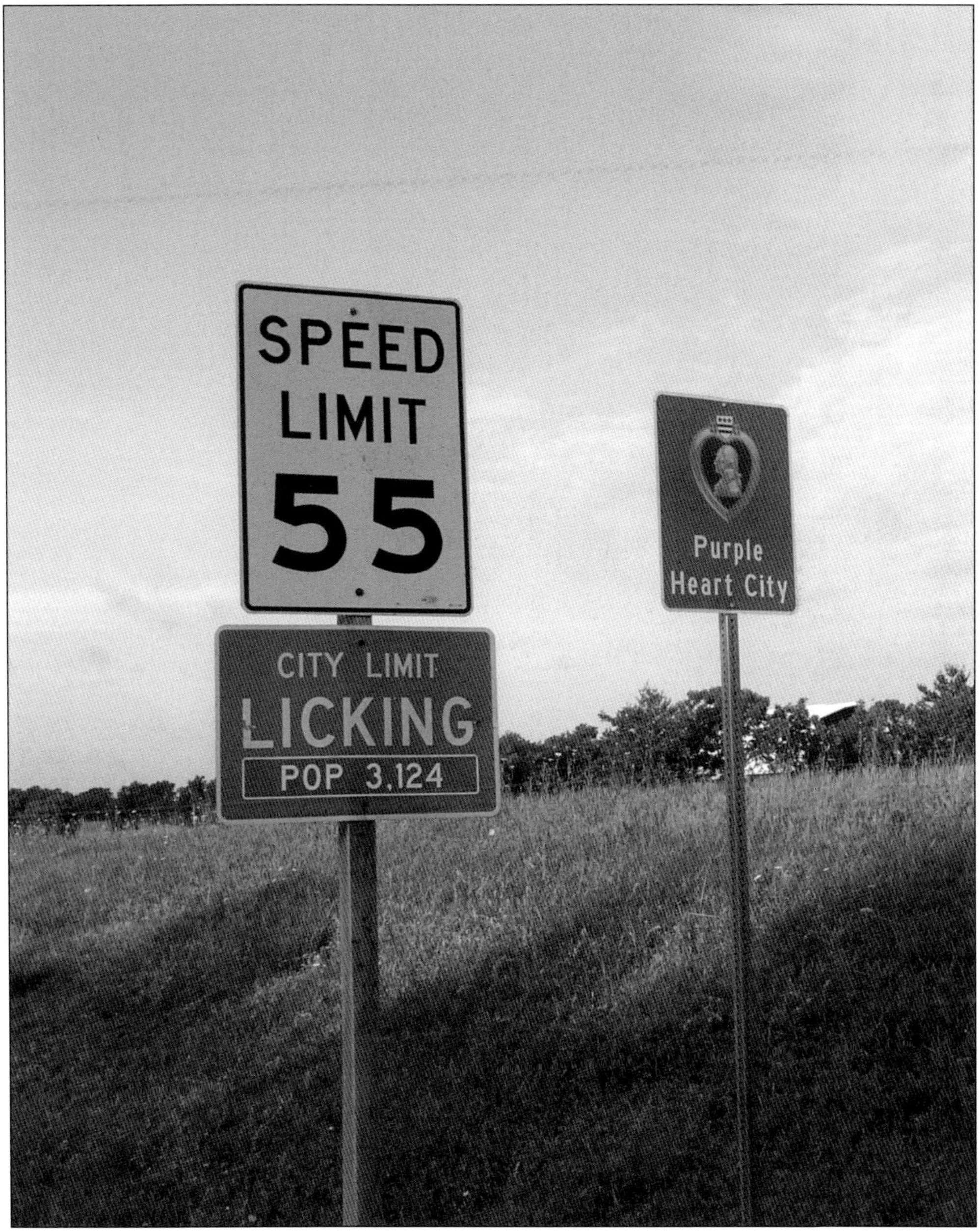

As motorists pass through the community of Licking on Highway 63 in Texas County, they may notice a sign that denotes the community as a "Purple Heart City." In this program of the Military Order of the Purple Heart, communities can receive such a designation by having the mayor or governing board sign a proclamation denoting their support for Purple Heart veterans.

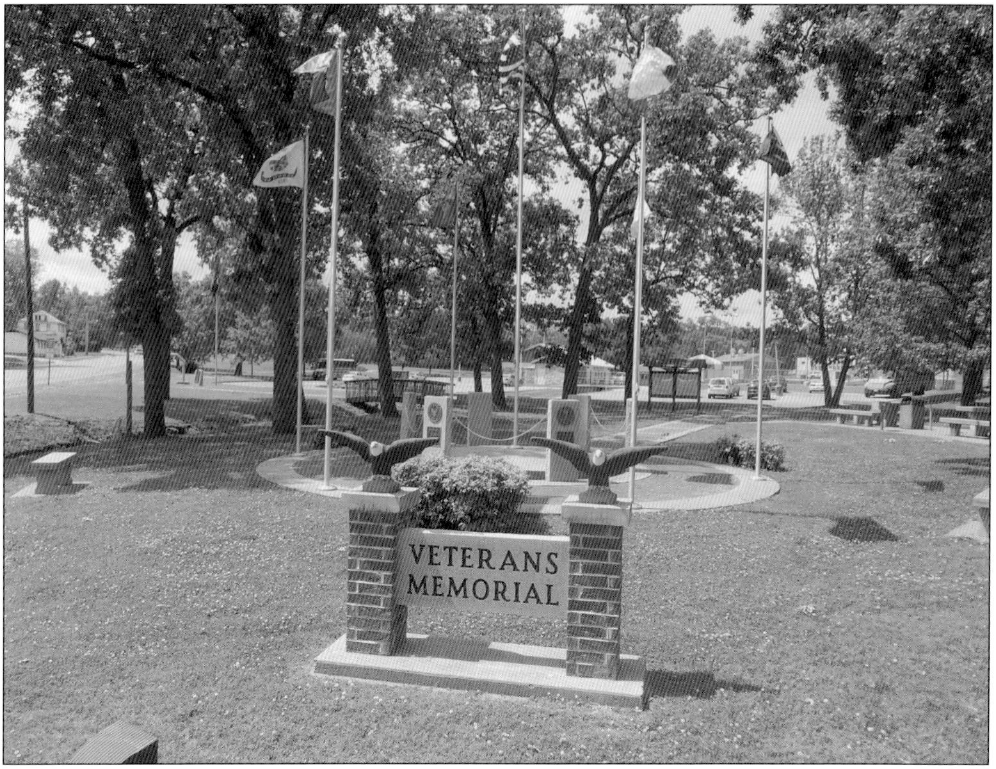

The city of West Plains in Howell County has chosen to honor its local veterans through a memorial erected in People's Park. The memorial was dedicated on May 27, 2002, and consists of columns arranged in a circular pattern that are dedicated to each branch of the military. Additionally, the tribute has a section honoring Gold Star Mothers, with the names of their fallen sons and daughters listed on memorial bricks.

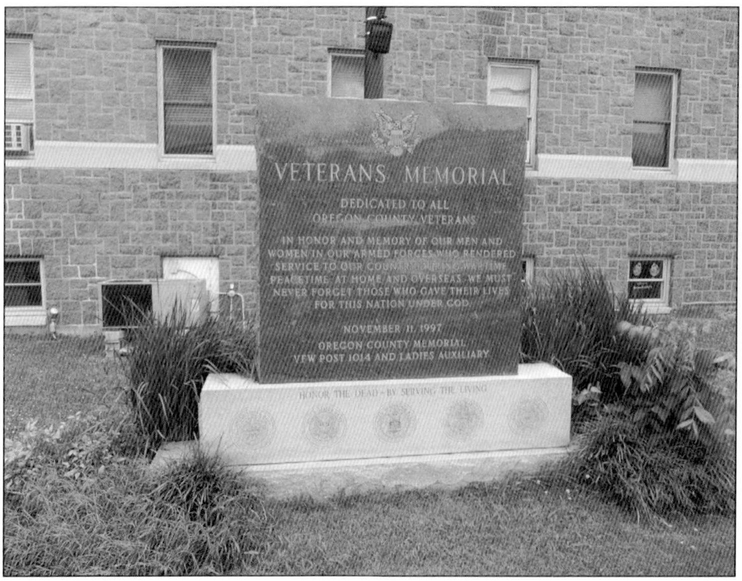

The Oregon County Veterans Memorial is located on the lawn of the courthouse in the small southeastern community of Alton. Constructed from red granite, the monument was dedicated in honor of all veterans on November 11, 1997, and sponsored by the county, the local Veterans of Foreign Wars post, and its auxiliary.

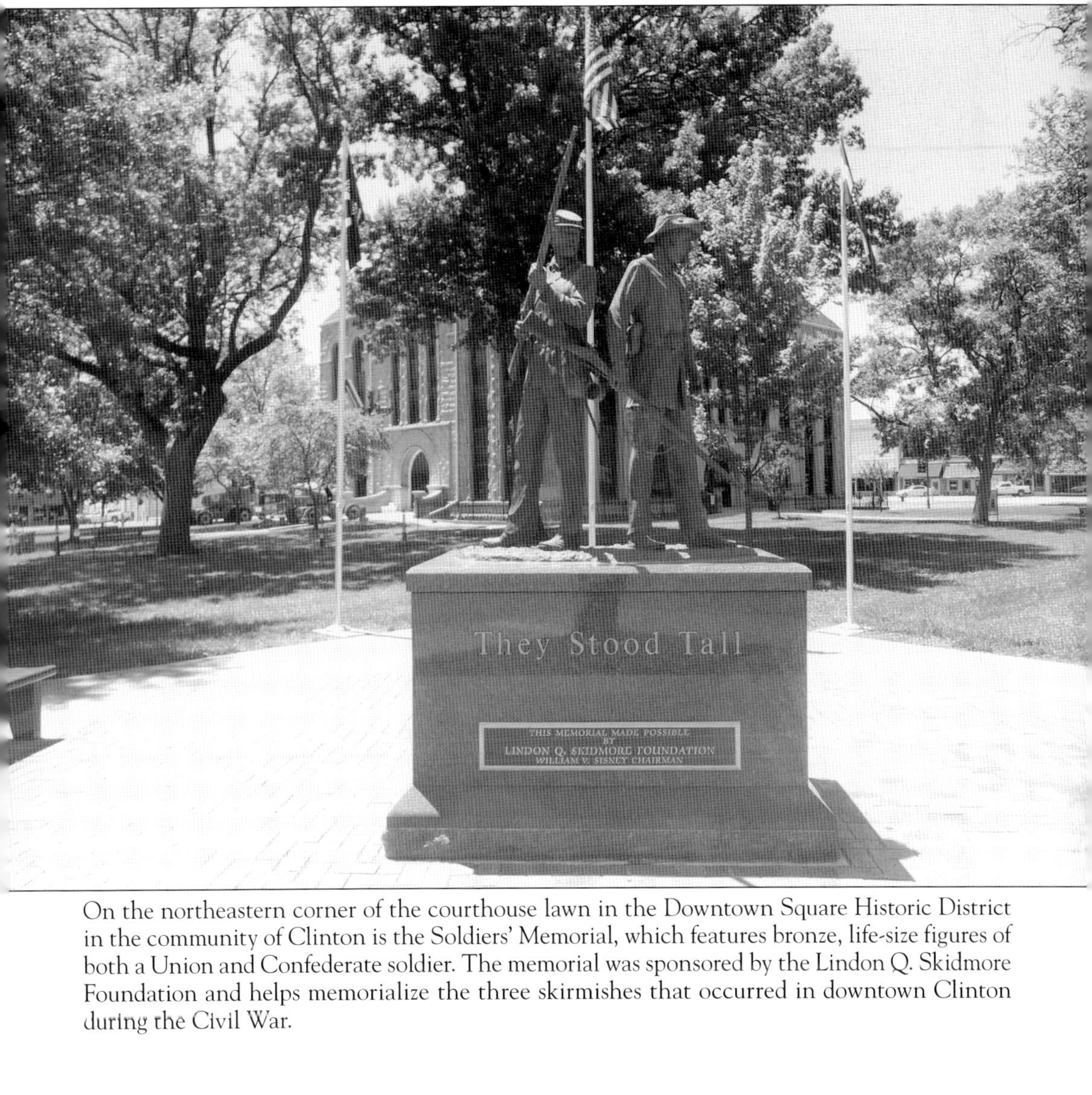

On the northeastern corner of the courthouse lawn in the Downtown Square Historic District in the community of Clinton is the Soldiers' Memorial, which features bronze, life-size figures of both a Union and Confederate soldier. The memorial was sponsored by the Lindon Q. Skidmore Foundation and helps memorialize the three skirmishes that occurred in downtown Clinton during the Civil War.

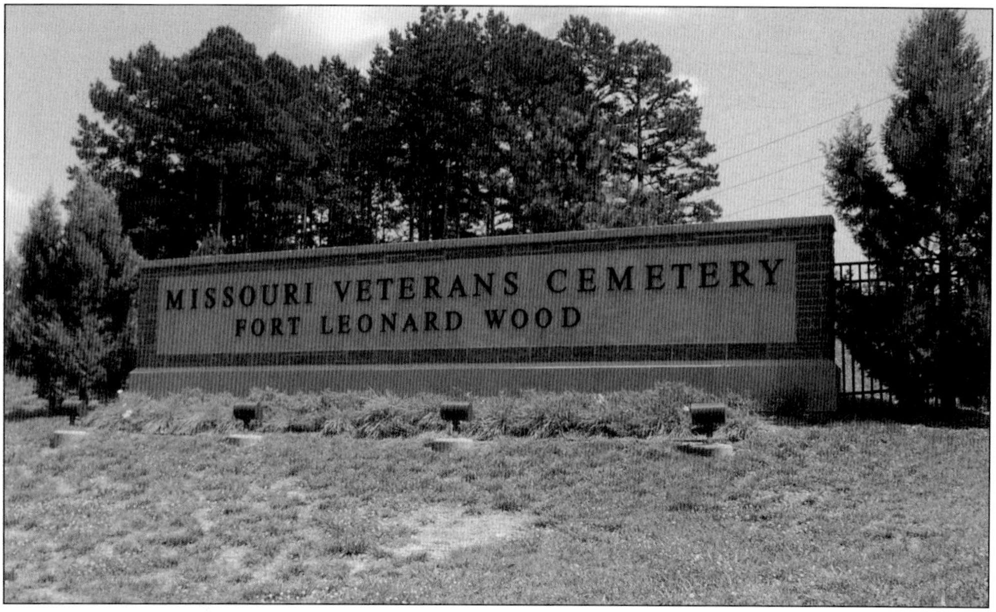

The ground breaking for the Fort Leonard Wood Veterans Cemetery was held on November 7, 2008, and was officially dedicated on September 13, 2010. The cemetery is one of five in the state operated by the Missouri Veterans Commission and is situated on 229 acres donated by the US Army Maneuver Support Center and Fort Leonard Wood.

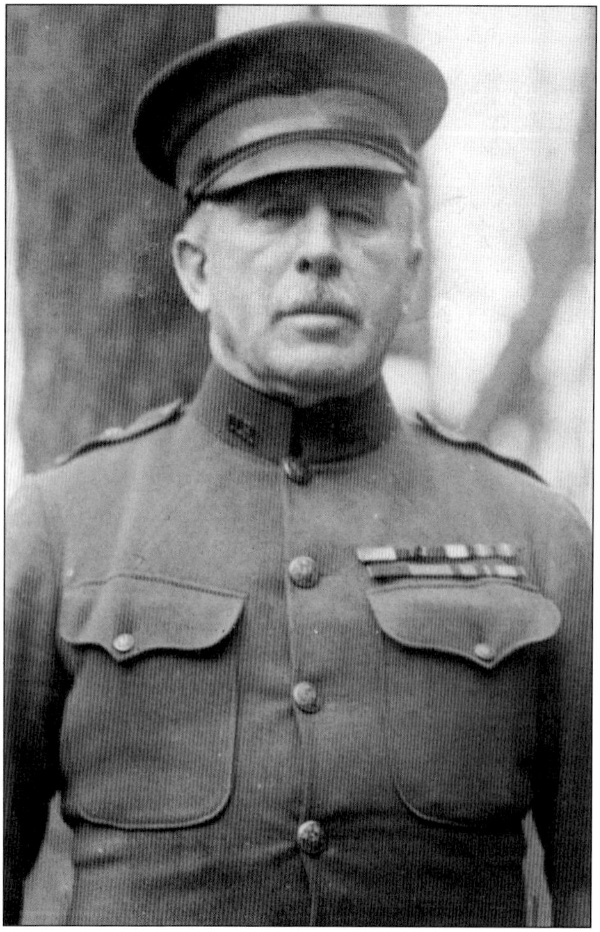

Leonard Wood graduated Harvard Medical School and later earned a Congressional Medal of Honor for his service in the campaign against Geronimo. During the Spanish-American War, he commanded the 1st Volunteer Cavalry alongside future president Teddy Roosevelt. Wood went on to serve as military governor of Cuba and chief of staff of the Army and helped train the 10th and 89th Divisions for service in World War I. The major general passed away in 1927 and was laid to rest in Arlington National Cemetery. Fort Leonard Wood in Pulaski County was named in his memory in 1941.

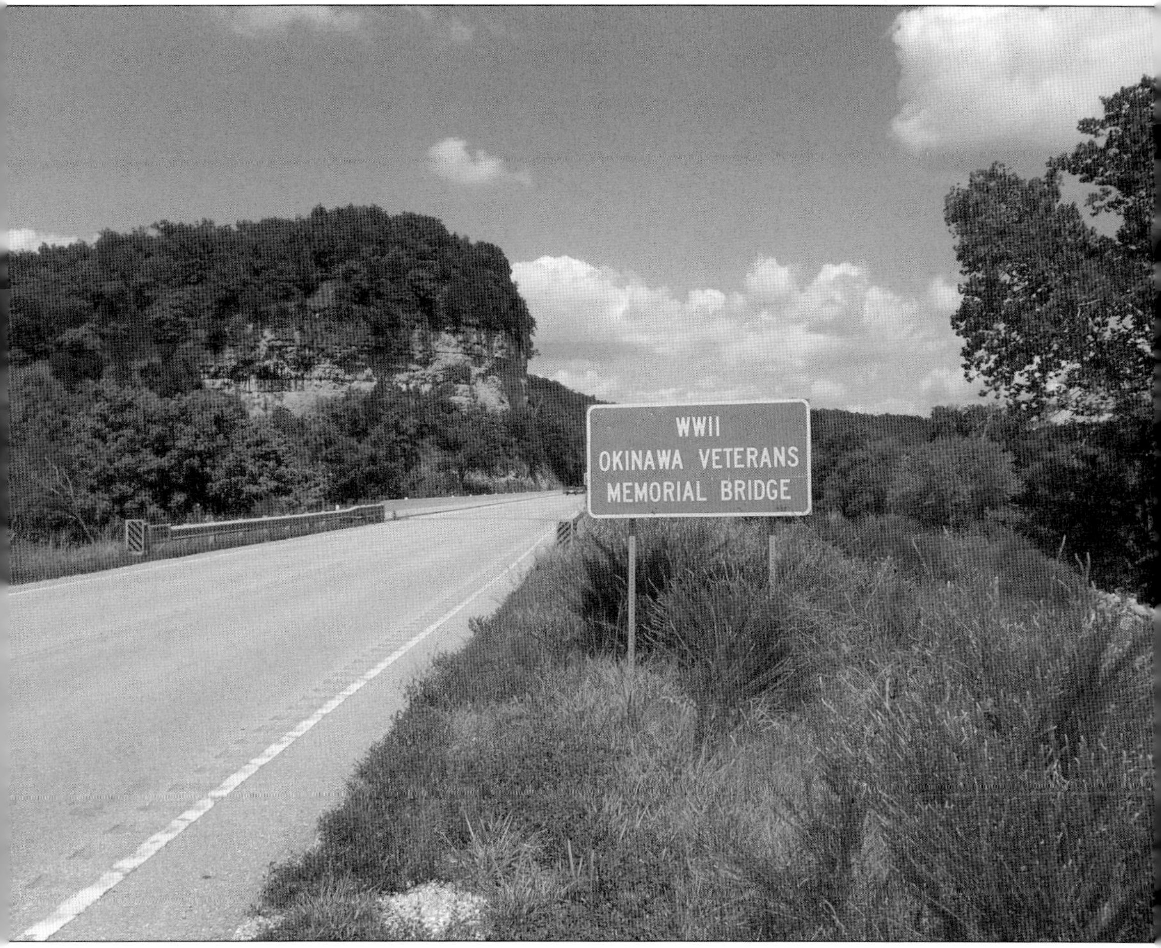

The service of Missouri veterans has been memorialized in many forms throughout the state, which includes the naming of stretches of highways and bridges to honor individuals and groups of veterans. Along Highway 17 near Waynesville, the bridge crossing the Gasconade River was designated the World War II Okinawa Veterans Memorial Bridge in 2009.

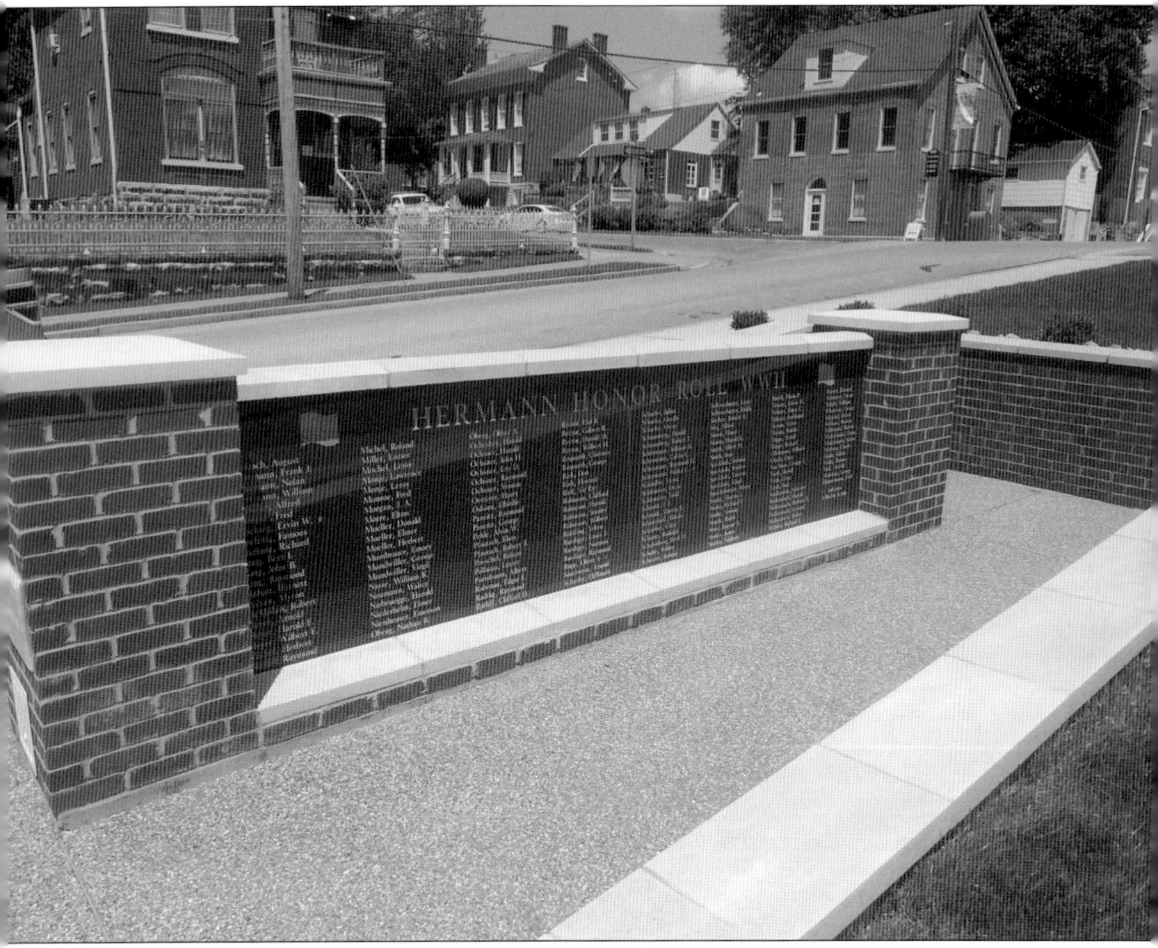

A World War II memorial is located in the parkway that divides Market Street south of the Old Firehouse and Hermann City Hall in the Gasconade County. The current monument was erected in 2016 to replace the original monument, which was donated by the American War Mothers in 1944.

Four

Kansas City Region

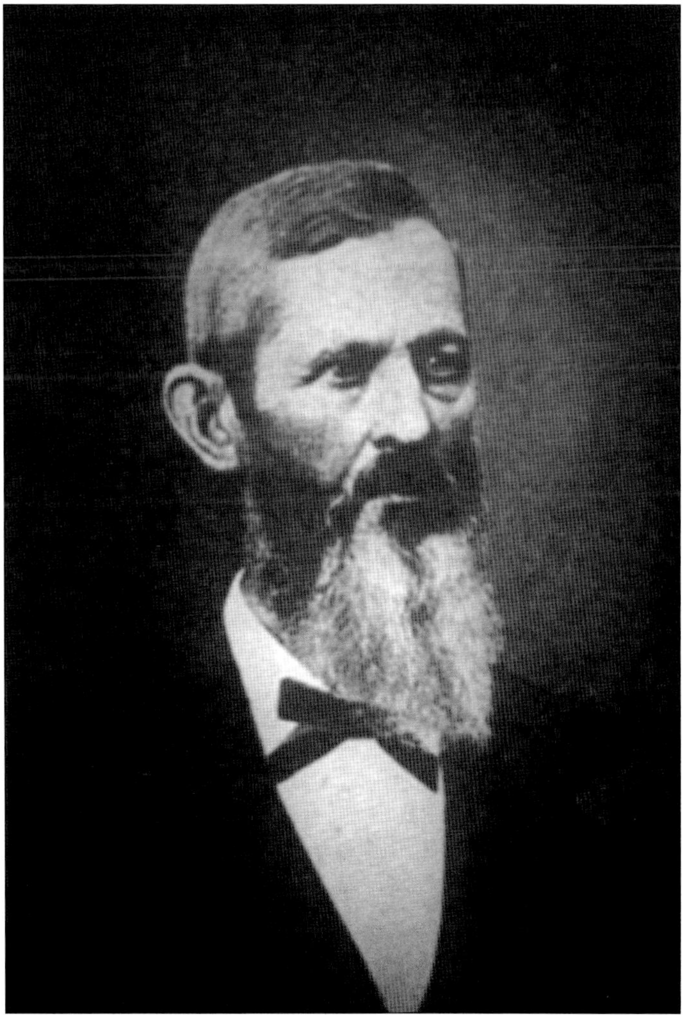

Born in Williamstown, Massachusetts, on October 10, 1811, Stephen G. Wentworth became well known throughout the Lexington, Missouri, community; however, his name carried on in perpetuity when he established the Wentworth Male Academy—the forerunner to Wentworth Military Academy—in 1880 as a memorial to his late son. Wentworth passed away in 1897 and was laid to rest in the Machpelah Cemetery in Lexington. Wentworth Military Academy shut down in May 2017.

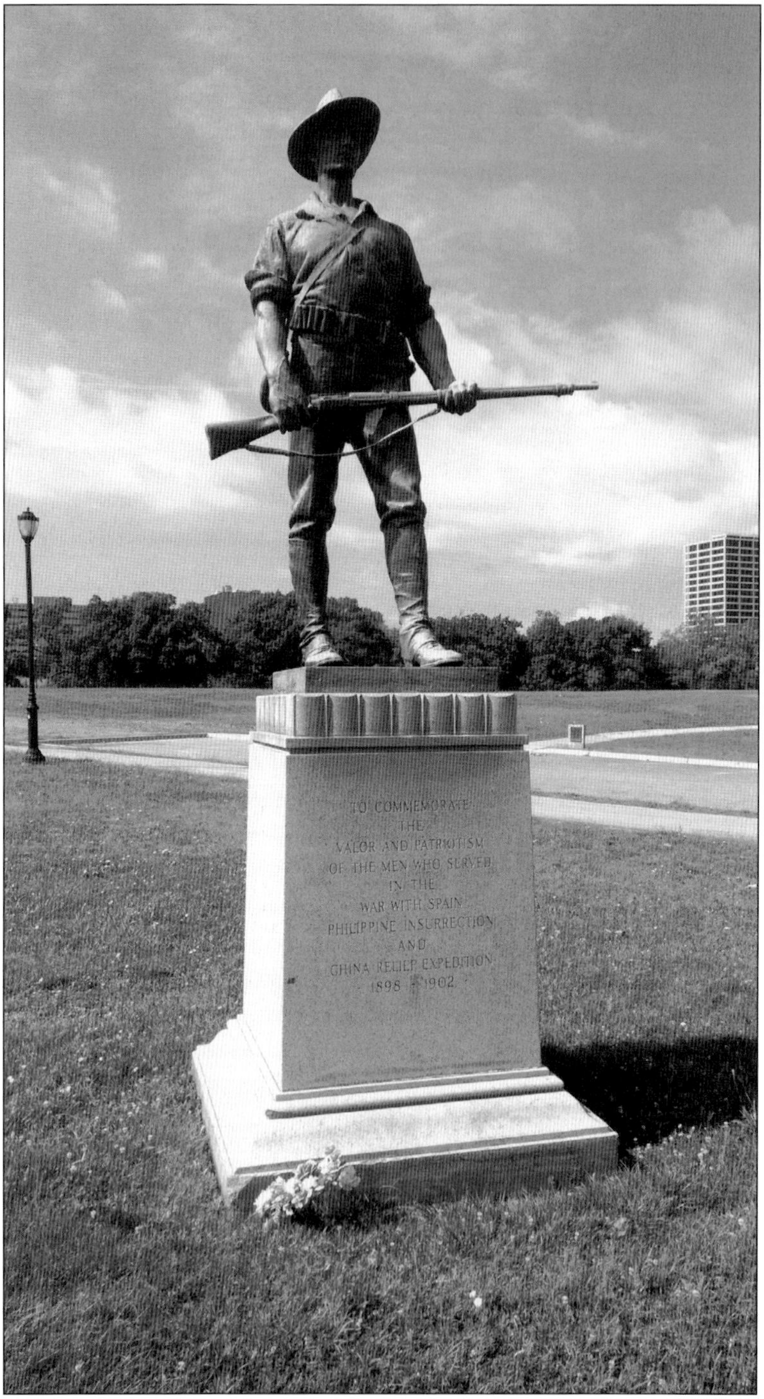

The Hiker is a Spanish-American War statue dedicated in Kansas City's Penn Valley Park south of the Liberty Memorial in 1947. The bronze statue was sculpted by Theo Alice Ruggles Kitson and is identical to Spanish-American War tributes that she created for other communities throughout the United States. It is believed that more than 50 replicas of the 8-foot-plus-tall *The Hiker* were sold between 1906 and 1965.

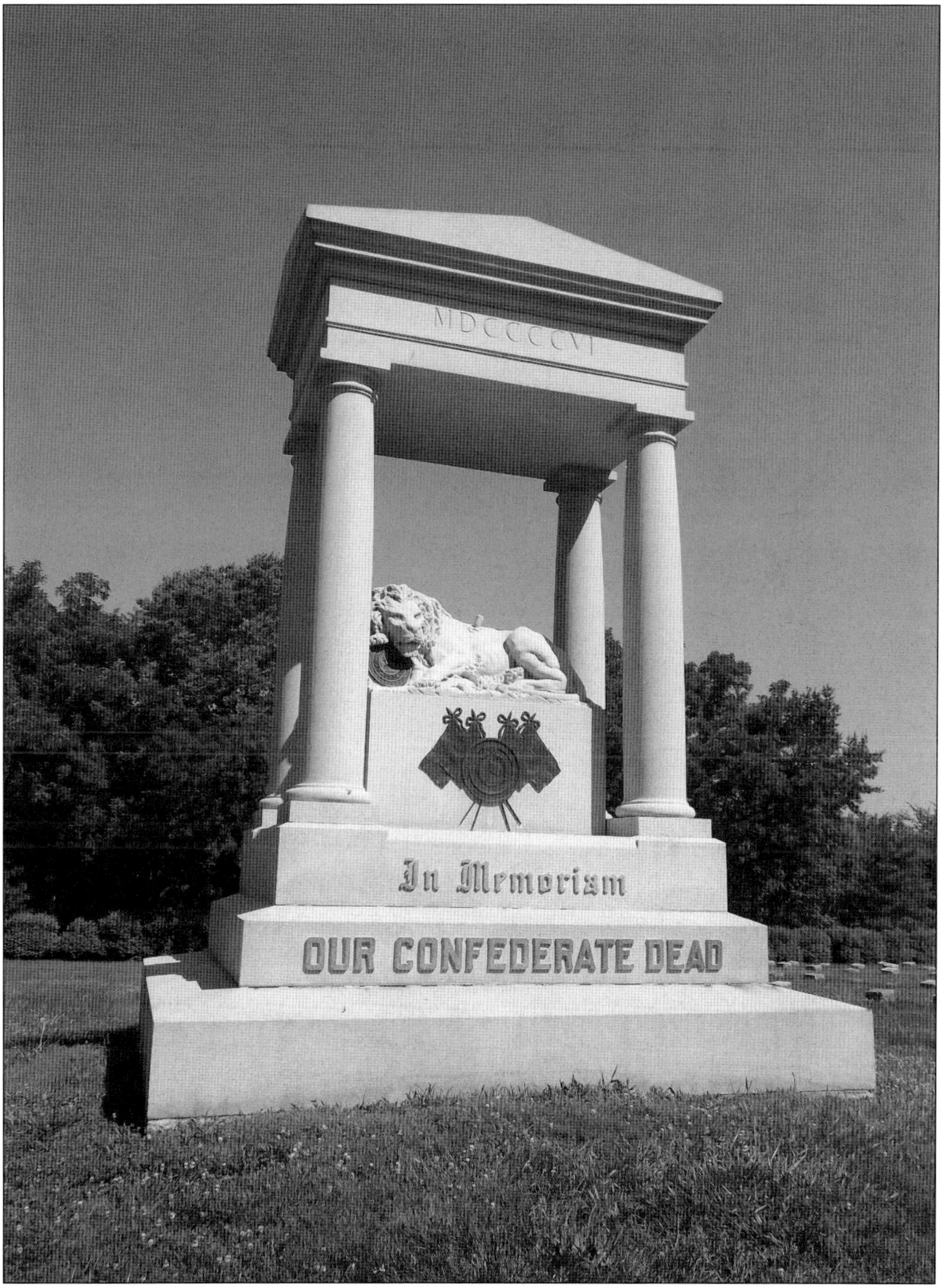

This memorial to the soldiers of the Confederacy who lost their lives during the Civil War was dedicated in 1906 in the Confederate Memorial Cemetery in Higginsville by the Missouri Division of the United Daughters of the Confederacy. At a cost of $5,000, it was constructed from Barre granite and features a lion resting his right paw on the seal of the Confederacy, symbolizing the proud yet defiant nature of those who fought for the Confederate states. (David Keckler.)

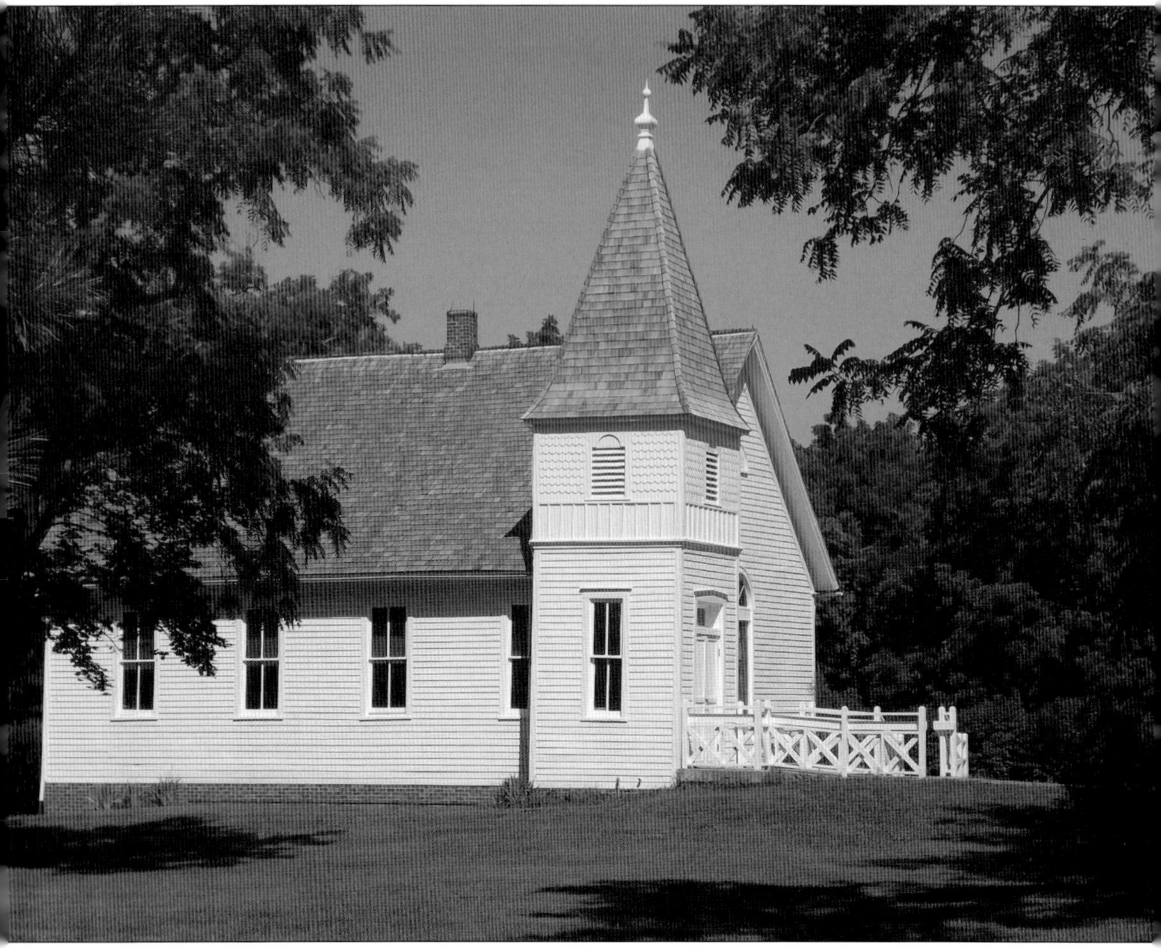

Both a chapel and cemetery are located on a 135-acre site that was once the Confederate Soldiers Home of Missouri—a project to provide housing, food and health care for Missouri's aging Confederate veterans that came to fruition in 1893 through the fundraising efforts of a group called the Daughters of the Confederacy. A few years later, the State of Missouri assumed control of the home, which remained in operation until it was closed in 1950. In 1952, the site became a state park and is now operated as the Confederate Memorial State Historic Site. (David Keckler.)

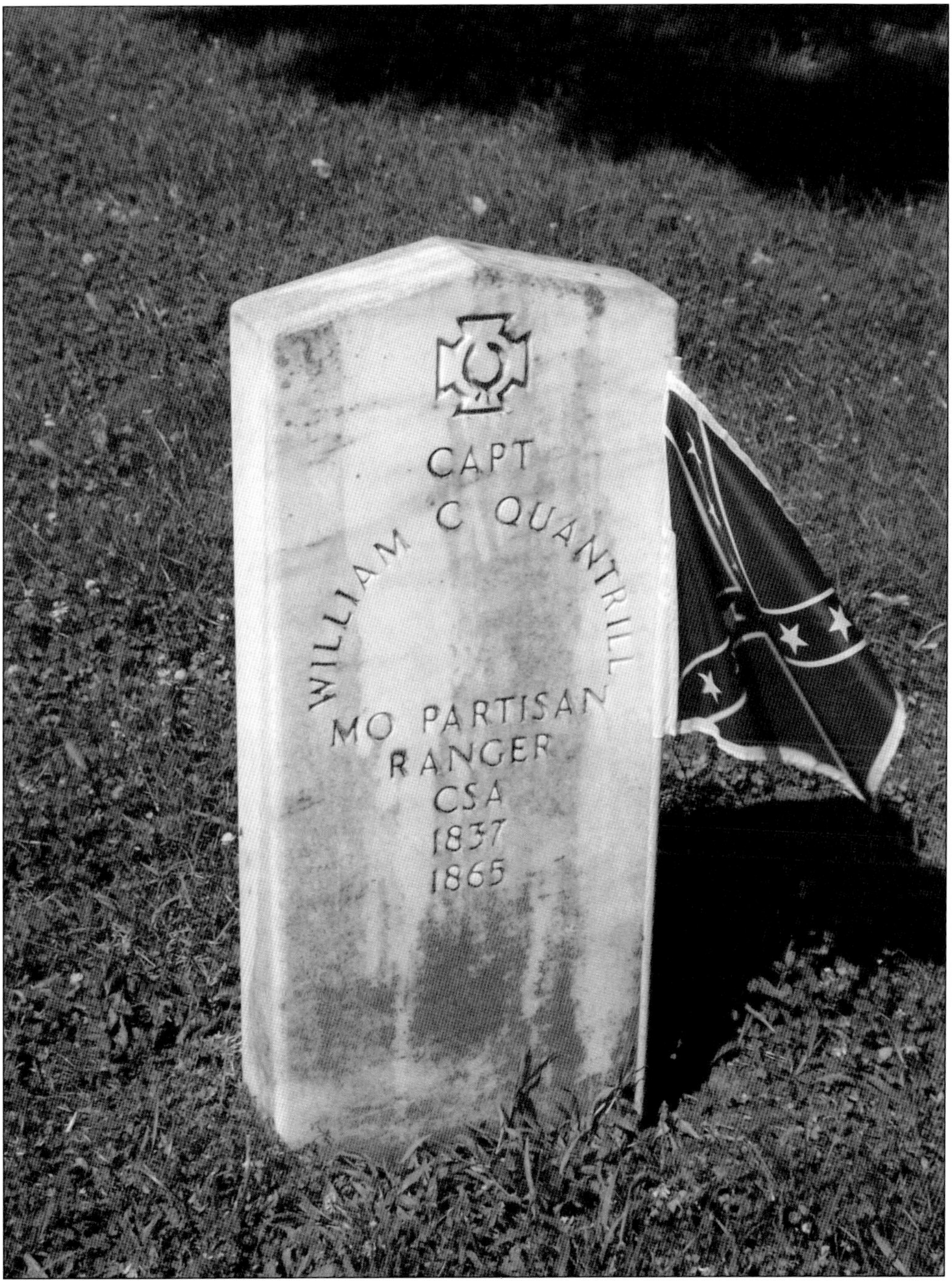

Within the cemetery of Confederate Memorial State Historic Site is the grave containing some of the remains of Capt. William Quantrill, one of the most notorious guerrilla leaders during the Civil War. Quantrill died on June 6, 1865, from wounds received during a skirmish with Union forces nearly a month prior. His remains were initially interred in Louisville, Kentucky; however, his grave was later exhumed and some of his remains reburied in his hometown of Dover, Ohio. Years later, amid some controversy, three arm bones, two leg bones, and some hair from Quantrill's remains were later interred in Higginsville. (David Keckler.)

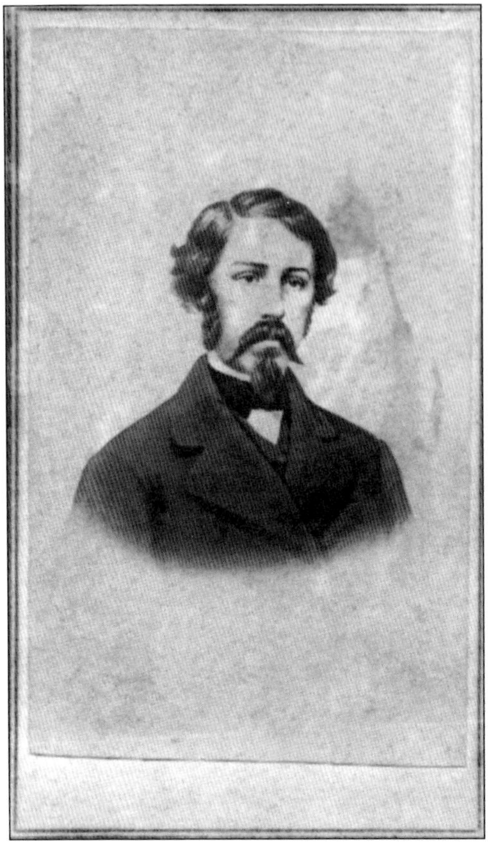

Born in Ohio in 1837, William Clarke Quantrill served many years as a schoolteacher and later made a living as a gambler in Utah. Prior to the Civil War, he moved to Kansas after warrants were issued for his arrest with regard to his alleged involvement in murder and theft. During the Civil War, he led a group of guerrillas known as Quantrill's Raiders who harassed and killed Union soldiers and sympathizers along the Kansas-Missouri border. He is perhaps best known for his participation in the Lawrence Massacre—an event that occurred on August 12, 1863, during which he commanded a raid on pro-Union Lawrence, Kansas, resulting in the deaths of more than 160 men and boys in the town. (Museum of Missouri Military History.)

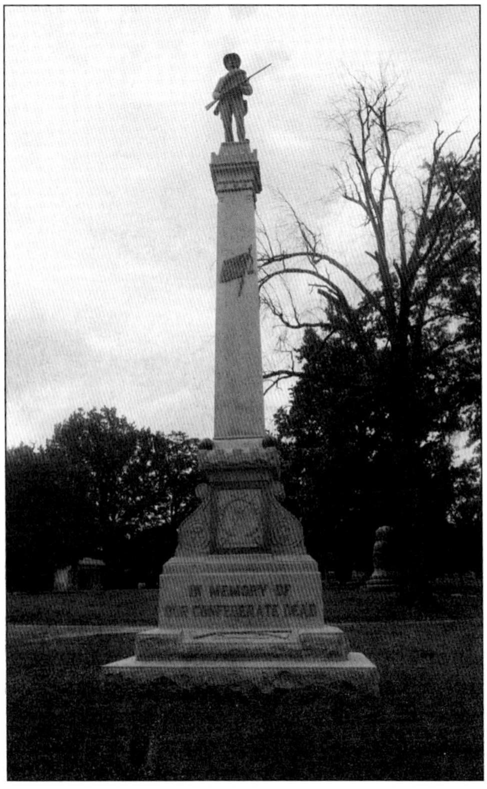

In 1902, the Kansas City, Missouri, Chapter 149 of the United Daughters of the Confederacy erected in Forest Hill Cemetery this massive pillar topped by a Confederate soldier as a memorial to the Confederate soldiers who were killed during the Battle of Westport on October 23, 1864. Several Confederate soldiers who lost their lives during the battle are buried near the 36-foot-high monument, including some who fought with Capt. William Quantrill. (Tina Amick.)

Joseph Shelby was born in Kentucky but in later years moved to Lexington, Missouri. During the Civil War, he became a veteran of the Battle of Wilson's Creek near Springfield and the Battle of Pea Ridge, Arkansas. It was during the Battle of Westport in Kansas City, however, that Shelby, who was in command of the Iron Brigade and supporting Gen. Sterling Price's Missouri Expedition, was outnumbered by Union troops and forced to retreat south. Shelby survived the war and after living briefly in Mexico, returned to Missouri in 1867. He passed away in 1897 and is buried near the Confederate monument in Forest Hill Cemetery in Kansas City. (Museum of Missouri Military History.)

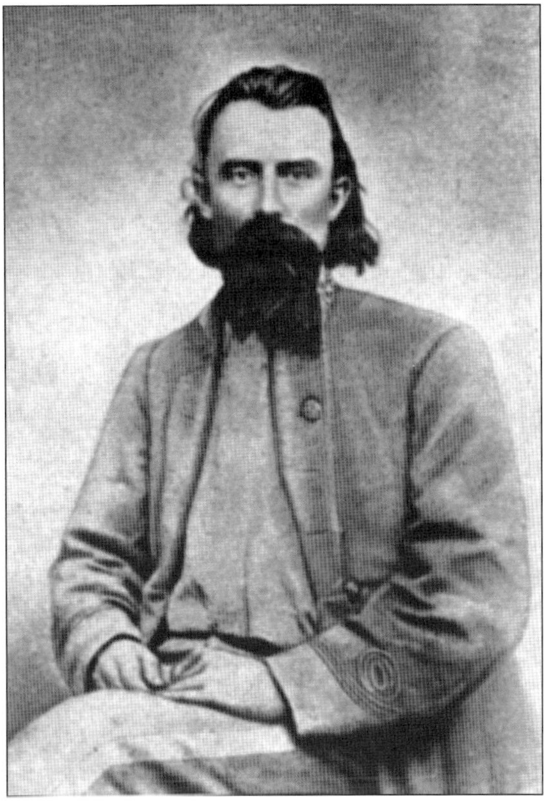

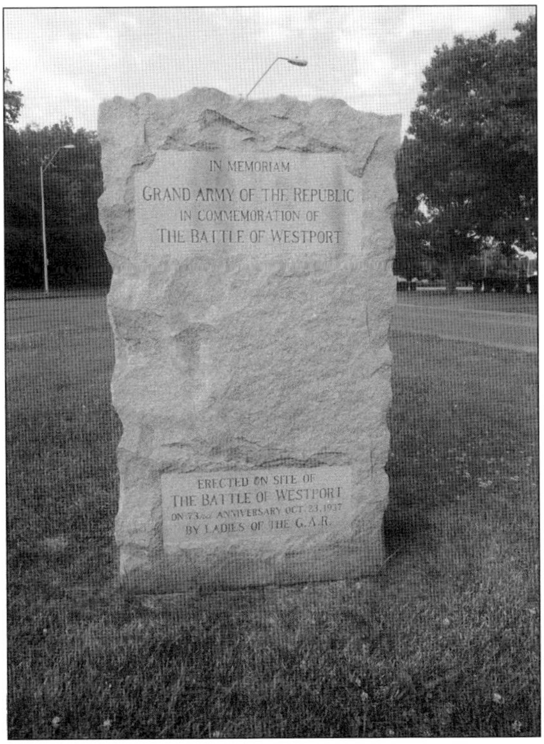

On October 23, 1937, the Ladies of the Grand Army of the Republic dedicated a light gray granite monument in honor of the Union soldiers who served in the Battle of Westport during the Civil War. The small monument cost $350 to build and is located in a small grassy area at the intersection of Sixty-Third Street and Paseo Boulevard in Kansas City.

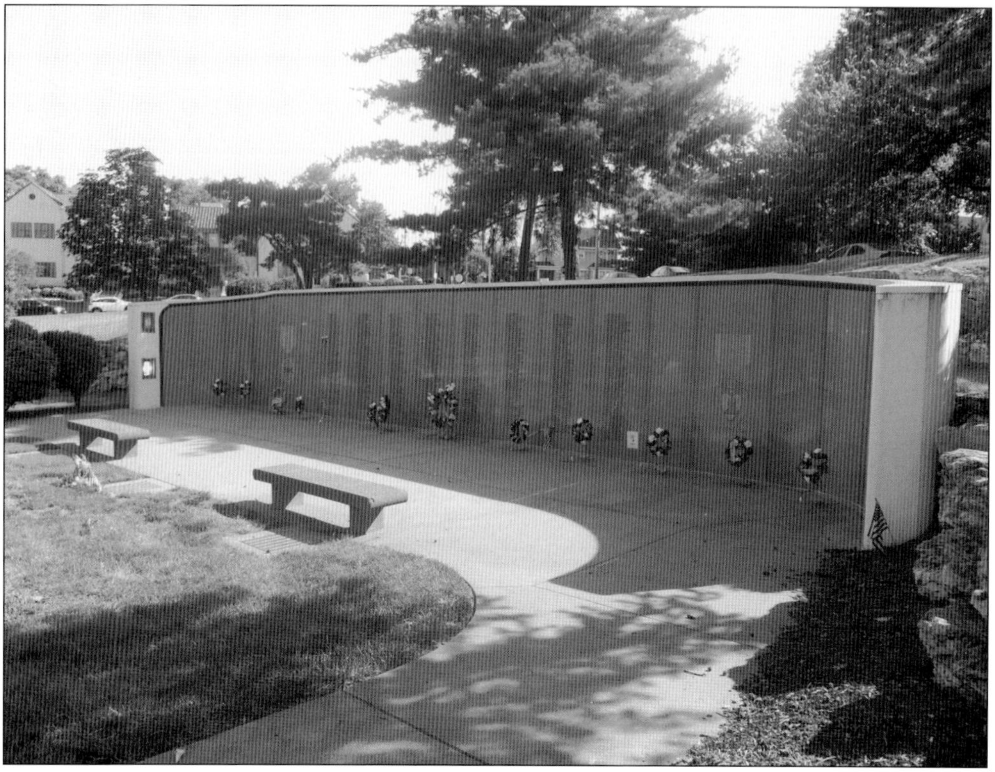

The Vietnam Veterans Memorial Fountain was installed at Broadway and West Forty-Second Street in Kansas City in 1985. In addition to fountain pools, one striking feature of the memorial is a semicircular wall that lists the names of 451 casualties of the Vietnam War who were from the Kansas City community inscribed upon it. (Tina Amick.)

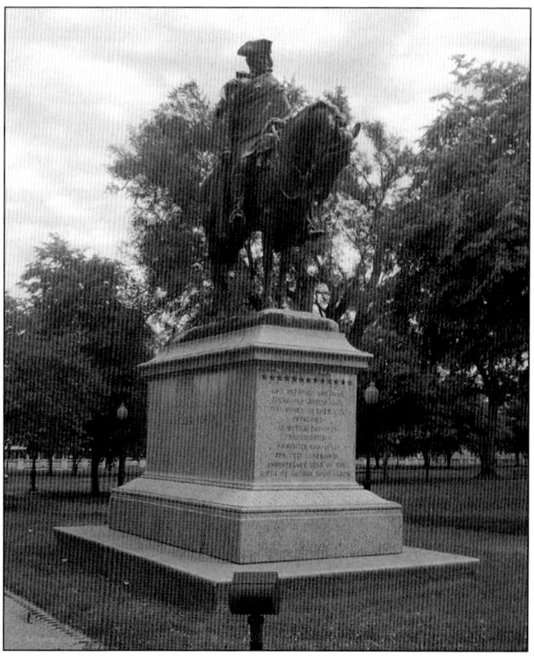

This monument in Washington Square Park in Kansas City was dedicated on November 11, 1925, to honor Gen. George Washington's role in the American Revolution. The statue is a replica of one found in Brooklyn, New York, and cost more than $30,000 to erect. The monument was purchased using public donations and measures an impressive 16 feet, 7 inches in height. (Tina Amick.)

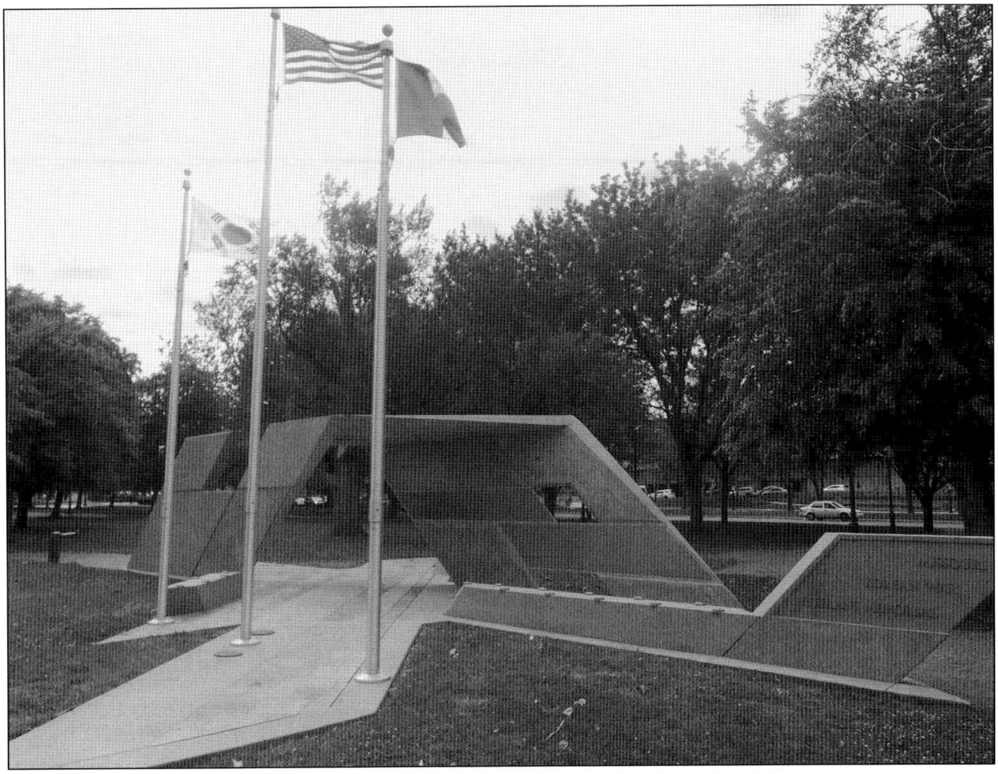

The Missouri Korean War Veterans Memorial was dedicated in September 2011 in the southwest corner of Washington Square Park in Kansas City. Funded through private donations, the memorial has several notable features that include a map of Korea and a listing of names of the more than 900 Missourians who were killed during the war.

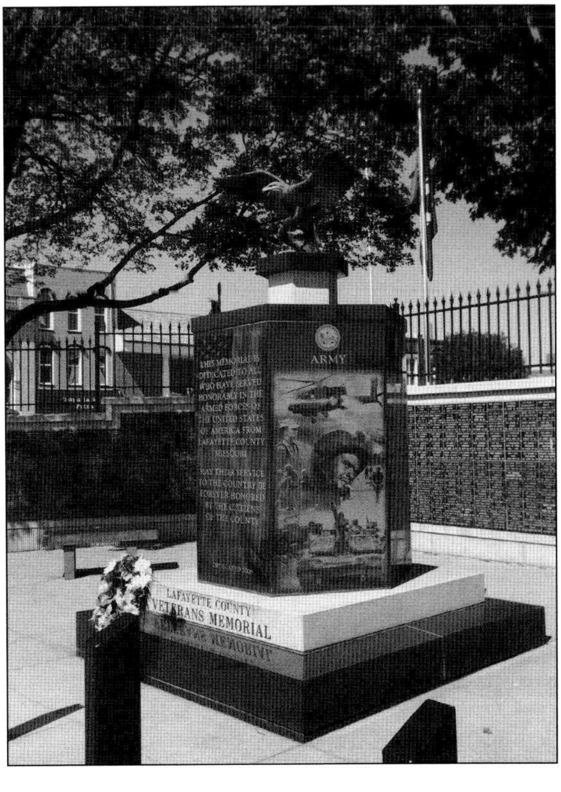

The Lafayette County Veterans Memorial is located on the courthouse square in the historic community of Lexington. Dedicated in 2006 to honor veterans of all wars, the memorial features a six-sided column with graphics specific to each branch of service in front of a semicircular black marble wall listing the names of county citizens who have served in the US military. (David Keckler.)

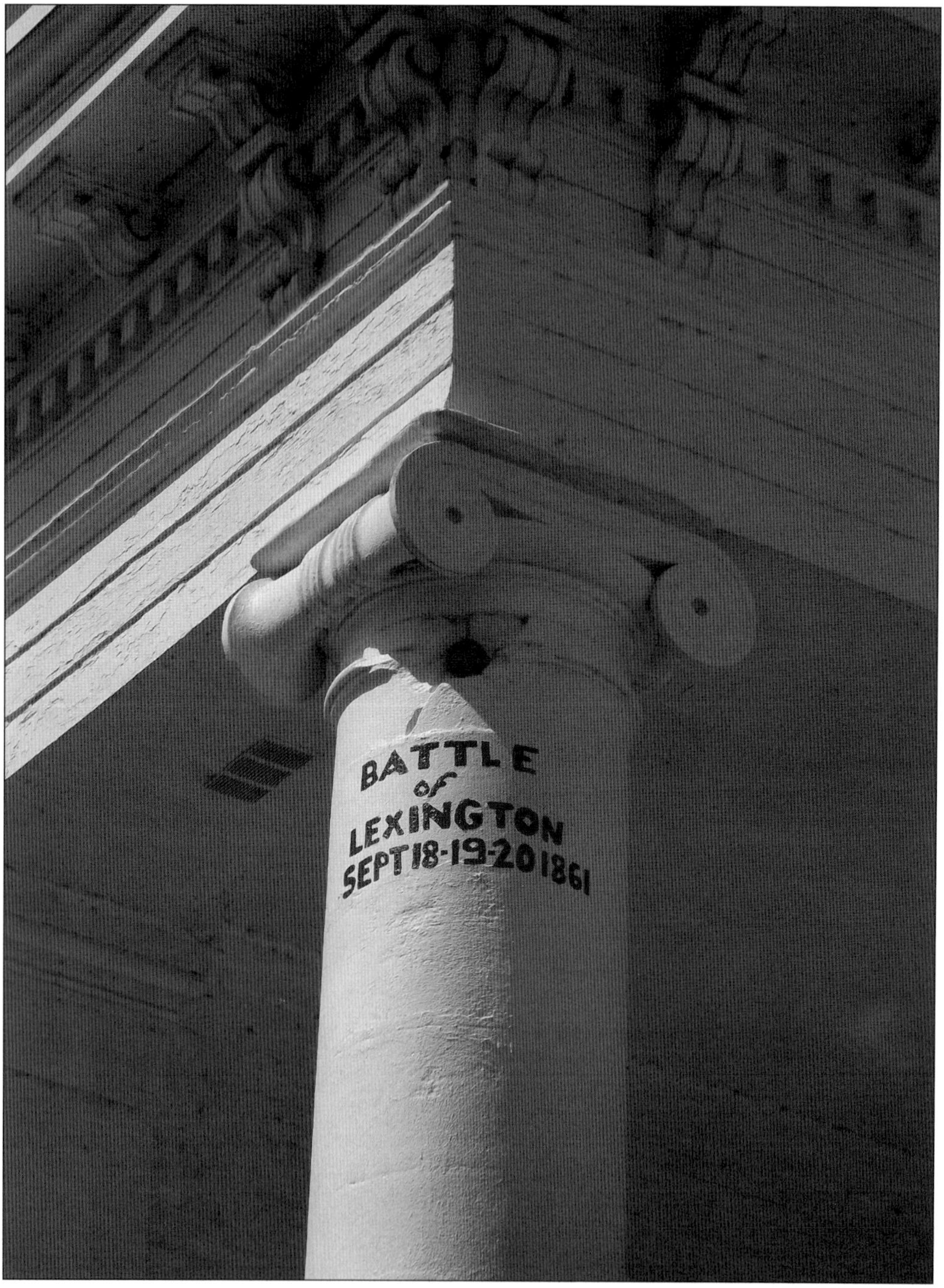

The Lafayette County Courthouse in Lexington, which was built in 1847 and is the oldest Missouri courthouse in continued use as a courthouse, was struck by a cannonball possibly fired from Hiram Bledsoe's Missouri Battery during the Battle of Lexington in the Civil War. The original cannonball has since been replaced but evidence of the damage remains clearly visible in the upper section of the east column of the courthouse. (David Keckler.)

The Lafayette-Lexington Chapter of the Daughters of the American Revolution erected this monument in 1928 on the site of the now closed Wentworth Military Academy. The small concrete pillar has a plaque denoting the site from where troops under the command of Capt. Henry Guibor—a Confederate artillery officer from St. Louis—shelled Union troops entrenched on nearby Masonic College Hill, which is now the site of College Park.

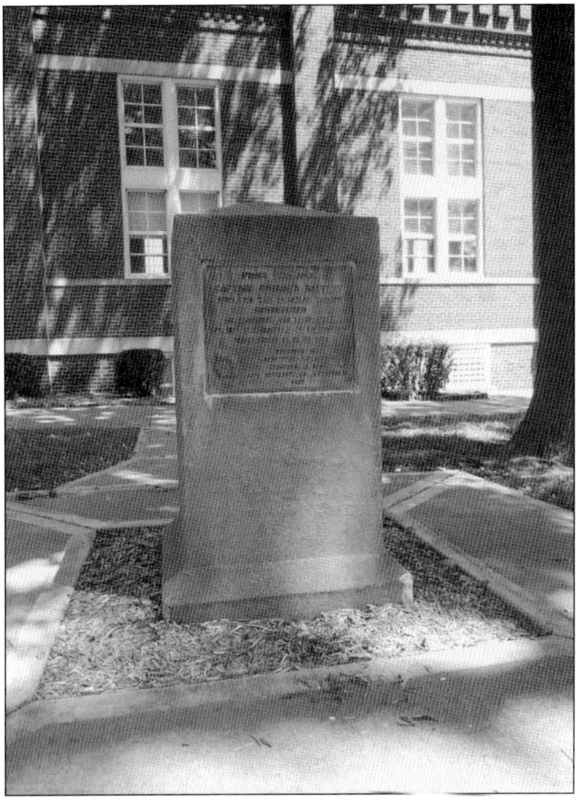

While a road was being built through College Park in Lexington in October 1932, the remains of five Union soldiers killed during the Battle of Lexington were discovered. The identities of the soldiers were never established but they are believed to have been members of Col. Thomas A. Marshall's 1st Illinois Cavalry. The remains were reburied in a common grave inside the entrance to the Lexington battlefield.

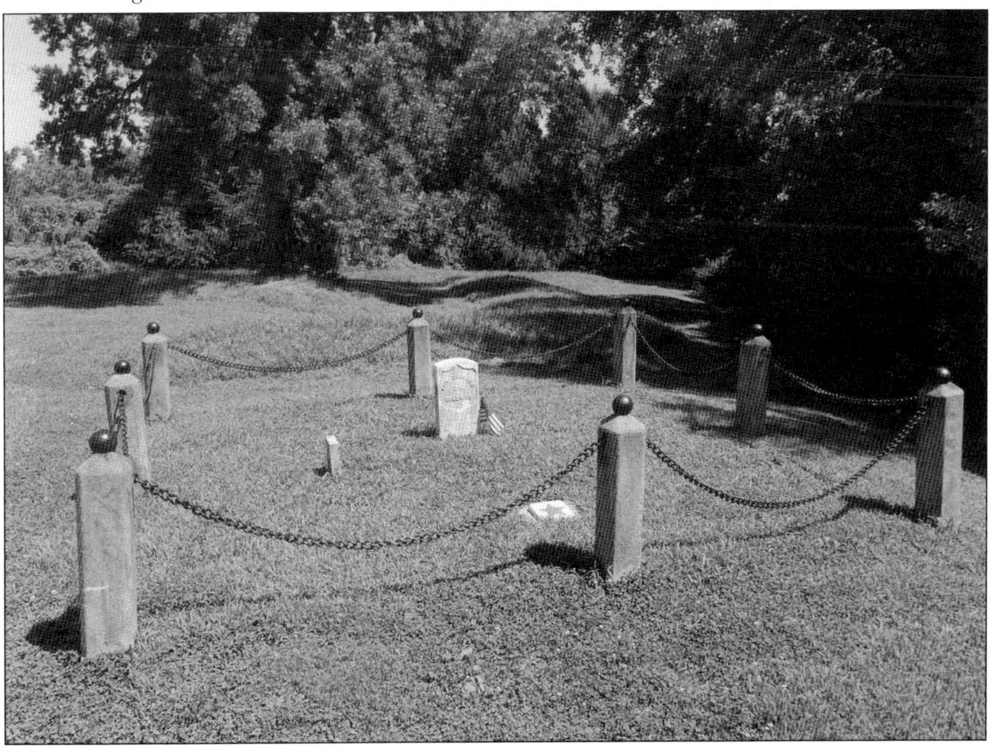

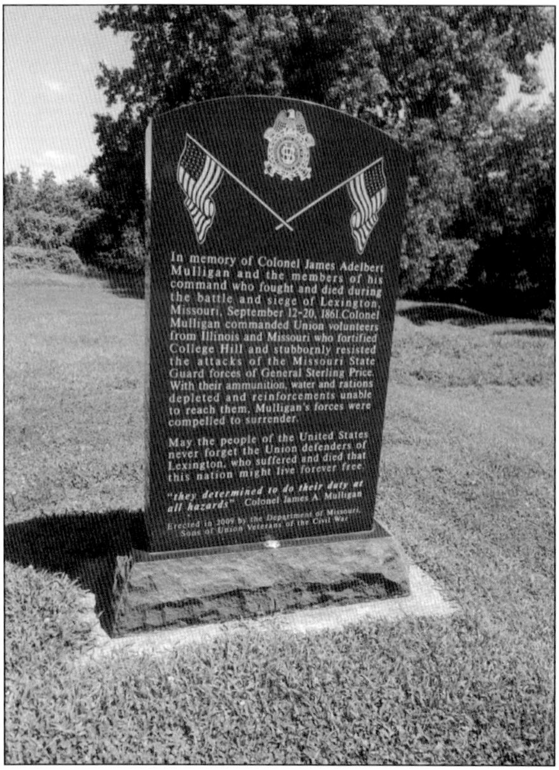

The Department of Missouri, Sons of Union Veterans of the Civil War placed this marker in 2009 at the site of the Battle of Lexington to honor Col. James Mulligan. Mulligan surrendered his forces to Confederate general Sterling Price on September 20, 1861, and remained a prisoner of war until October 30, 1861. During the Second Battle of Kernstown, Virginia, on July 24, 1864, he was mortally wounded and died two days later.

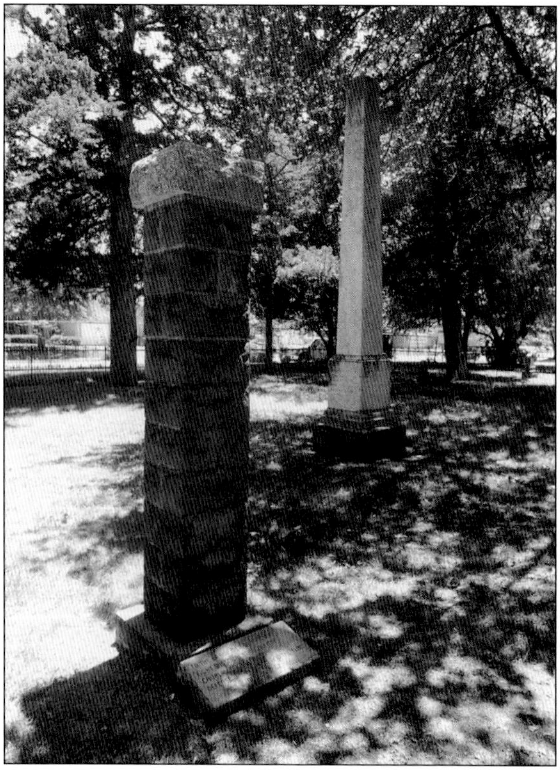

Memorials dedicated to the remembrance of the fallen from the Battle of Lone Jack, which occurred during the Civil War on August 16, 1862, are located in the Soldier's Cemetery adjacent to the Lone Jack Battlefield Museum. In the foreground is a memorial column dedicated to the Union dead, and in the background is the column dedicated to the Confederate dead. Most of the 270 killed during the battle were buried in trenches inside and near the cemetery.

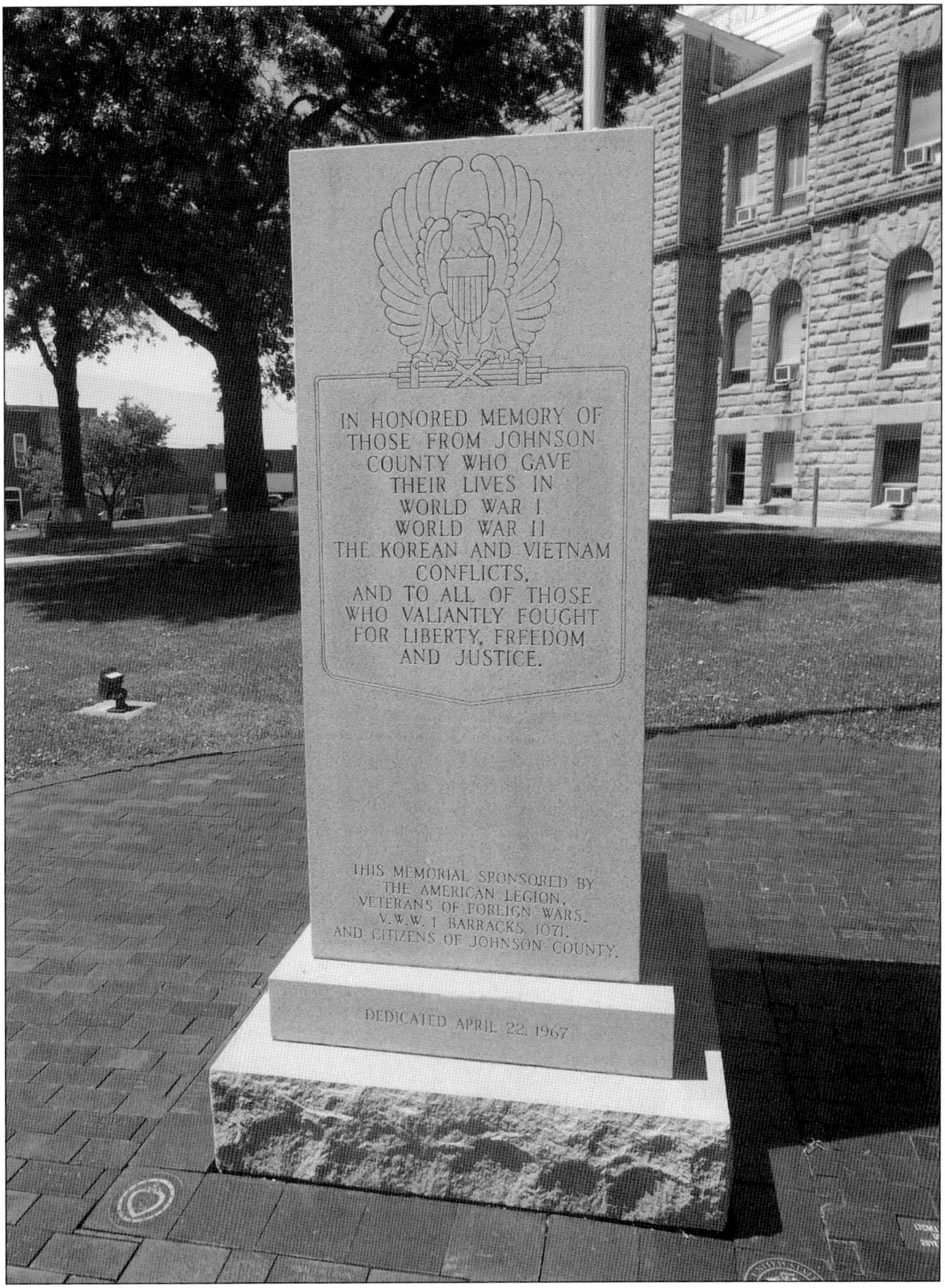

A memorial honoring Johnson County residents who made the ultimate sacrifice in World War I, World War II, Korea, and Vietnam was dedicated on the lawn of the county courthouse in Warrensburg on April 22, 1967. The names of those from the county who lost their lives during these conflicts are listed on the sides and back of the granite monument. (Tina Amick.)

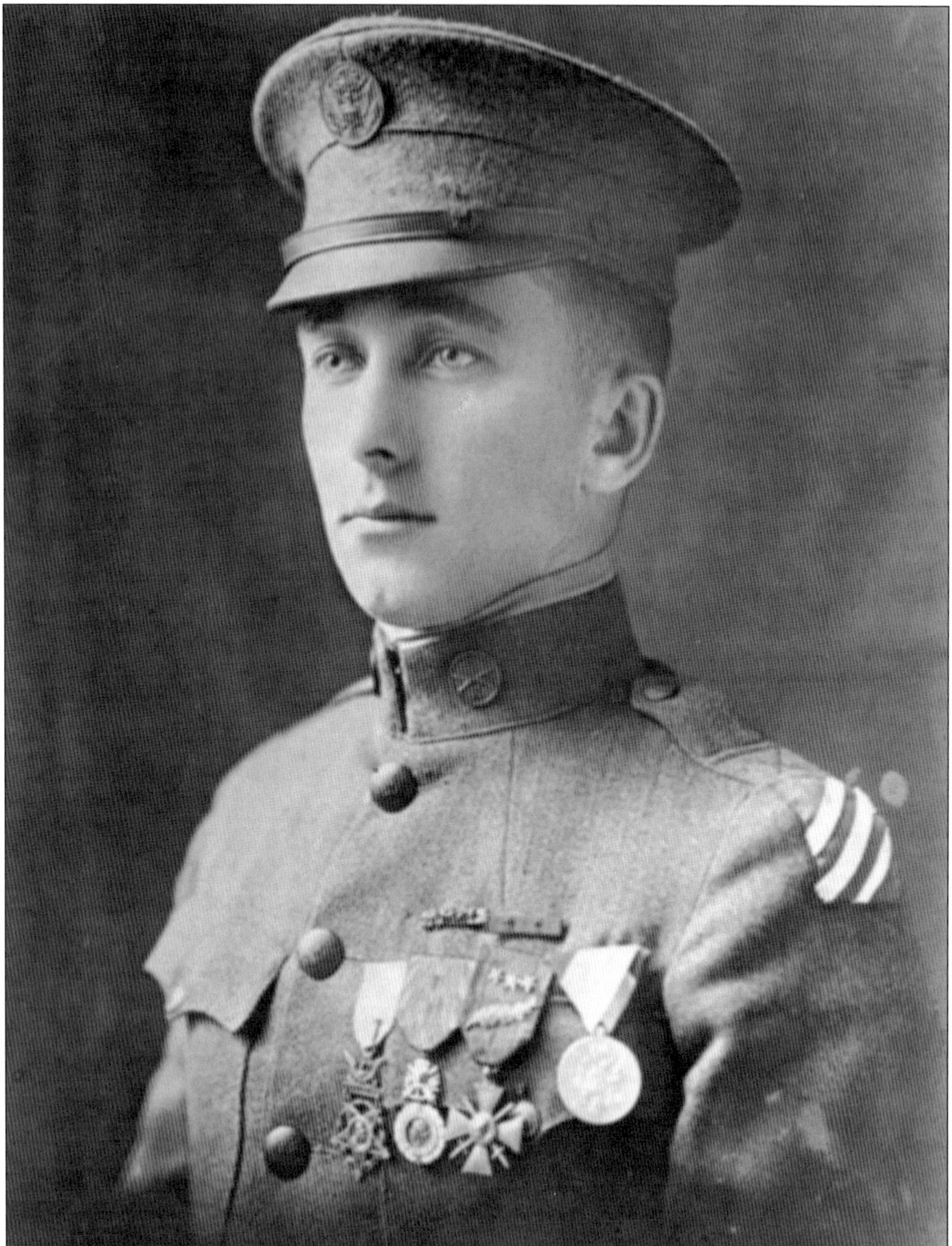

John Barkley was serving with the US Army at Cunel, France, during the Meuse-Argonne Offensive on October 7, 1918, when he was able to repair a captured enemy machine gun, mount it on a French tank, and then twice repel German counterattacks. This brave action is what earned him the Medal of Honor. The soldier's service has been memorialized through a large framed poster that hangs inside the entrance of the Johnson County Courthouse in Warrensburg. (Museum of Missouri Military History.)

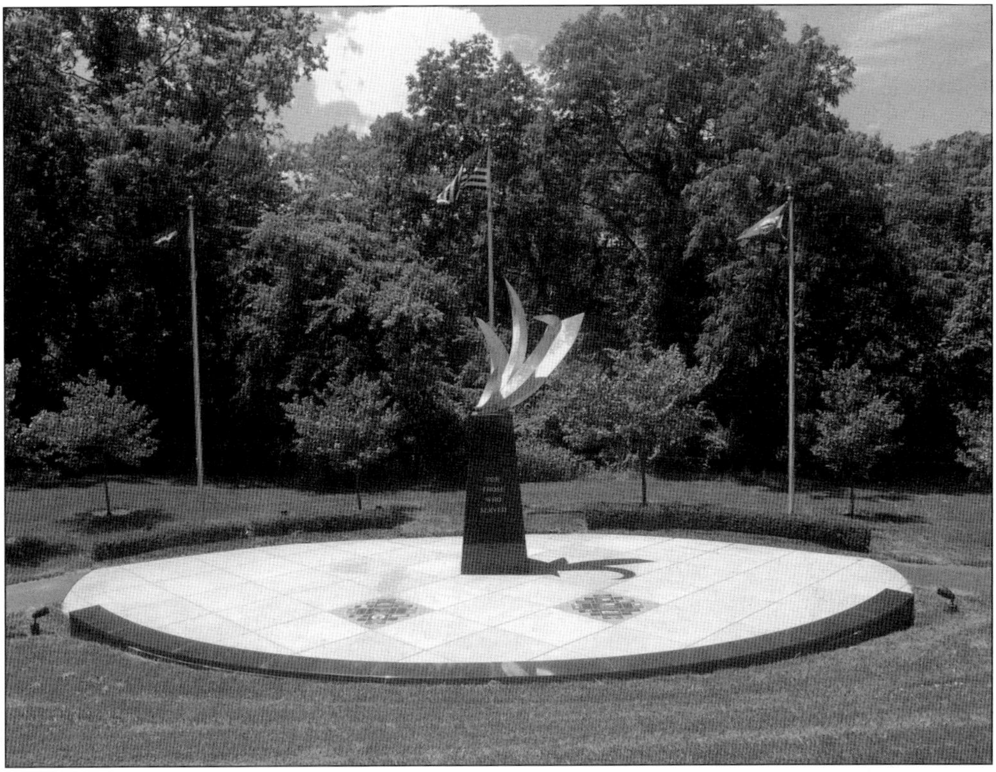

A ceremony was held in April 2013 to dedicate the Blue Springs Veterans Way Memorial inside Pink Hill Park in Blue Springs. The memorial was funded through private donations collected through the work of the Veterans Way Memorial Committee and is located on the site where the "The Wall That Heals"—a half-scale replica of the Vietnam Veterans Memorial in Washington, DC, that travels to communities throughout the country—was exhibited in 2010. (Tina Amick.)

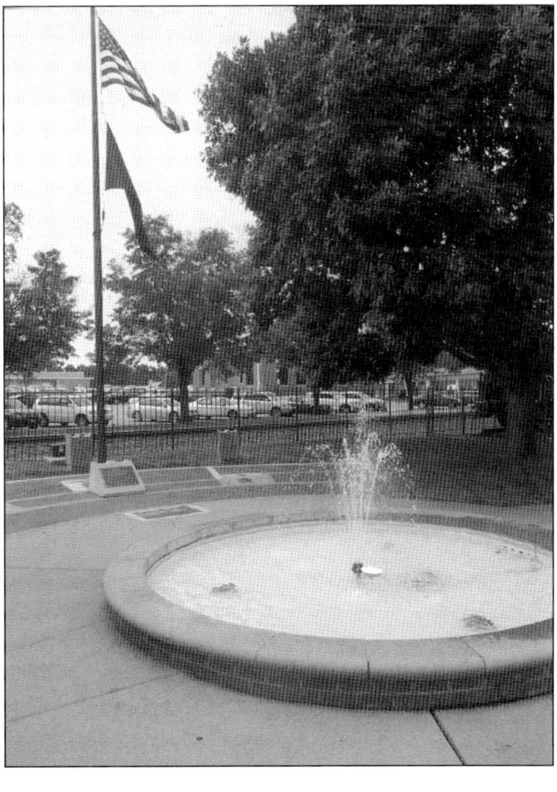

The Veterans Memorial in William B. Howard Station Park in Lee's Summit was initially launched in 1995 by the Lee's Summit Patriotic Council. The memorial has been expanded in recent years and now features a fountain and flagpole in addition to memorial bricks that have been purchased to honor veterans both past and present. (Tina Amick.)

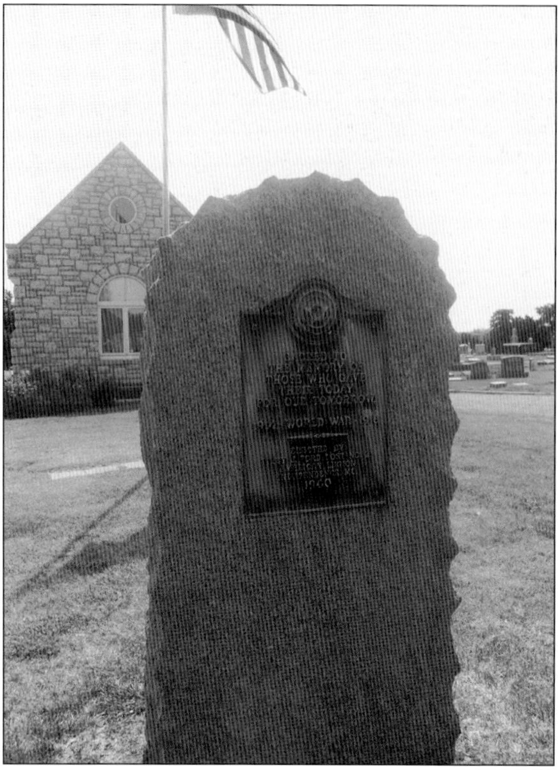

Inside the entrance to the Woodlawn Cemetery in Independence is this red granite marker that is approximately four feet tall with an affixed bronze plaque containing an American Legion seal. The memorial is dedicated to those who gave their lives in World War I and was placed in 1940 under the sponsorship of the American Legion Post 21, which was named for Tirey J. Ford—an Independence soldier killed in the war.

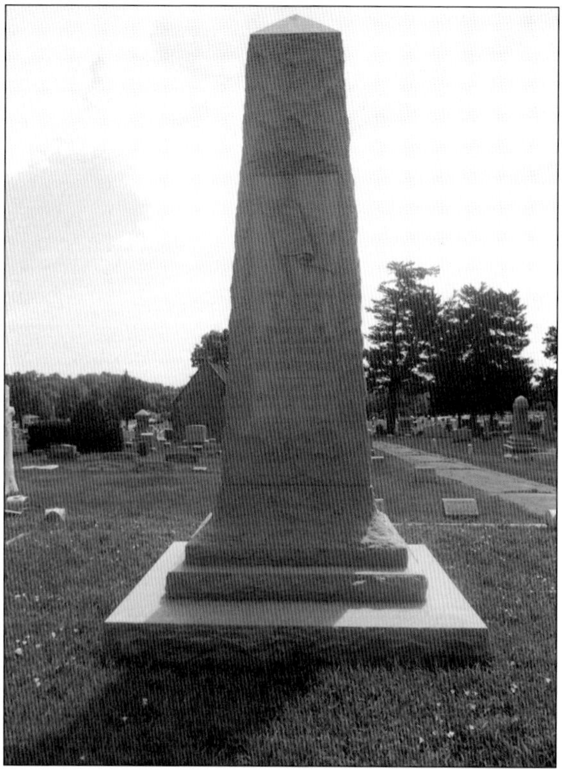

The Independence Chapter 710 of the United Daughters of the Confederacy erected this monument in Woodlawn Cemetery in Independence in 1924 "to the memory of the soldiers of the Confederacy." This granite obelisk features a Confederate battle flag and is located near the gravesite of Brig. Gen. John Taylor Hughes, a Confederate officer who was killed during an attack against a Union garrison in Independence in 1862.

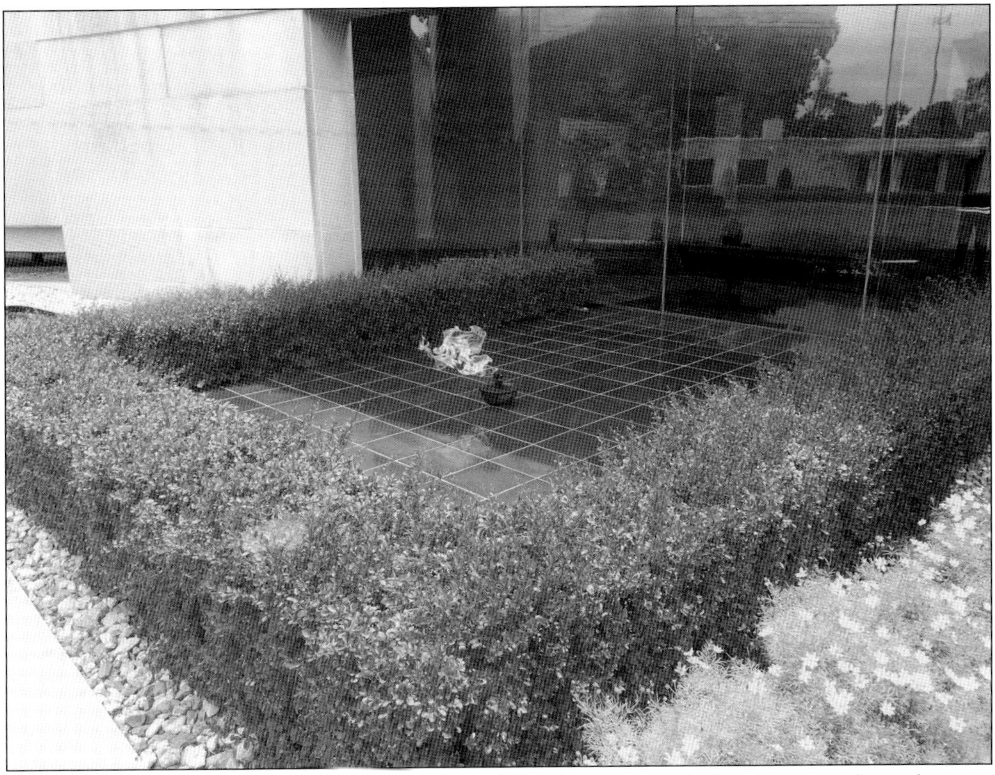

In the courtyard of the Harry S. Truman Presidential Library and Museum in Independence is an eternal flame dedicated on March 15, 1991. The memorial was sponsored by the Tirey J. Ford American Legion Post 21 of Independence to honor the late president's service to the country as a soldier and president, while also acknowledging his membership in the American Legion.

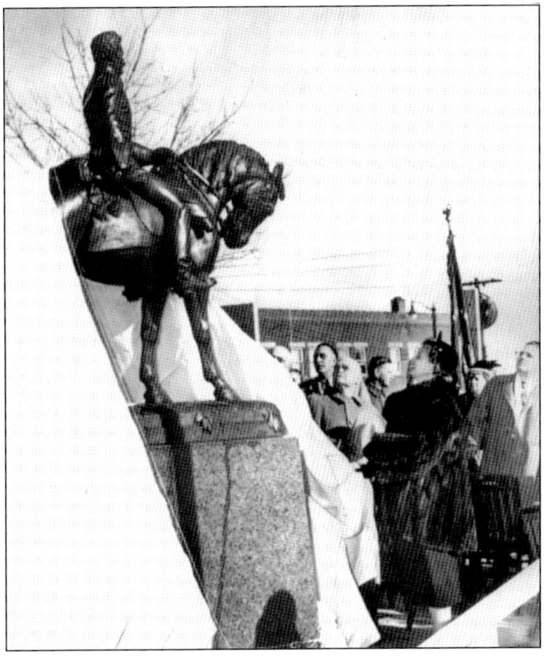

Margaret Truman is pictured during the unveiling of the statue of Gen. Andrew Jackson—who gained famed in the Battle of New Orleans during the War of 1812—in front of the Jackson County Courthouse in Independence on December 26, 1949. The statue was a gift from Pres. Harry S. Truman to the county and is a half-size reproduction of the statue in front of the county courthouse in Kansas City, Missouri.

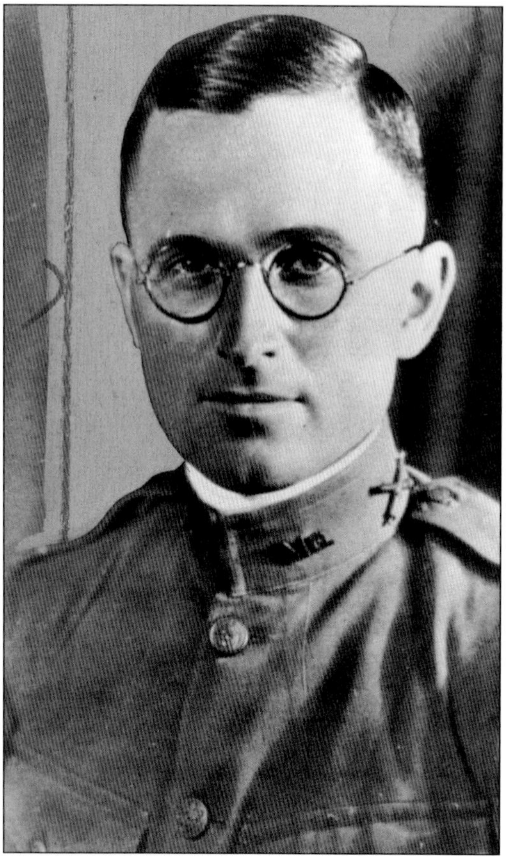

A young Harry S. Truman is pictured as a first lieutenant with Battery F, 2nd Missouri Field Artillery in 1917. In 1905, Truman first enlisted in the Missouri National Guard, with whom he served for the next six years. After the United States joined World War I, Truman rejoined his Guard unit before it was federalized as the 129th Field Artillery. The future president served overseas from March 3, 1918, through April 20, 1919, as an artillery officer, rising to the rank of captain.

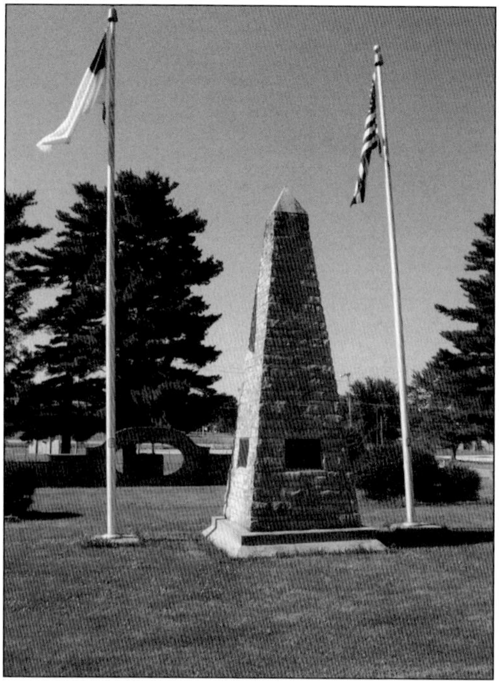

During the Civil War, there were many members of the congregation of St. Paul's Lutheran Church in Concordia who were killed as a result of guerilla activity, many of whom are buried within the church's cemetery. Also within the cemetery is this substantial stone obelisk erected in 1952 that recognizes not only the 175 congregation members who served during World War II but also those who served during the Korean and Vietnam Wars. (David Keckler.)

Charles Denver Barger was born in Lawrence County in southwest Missouri in 1892 and, as a young boy, was adopted by the Barger family after his father went to prison and his mother placed him in an orphanage. During World War I, he was drafted into the 89th Infantry Division and distinguished himself during the Meuse-Argonne Offensive when he and a fellow soldier went into enemy territory to rescue three wounded soldiers. For his bravery, Barger was later awarded a Congressional Medal of Honor by Gen. John J. Pershing.

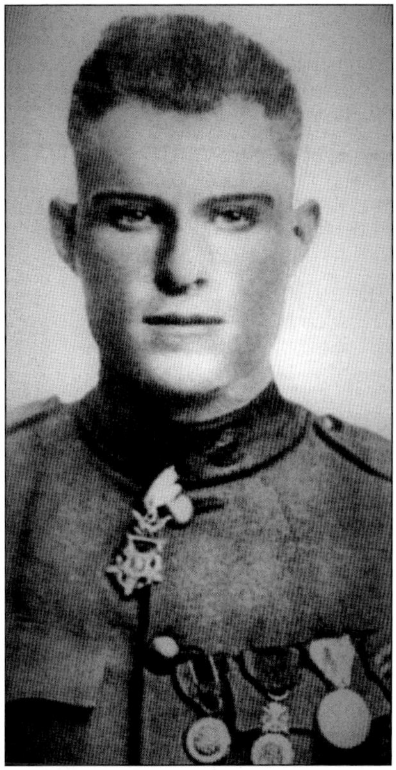

Barger encountered hard times after the war and struggled with the effects of his combat service. He died in Kansas City on November 25, 1936, when only 44 years old and was laid to rest in the Blue Springs Cemetery. In 2016, a special memorial honoring the Medal of Honor recipient's service was placed near the cemetery's veterans memorial during a ceremony attended by some of Barger's descendants.

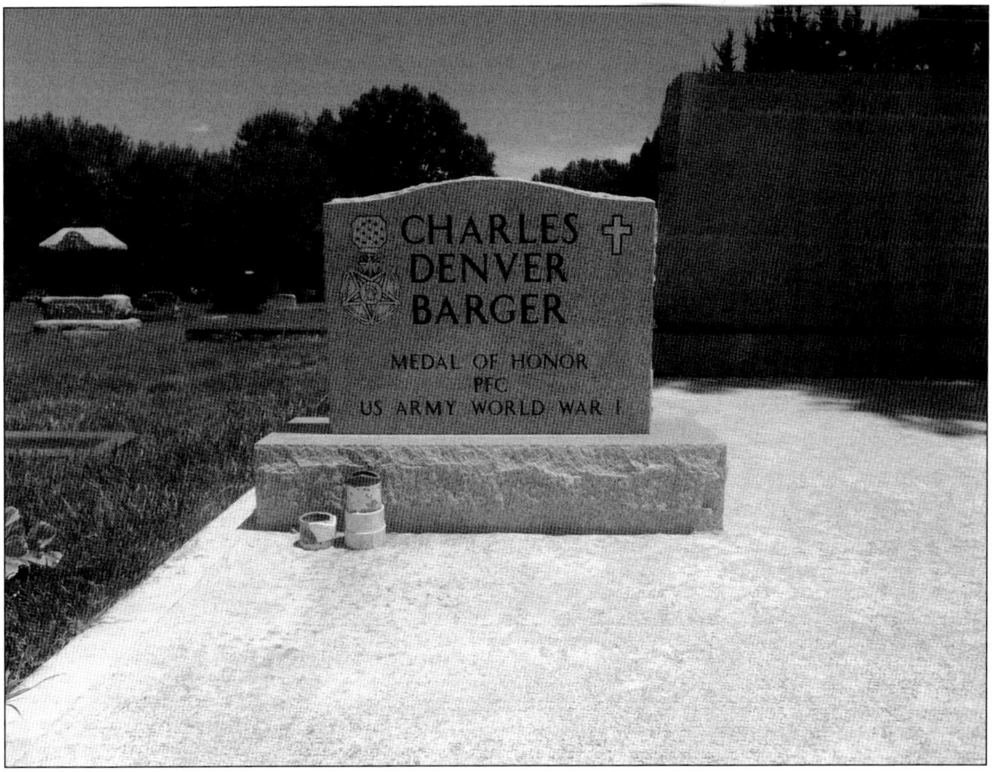

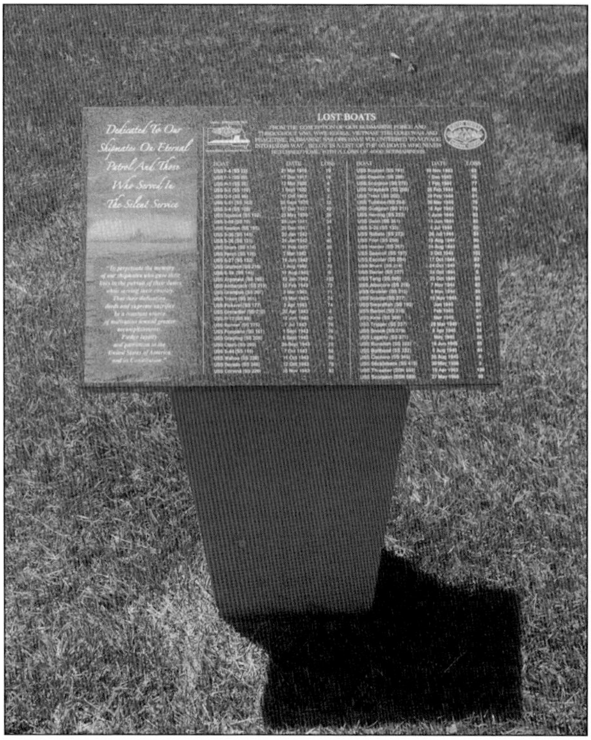

The Topeka-Jefferson City Base of the United States Submarine Veterans, Inc. was integral in the placement in Pink Hill Park in Blue Springs of this memorial honoring the memory of submarine veterans who lost their lives in the service. Consisting of a plaque situated on top of a pedestal, the memorial was funded through donations received from local civic organizations, businesses, and community members and lists the names of the 65 submarines that never returned home.

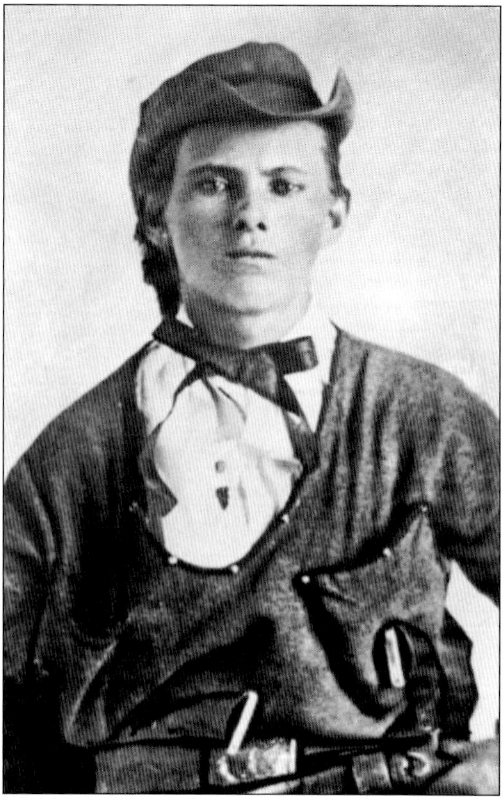

Jesse James was born in 1847 near the western Missouri community of Kearney and rose to fame after the Civil War as a member of the James-Younger Gang—outlaws who robbed banks, trains, and stagecoaches. During the Civil War, both Jesse and his brother Frank served as guerrilla fighters with William Quantrill and "Bloody Bill" Anderson.

After Robert Ford shot and killed Jesse James in St. Joseph, Missouri, on August 3, 1882, James was laid to rest in the yard near the farmhouse on the family farm near Kearney, but his remains were later moved to nearby Mt. Olivet Cemetery. Two stones now mark James's grave, with one describing his service to the Confederacy during the Civil War. (Tina Amick.)

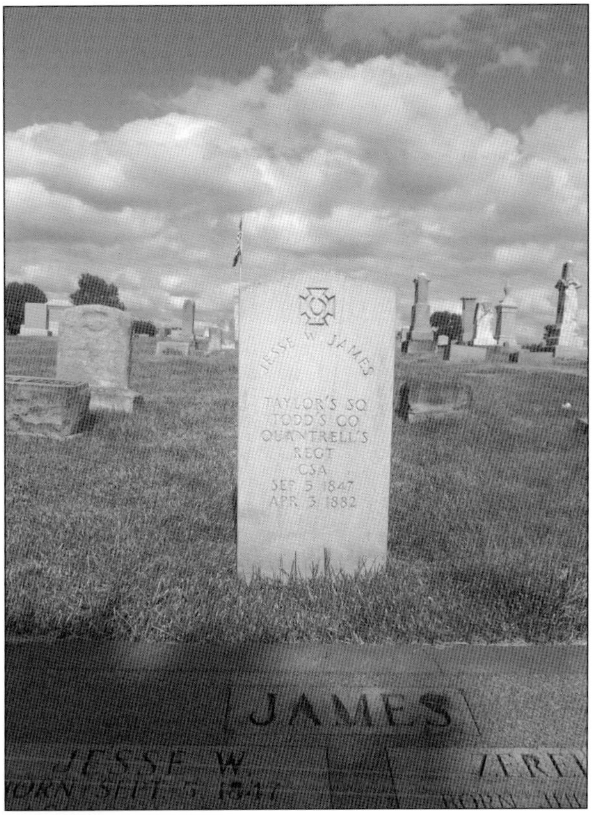

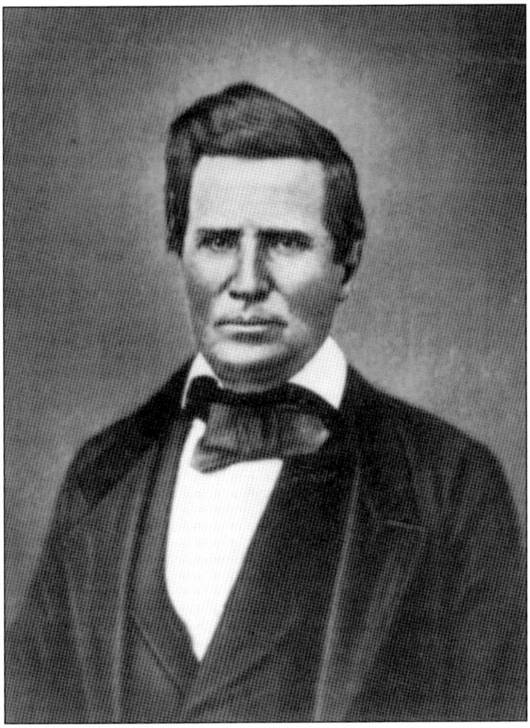

Alexander William Doniphan was born in Kentucky in 1808, became an attorney, and later moved to Liberty, Missouri. Doniphan was serving as a brigadier general in the Missouri Militia and refused an order to execute Joseph Smith and other leaders of the Mormon Church during the Mormon War of 1838. During the Mexican War, he served as colonel of the 1st Regiment of Missouri Mounted Volunteers and led his men on a march of nearly 5,500 miles during the military campaign, which is considered the longest since the times of Alexander the Great. (Museum of Missouri Military History.)

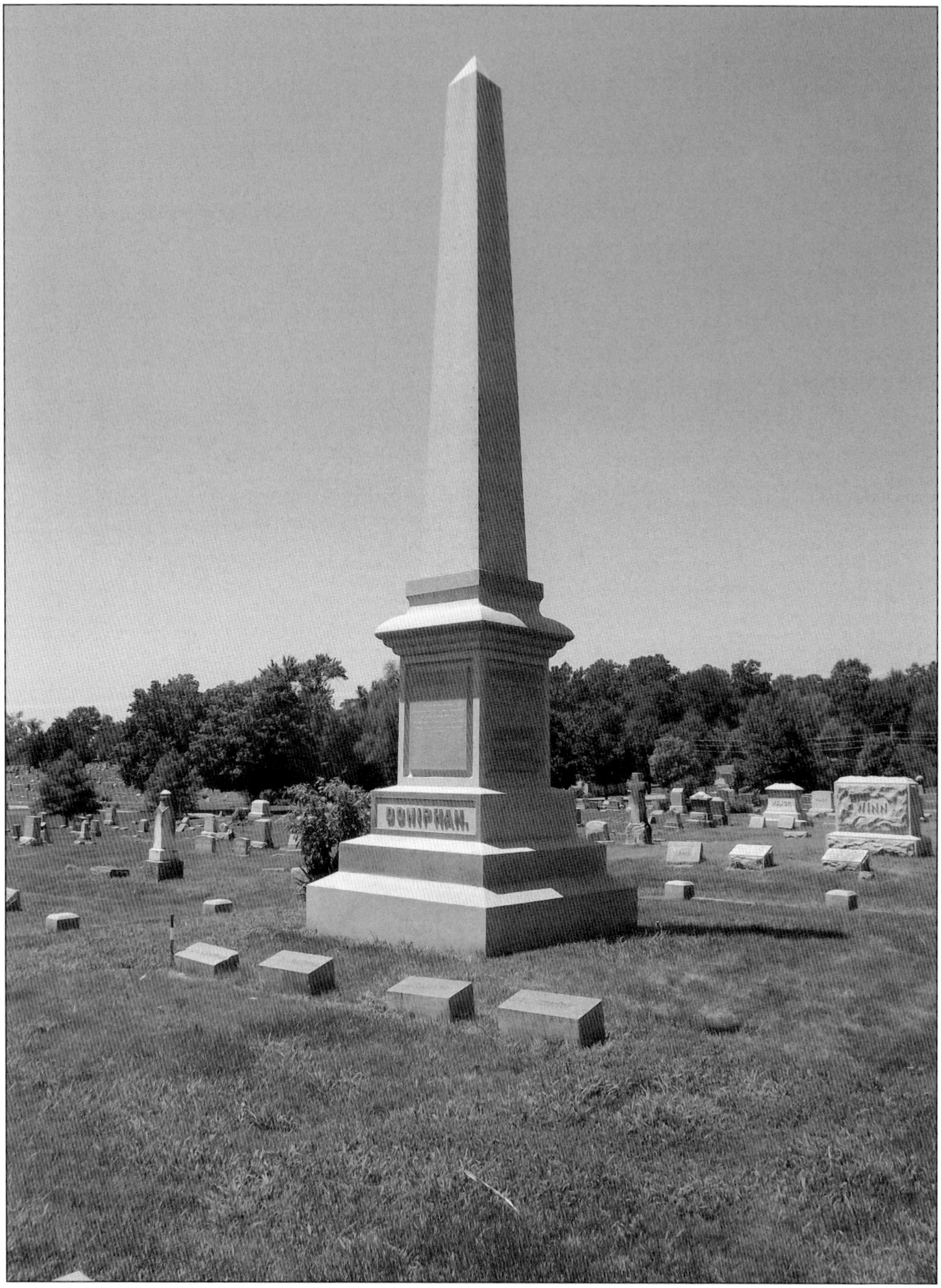

During the Civil War, Doniphan moved to St. Louis and processed pension applications for the Missouri Claims Commission. In the years after the war, he operated a law office in Richmond, Missouri, until his death in 1887. The former soldier was laid to rest under this massive obelisk in Fairview Cemetery in Liberty. The city of Doniphan in Missouri was named in his memory. (David Keckler.)

Five

St. Louis Region

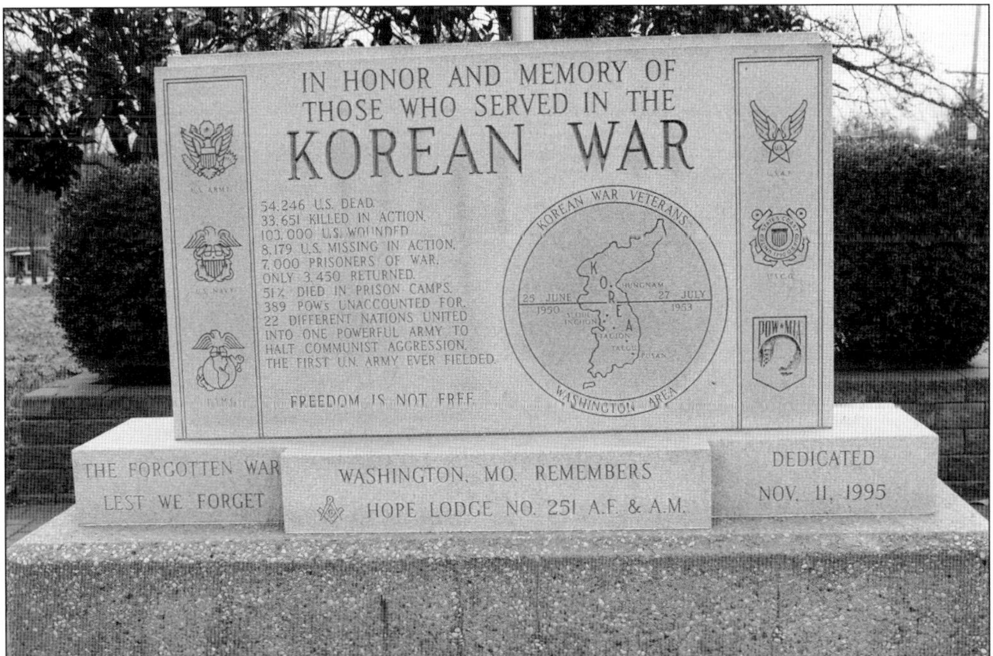

The Korean War Memorial in Krog Park in Washington, Missouri, was dedicated in 1995 from money raised by a committee of local Korean War veterans, with the local Masons contributing the most money toward the memorial. Several years later, in 2013, the Korean War Veterans Association, Washington Chapter 324 was formed and began holding meetings at the local American Legion. The newly formed grouped sponsored a ceremony on July 24, 2013, marking the 60th anniversary of the armistice of the Korean War, during which then governor Jay Nixon offered remarks and laid a wreath at the memorial. (Tina Amick.)

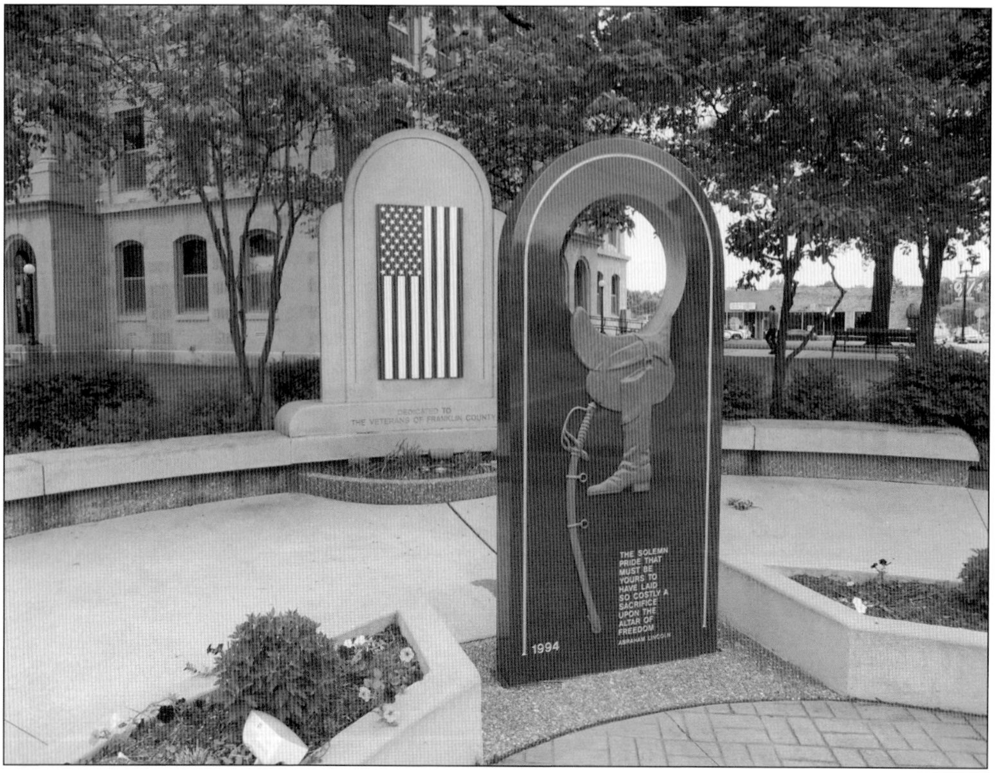

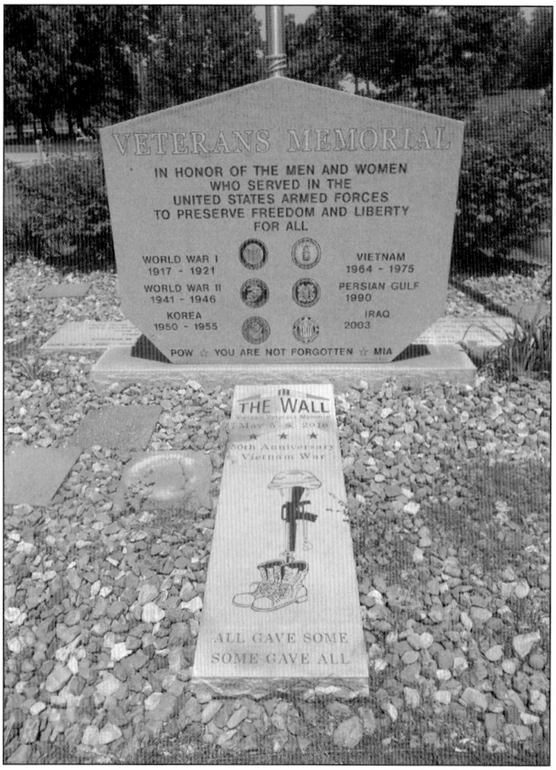

In 1994, the Franklin County Veterans Memorial was dedicated on the grounds of the county courthouse in Union. Features of the memorial include a light-colored column with a rounded top, on which an American flag is set. In front of this is situated a shorter, rounded-top black column, upon which is inscribed a picture of a saddle, pair of boots, and a saber, in addition to a quote from Pres. Abraham Lincoln.

While the Vietnam Traveling Memorial Wall—a smaller-scale replica of the Vietnam Veterans Memorial in Washington, DC—was on display in West City Park in Festus from October 5 to 8, 2006, the Jefferson City Wall Foundation dedicated a Veterans Memorial. It is located near the entrance to the park, recognizes veterans of all wars, and was made possible through the work and donations of several local sponsors.

A plain, gray granite monument was dedicated to Jefferson County veterans during a ceremony held at the county courthouse in Hillsboro on November 11, 1984. The monument was completed through the efforts of the Jefferson County Intervets—a coalition of the county's 11 veterans' organizations. As part of the memorial efforts, a plaque was installed in the courthouse listing the names of the 34 county residents who died in Vietnam and the 12 who lost their lives in the Korean War.

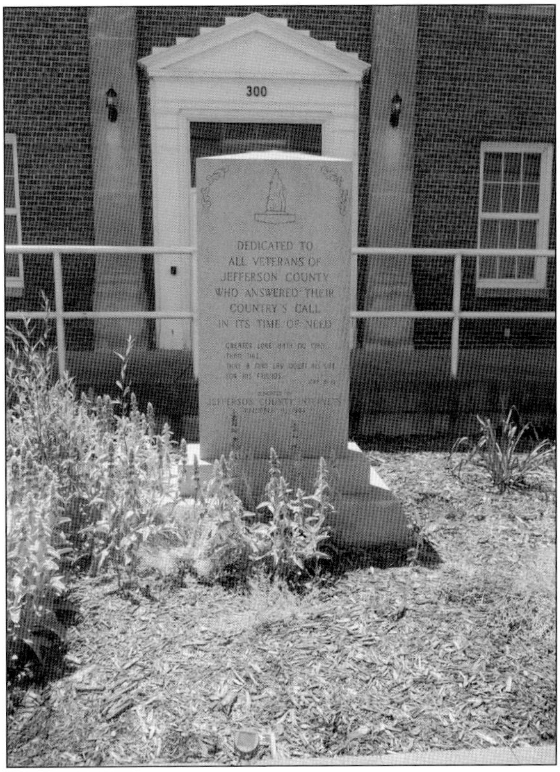

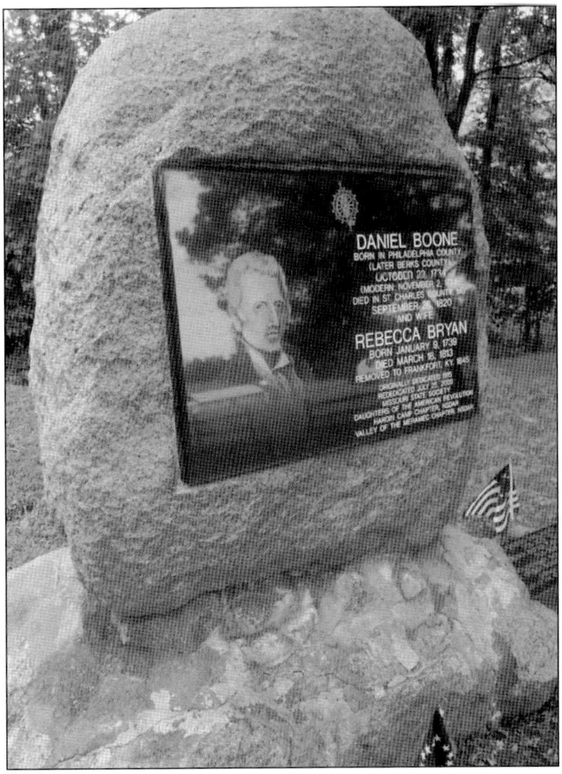

History knows Daniel Boone as a great explorer, frontiersman, and veteran of the Indian Wars; however, it remains uncertain whether his remains are actually interred in the Daniel Boone Burial Site (formerly known as the Old Bryan Cemetery) near Marthasville. Many stories continue to circulate claiming that Boone's body was exhumed in the years after his death and reinterred in Kentucky.

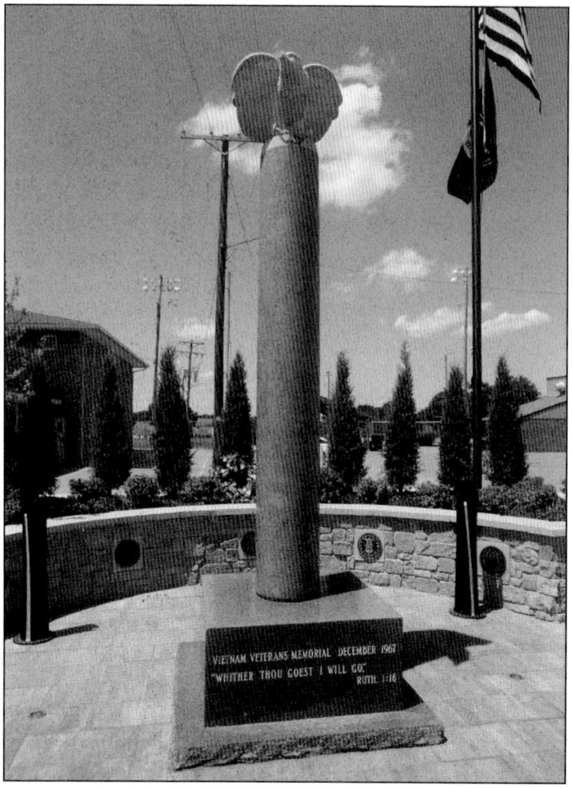

Wentzville acquired the distinction of being the home of one of the first memorials to honor Vietnam veterans when this monument was dedicated on December 19, 1967. The monument, which was funded through donations collected from local citizens, features a column of red Missouri granite topped by the carved figure of an eagle. (Tina Amick.)

In 1919, the Hardin Camp Chapter of the Daughters of the American Revolution and local citizens erected this pagoda in Jonesburg City Cemetery in the Montgomery County community of Jonesburg to honor local veterans who served in World War I. A plaque affixed to one of the stone columns on the structure lists the names of all Jonesburg men who served in the war, in addition to enumerating those who were wounded, killed in action, or died in the service.

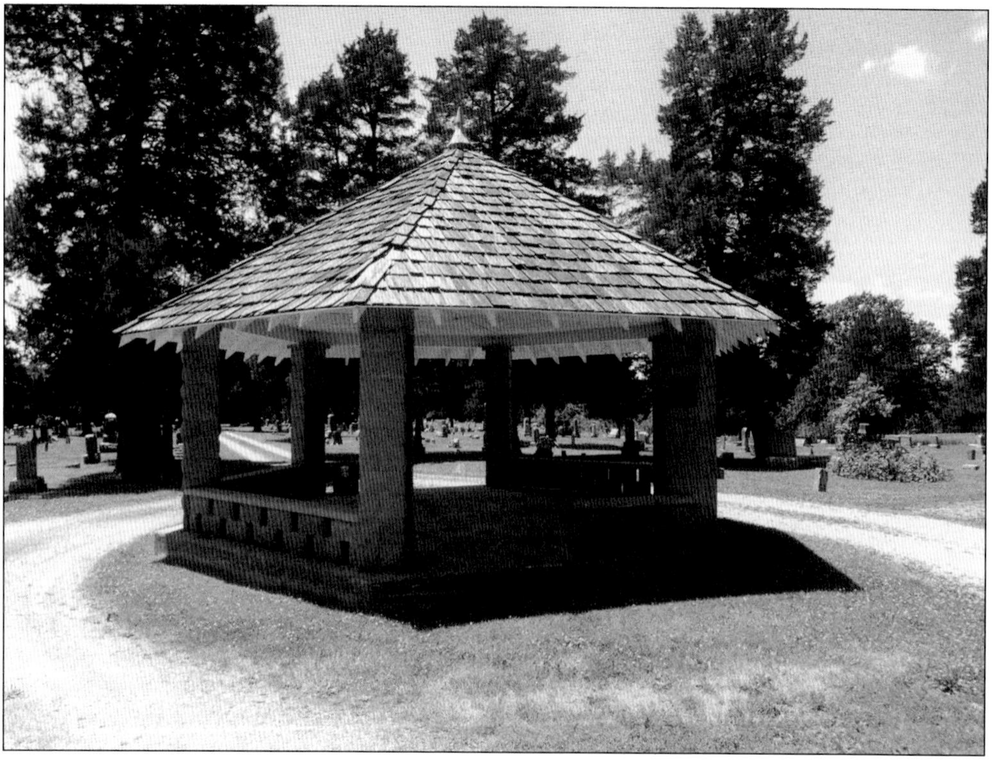

The Warren County Veterans Memorial was dedicated November 11, 1997, in front of the county courthouse in Warrenton. A brick veteran's memorial was first dedicated in 1970 in front of the previous courthouse but was demolished during the construction of the new courthouse in 1997. The new memorial was built using $10,000 raised among residents of the community.

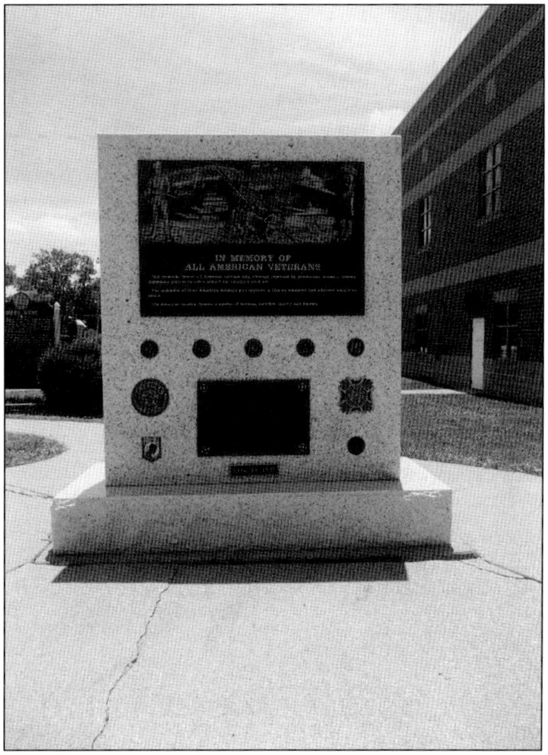

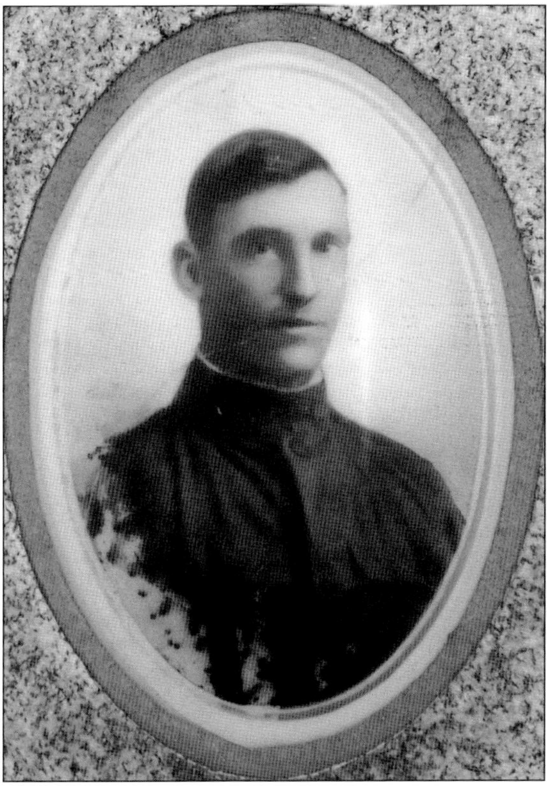

Archie Bowman was born on April 23, 1894, in the former community of Hamburg in rural St. Charles County. Hamburg was one of three communities in the area that were evacuated after the US government purchased the property to build a plant to manufacture TNT after the United States entered World War II. As a young man, Bowman worked at the local Weldon Spring Quarry until he was inducted into the US Army on April 28, 1918.

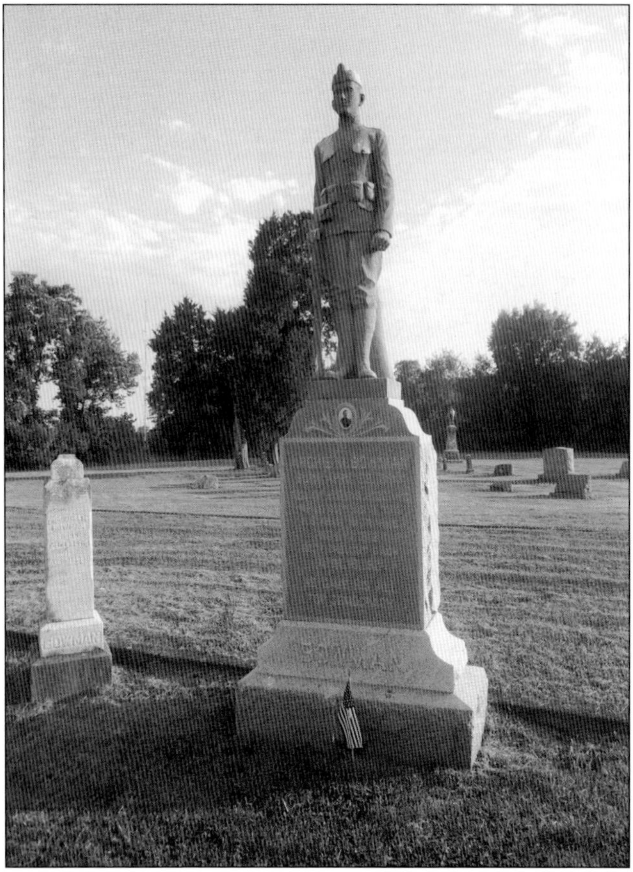

While serving with Company A, 356th Infantry Regiment during the Meuse-Argonne Offensive, Pvt. Archie Bowman was wounded during the first week of November 1918. On November 17, 1918, six days after the armistice, Bowman died from his wounds and was initially interred in France. His body was returned to the United States in April 1921 and reinterred in the Thomas Howell Cemetery near Weldon Spring, where his family erected this elaborate monument in honor of his service.

Though first mention of the 6th US Infantry can be found in the acts of Congress of July 16, 1798, and March 3, 1799, it began its lengthy stint at Jefferson Barracks when transferred there in April 1827. The regiment participated in several major conflicts to include the Civil War and World War I, but its tenure at Jefferson Barracks came to a close in 1940 when it became the 6th Infantry (Armored). This monument chronicling the legacy of the 6th US Infantry is located in front of the post headquarters on what remains of the military base at Jefferson Barracks.

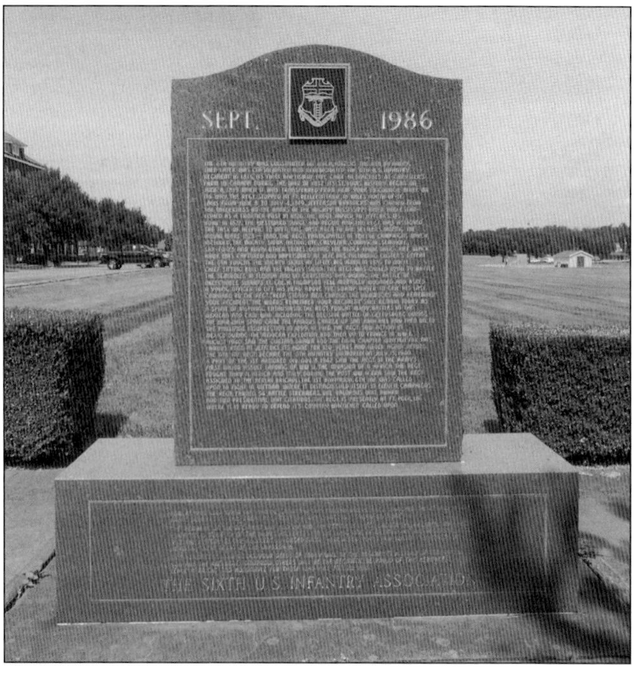

Hanging on the wall of a second-floor room in the Post Headquarters building at Jefferson Barracks is this painting that serves as a memorial that preserves the layout of the military post prior to World War II. This large, detailed painting was completed in February 1938 by Pvt. Ralph Rausch, who was stationed at the barracks with Company H, 6th US Infantry.

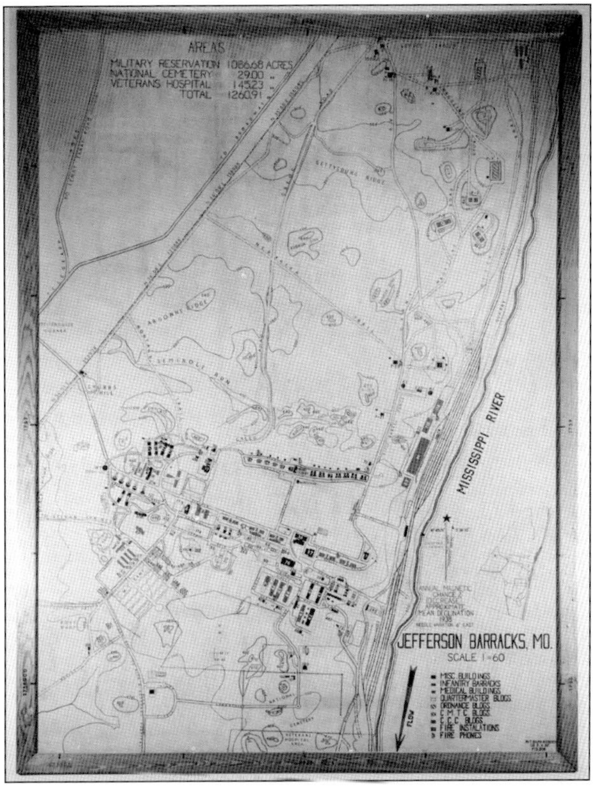

Several airborne units of the US Army sponsored this memorial located in a park across from the main entrance to the military base at Jefferson Barracks in St. Louis. The memorial denotes the site of the first parachute jump from an airplane, made by US Army captain Albert Berry on March 1, 1912.

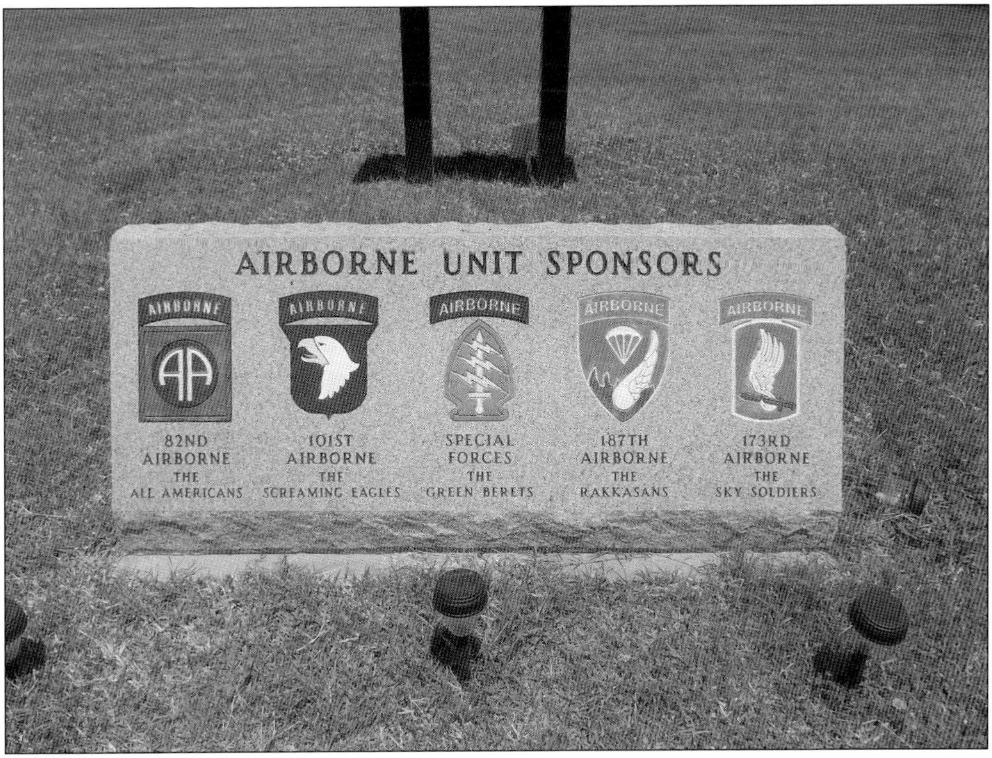

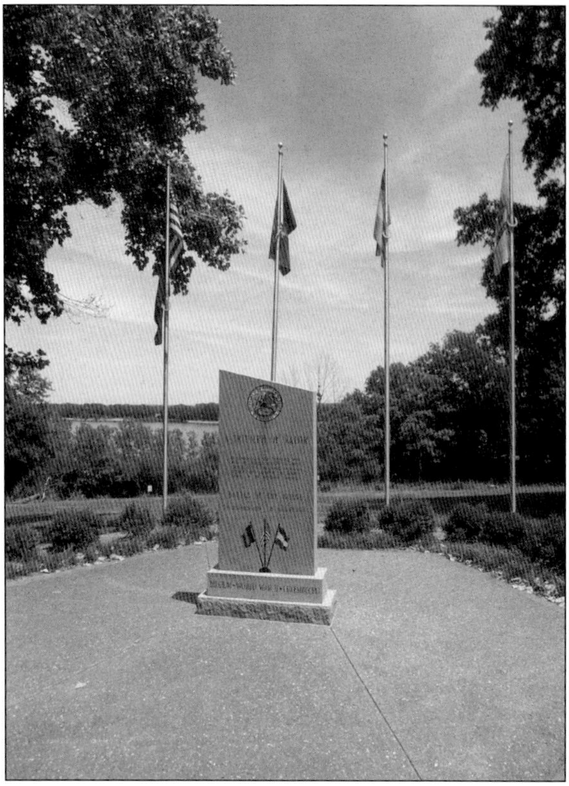

A tribute to those who served during the Battle of the Bulge in World War II overlooks the Mississippi River on a site at the Jefferson Barracks Historic Park. The monument was dedicated on October 12, 1997, by the St. Louis Gateway Chapter of the Veterans of the Battle of the Bulge, cost $20,000 to build, and is a replica—in shape only—of the National Battle of the Bulge Monument at the Valley Forge Military Institute in Wayne, Pennsylvania.

Within the Jefferson Barracks National Cemetery is a red granite memorial dedicated in November 1904 by the St. Louis Chapter of the Daughters of the American Revolution in honor of the memory of the unknown soldiers who died at Fort Bellefontaine between 1806 and 1826. The fort was located along the Missouri River in northern St. Louis County but was replaced by Jefferson Barracks in 1826.

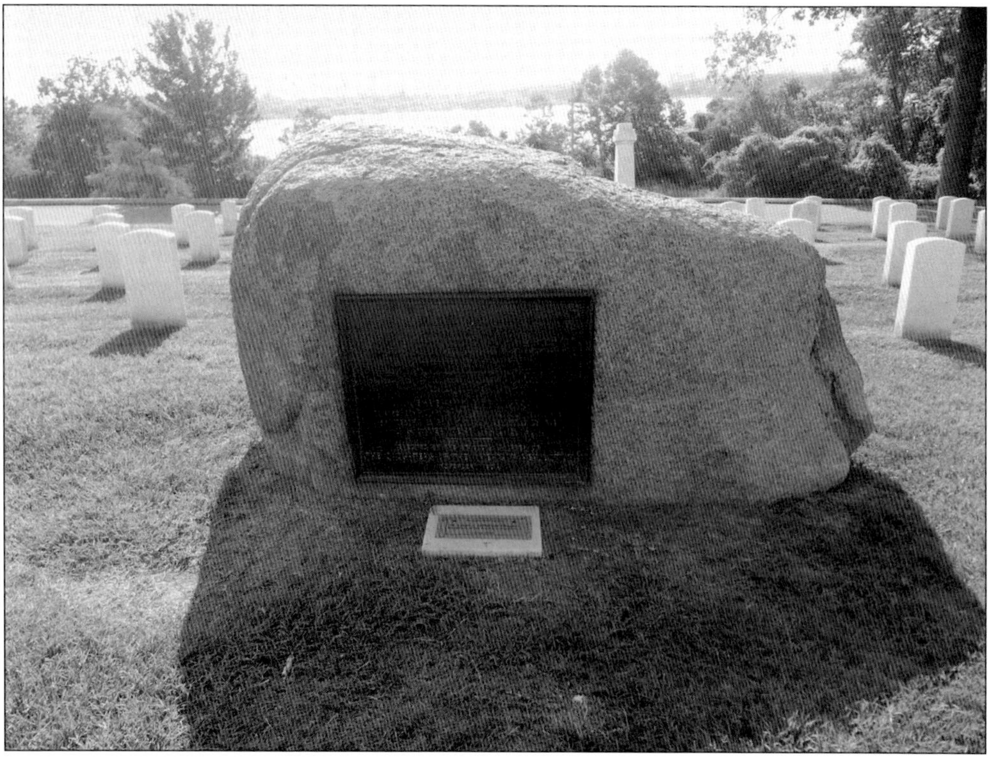

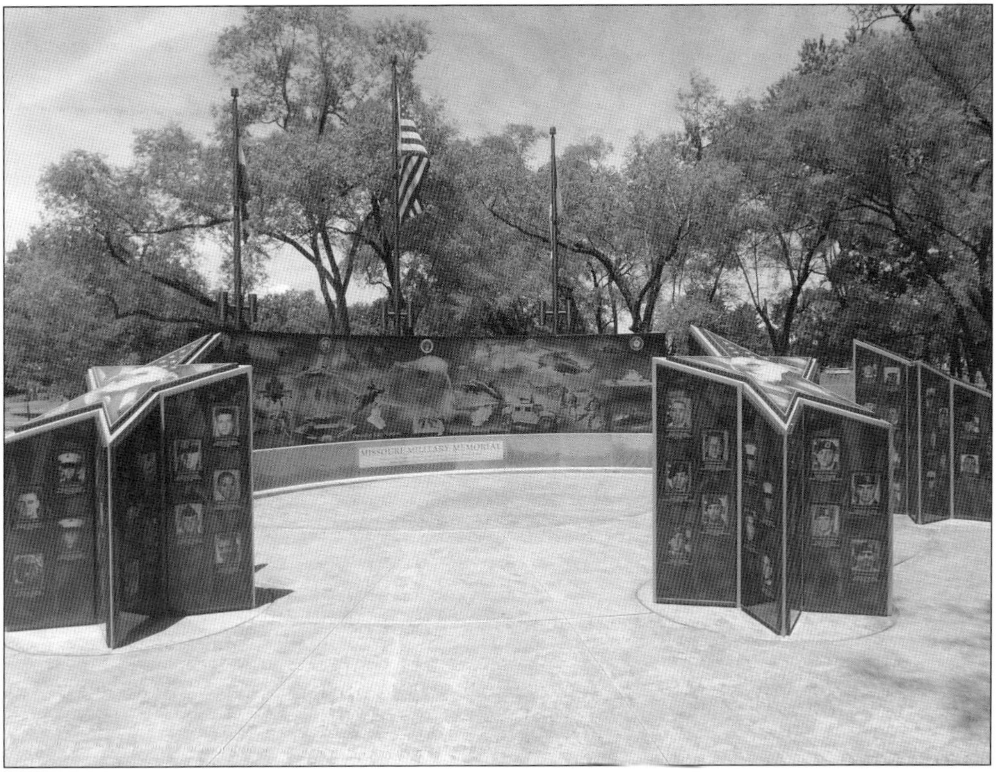

Ground breaking for the Missouri Military Memorial inside Jefferson Barracks Historic Park was held in April 2017. The memorial was built to honor the men and women of Missouri who lost their lives in Afghanistan and Iraq and was built using monies raised by local Gold Star families. It was constructed from 110,000 pounds of black granite and features three large granite stars adorned with pictures of the state's fallen warriors. (Tina Amick.)

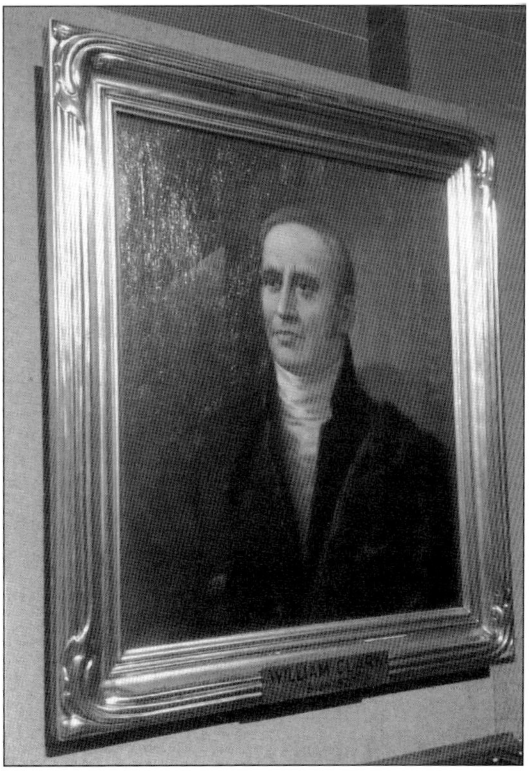

William Clark is best known for being a cocaptain with Meriwether Lewis during the famed Lewis and Clark Expedition. In the years after his westward journey, Clark would go on to make his home in St. Louis and was appointed a brigadier general of the militia and superintendent of Indian Affairs for the Territory of Upper Louisiana. Clark is featured here in his portrait hanging inside the Missouri State Capitol.

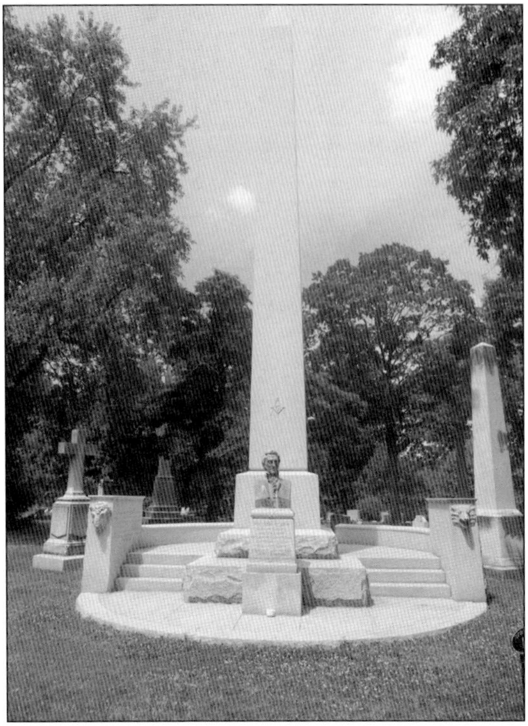

The grave and memorial site of William Clark is located in the historic Bellefontaine Cemetery in northern St. Louis. Clark passed away in St. Louis on September 1, 1838, and is reputed to have had a funeral procession extending more than a mile in length. Jefferson Kearny, who Clark's son by his second wife, provided the money for a monument to be erected over Clark's grave in 1904. (Tina Amick.)

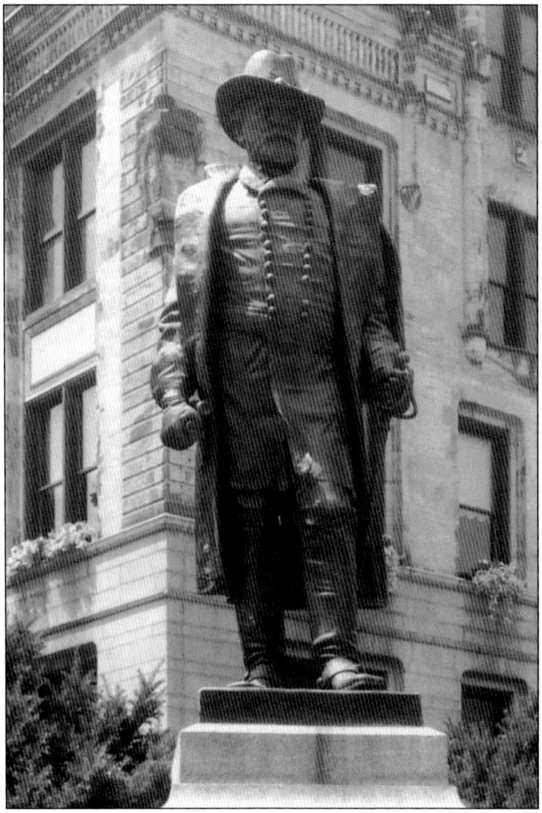

Nine feet in height, this memorial tribute to the Union Civil War general and 18th president of the United States, Ulysses S. Grant, was cast in 1888. It has been moved from its original location over the years but is now located on the southwest corner of Market Street and Tucker Boulevard next to St. Louis City Hall. The statue features Grant in military uniform with his left hand resting on his saber while clutching a pair of field glasses in his right hand.

The St. Peters Veterans Memorial Site was dedicated on October 3, 1998, at the City Centre Park in the City of St. Peters. In addition to a prominently displayed stone marker honoring all veterans, the memorial site also features fountains and statues honoring both servicemen and servicewomen. Pictured here is a statue within the memorial site that was commissioned to honor all women who served in the nation's armed forces.

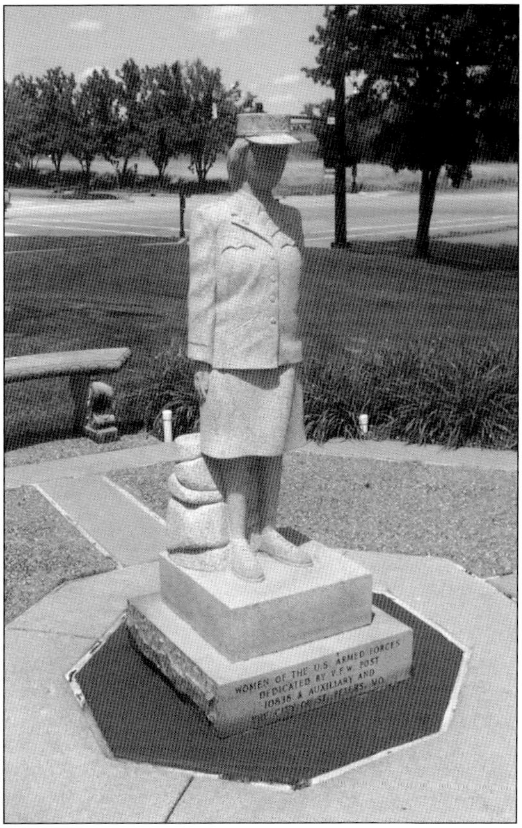

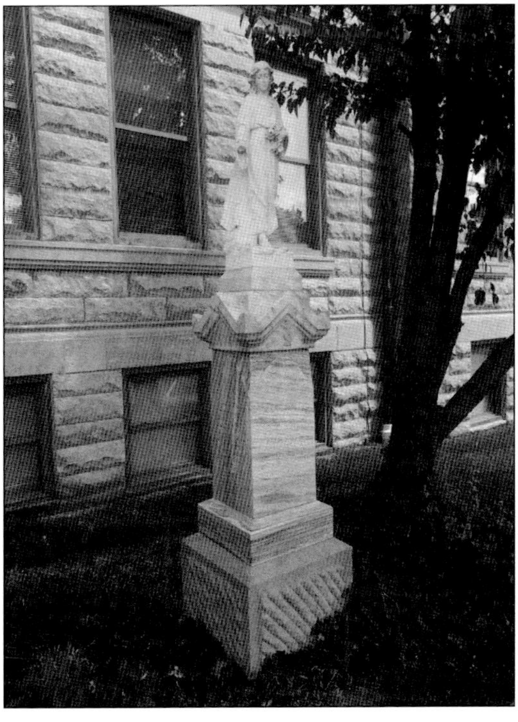

This World War I memorial was dedicated on the lawn of the old courthouse in the community of St. Charles on November 11, 1920. The monument was sponsored by the Gatzweiler Woman's Relief Corps—an auxiliary of the Grand Army of the Republic, Inc.—and consists of a pedestal topped by a woman in a long robe holding a bouquet of flowers in her left hand. On the base of the memorial, the names of county residents who were killed during World War I are listed.

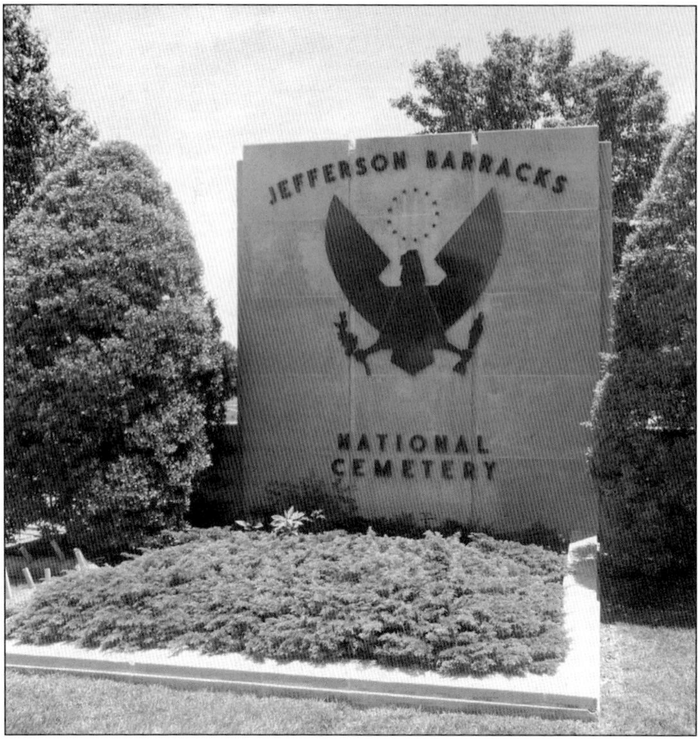

The Jefferson Barracks National Cemetery in St. Louis was officially established as a national cemetery in 1866; however, it is believed that the first burial actually occurred on August 5, 1827, a year after the founding the Jefferson Barracks military post. During the late 1930s and early 1940s, many improvements were made to the cemetery through the Depression-era program known as the Works Progress Administration.

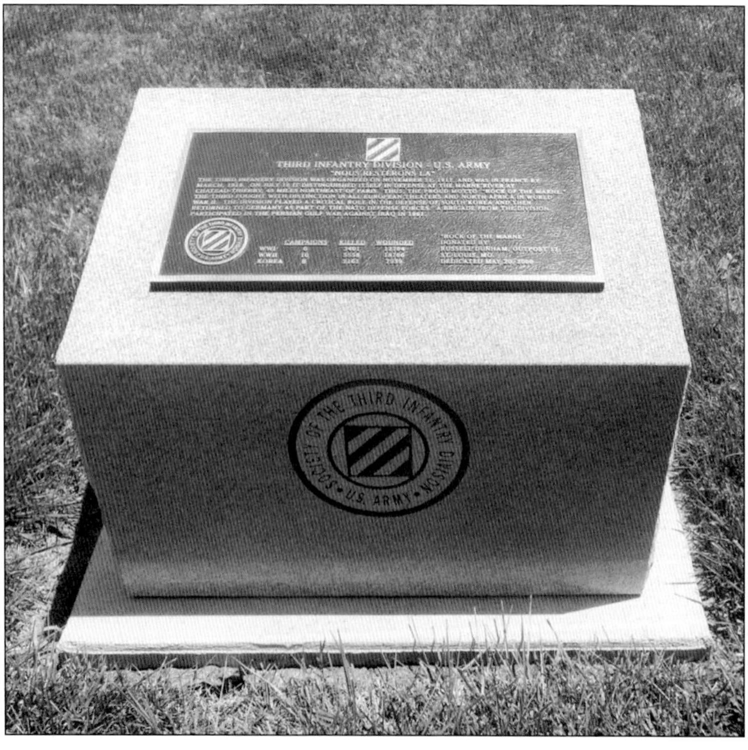

In a grassy area inside Jefferson Barracks National Cemetery, a polished marble marker honors the soldiers of the US Army's Third Infantry Division and was dedicated on May 20, 2000. Earning the title "Rock of the Marne" for its courageous performance during World War I, the Third Infantry Division included such notable veterans as Audie Murphy, one of the most decorated soldiers of World War II.

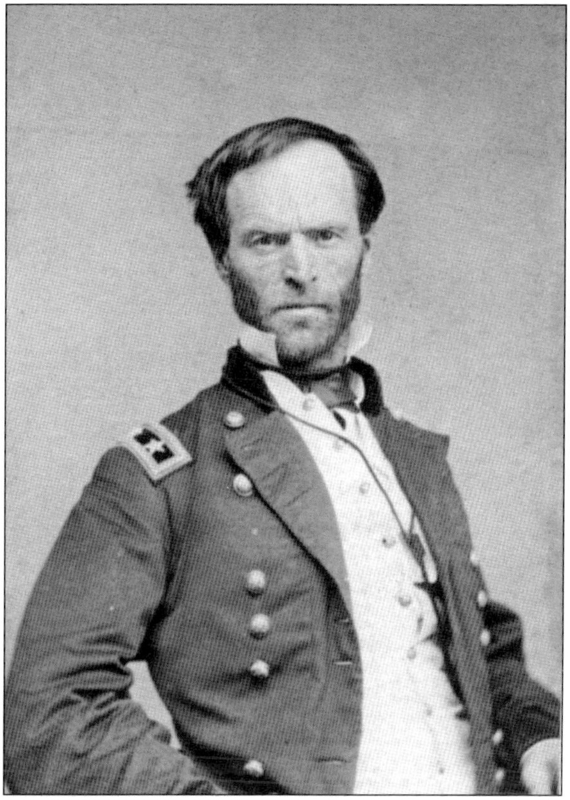

William Tecumseh Sherman was a native of Ohio and raised by a family friend following the death of his father. An 1840 graduate of West Point, Sherman resigned from the Army in 1853 and, throughout the next few years, worked as a banker, practiced law, and served as a headmaster at a military academy. In early 1861, he moved to St. Louis and was soon appointed a colonel with the 13th US Infantry. (Museum of Missouri Military History.)

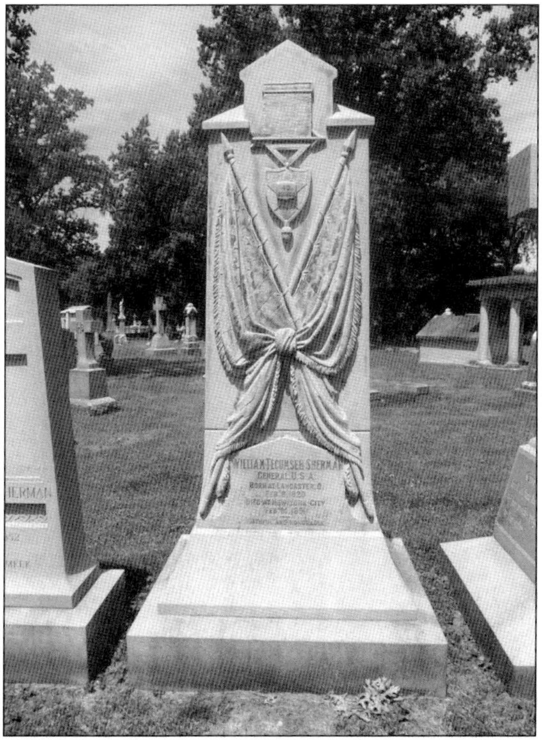

During the Civil War, Sherman rose to the rank of major general and became best known for his March to the Sea—a total war strategy designed to break the South's will to fight and leaving much destruction in its wake. After the war, Sherman remained in the Army until retiring in 1884. He eventually moved to New York City, where he died on February 14, 1891. Per his wishes, Sherman was interred in Calvary Cemetery in St. Louis. (Tina Amick.)

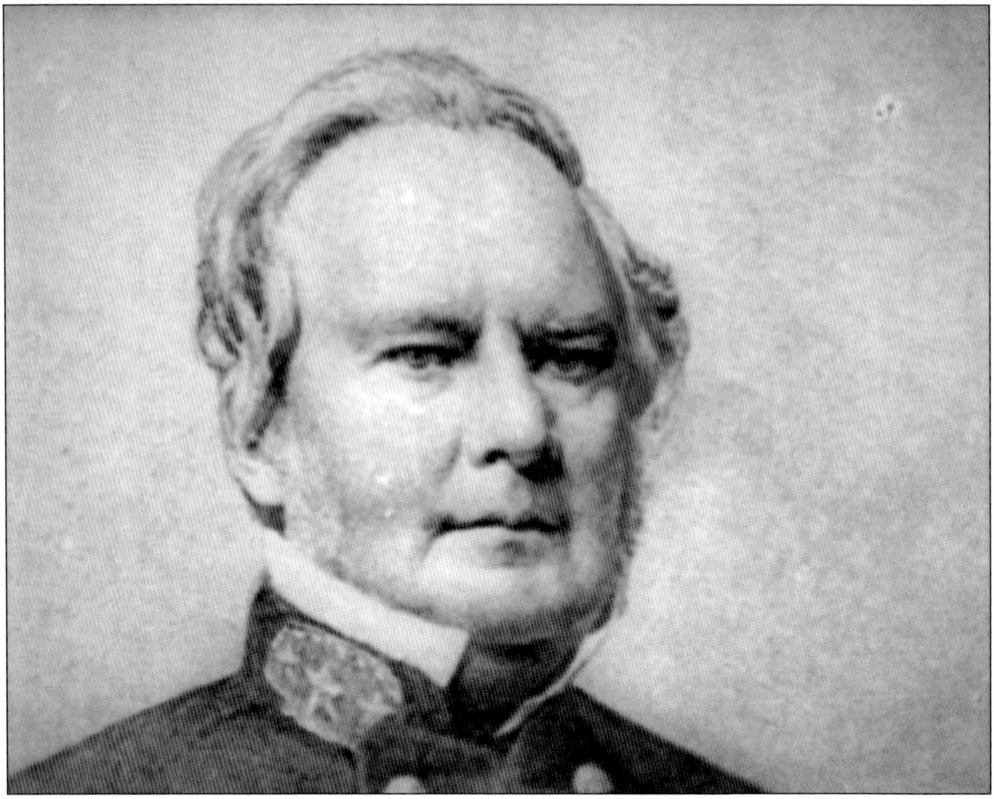

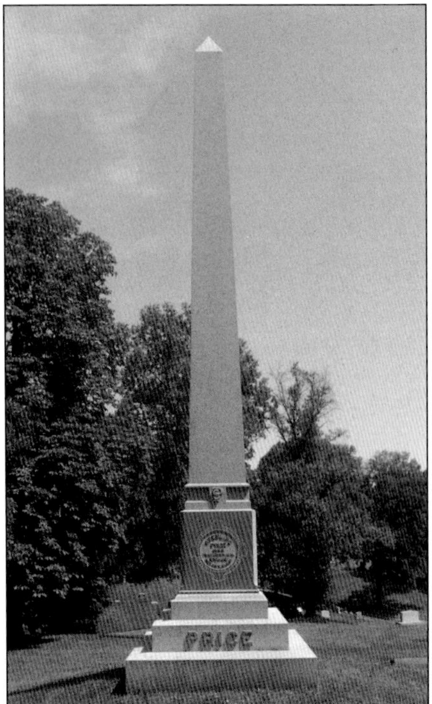

A native of Virginia, Sterling Price later relocated to Missouri with his family and went on to lead a regiment during the Mexican War. He served as a congressman for Missouri from 1845 to 1846 and Missouri's governor from 1853 to 1857. Although he served as a brigadier general and participated in several engagements of the Civil War, Price is perhaps best known for the force of 12,000 troops he led on a raid of Missouri during the fall of 1864. (Museum of Missouri Military History.)

Coming to the realization that the war was lost, Confederate general Sterling Price decided to emigrate to the country of Mexico in June 1865. In January 1867, he returned to Missouri, where he was provided with a home and other financial considerations from various admirers and supporters. Price passed away on September 29, 1867, and was interred in Bellefontaine Cemetery in St. Louis. (Tina Amick.)

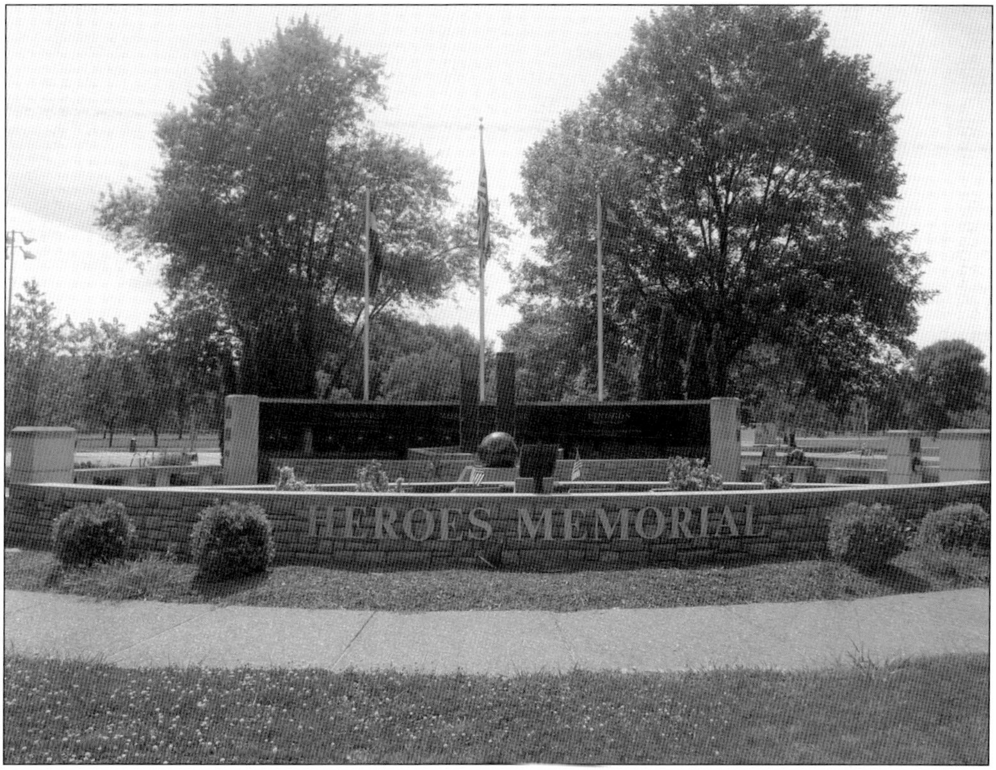

The Fenton City Park in the St. Louis County community of Fenton is home to the Heroes Memorial, honoring police, firefighters, EMS personnel, and all veterans. The memorial has several features, such as a globe that appears to float on a thin curtain of water, a sculpture symbolizing the Twin Towers, a black granite wall honoring the victims of the terrorist attacks of September 11, 2001, and plaques honoring veterans and other local personnel who serve the community.

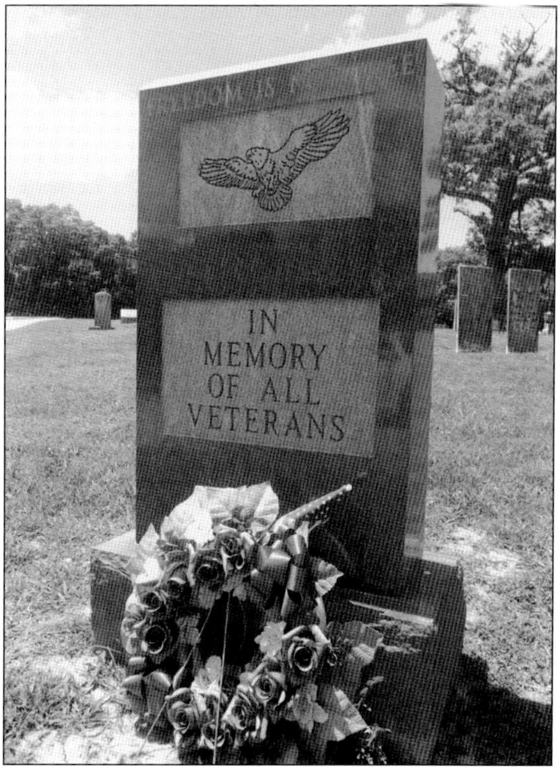

Located just north of Interstate 70 in the Warren County community of Wright City is this small, square marker that was dedicated to the memory of all veterans on Memorial Day 2006. The memorial sits beneath the flagpole inside the Wright City Cemetery and was sponsored by the Lee Singer Memorial Veterans of Foreign Wars Post 10687.

Consistent with our mission to preserve history on a local level, this book was printed in South Carolina on American-made paper and manufactured entirely in the United States. Products carrying the accredited Forest Stewardship Council (FSC) label are printed on 100 percent FSC-certified paper.

MADE IN THE USA